DYSTOPIA BY STEALTH

A True Account

Book 1:
My World Turned Into Theirs

S. A. Clark

Dystopia by Stealth, Book 1: My World Turned Into Theirs

Copyright © 2021 by Sharon Clark

All rights reserved. Permission granted to reproduce without modification.

Some readers may find the contents of this book disturbing.

This is based on the journal of Sharon Clark. Most names have been changed.

First Edition: June 2021

CONTENTS

1

PUT UNDER SURVEILLANCE AT PORCFEST

P*orcfest 2017, New Hampshire.* Friday, the first lecture was about helping the poor. I took notes and afterwards looked over the books at the table by the front. A man was there watching me look at the books. I saw that man several times during later lectures. He often asked questions during the Q/A period, and while he seemed to be generally interested, he did not seem to have an in-depth knowledge of the movement.

As I was walking out of a class, he came up to me, noticing the copious notes I was taking. He introduced himself as Brian Andrews. He told me briefly about himself. He is a writer. His background is in medicine, although he never practiced. He wrote two scholarly papers about how religion is the result and reflection of people trying to soothe a childhood trauma. He is an atheist. I told him I was moving to New Hampshire looking for a job at Bensonwood. I was in manufacturing. He asked why a girl would be into that. I hadn't really thought, "Hey, I'm a girl, what should I do." I just always loved designing and building, and I wanted to learn timber frame building and design multipurpose furniture to make housing more affordable for the poor. He perked up at that.

We talked a little. It seemed strangely easy to talk to him. He lingered on, picking out a few more pieces of information. "Can you stay and talk a little longer or do you have somewhere to go?" I ended up talking to him for 40 minutes. It was during Seth Hipple's lecture. I can't remember everything we said... I said I liked to listen to Tom Woods and Stefan Molyneux. I mentioned I was a Christian. He seemed concerned he had just been insulting, and hedged his argument in his papers saying that childhood traumas had made some beliefs more appealing than others. We exchanged emails, and he said he would send me his papers. I found him intelligent, and rather academic. He is Jewish. He said perhaps we would come up with some other questions for each other, and we went our separate ways.

The next time I saw him he seemed discouraged. I explained I had not read his papers because I wasn't on the local WIFI. He left, and I didn't see him for a while. Then I ran into him again. He told me he had heard a really great talk on *redacted*. He was really enthusiastic about it. *As I think back, it did not appear to be sincere enthusiasm. -2/13/20* I said he should send me some of their videos. I pointed out Lyn Ulbricht, who had just finished speaking. I said I regretted not being in her lecture. I told him she was The Dread Pirate Robert's mother, and told him a little bit about the significance of the case. He was shocked and said DPR had tried to kill someone, and I responded that charge was only used to gain pre-trial advantage, and was dropped and never prosecuted in court. I told him even though the Silk Road was used to sell drugs, and those may be harmful, it was still a really significant point in humanity, doing something we had not previously been capable of doing--creating a truly free market. I also noted her talks were about how the judge made up new definitions to the laws to convict DPR, and there was good reason to question whether judges should be able to do that. It was like making Craigslist responsible for what people posting to Craigslist do. He said he would be sure to attend next year.

Brian followed me as I walked. Tonight was the Liberty Ecclesia game night. I wanted to attend. He apologized for coming off as insulting towards my religion. I said it was fine. I appreciated people disagreeing for rational reasons. He said he wondered why a rational person such as myself had become a Christian. I told him how I had been saved when I was four. I was very resistant at first. My parents would talk about it all the time. But I didn't want to be involved. I protested having to pray with the rest of the family when I was three, since I wasn't even a Christian. But I became convinced that they were in the right and I was wrong. I hadn't had the opportunity to study all the apologetics for it. He knew what that term meant. But I believed it was genuine. It became a part of me—a very important part, and it shaped how I thought and what my values were. It was only when I got a little older, around age 9, that I began to understand the other reasons for it. I could see that there was good evidence. I'm still not sure of everything, but I would rather have a weak faith in a true God than a strong faith in a false one. He asked if I was a believer in evolution. I said I had yet to be convinced. I believed in natural selection. "That's evolution," he offered. I told him that I didn't believe that all species originated from one, and that natural selection reduced complexity in the genetic code, and didn't build on it. When I'd heard expert evolutionists try to defend it, Richard Dawkins thought it might be aliens.

He started to explain his papers. He said that the thought of hell was so traumatizing that anyone presented with it cannot think rationally. *Another thing he said was that children could not hide their thoughts, so they would be pressured to conform them. He seemed to want me to understand this. -2/13/20* I said the one most important rule for me is to tell myself the truth. He continued if the thumb screws were brought out, people would break. Imagine a child watching a video of his parents being dragged screaming down into hell. Children are so warped by this. This is why people are biased. I countered that if the trauma could alter my beliefs so that I could be wrong, and there was no way to tell, then how could I trust my capacity to reason to even know if the trauma was affecting it? He backed off a little, saying it didn't completely rob me of my ability to reason. I came up with a counter argument. Global warming was an example of something alleged to have dire consequences if action was not taken. Telling children that the polar bears will die and all of humanity will come to an end might upset them, and might induce them to believe. But global warming still might be true. Even if people are influenced by the appeal to force argument, the conclusion might still be a reality, just not proven by those means. I was leaning on the side of the men's restroom. It was on the way to Liberty Ecclesia, so we had stopped there for him. He asked me if I'd ever had a conversation on the lintel of a men's restroom. I stepped away so he could have a little privacy. When he came out, he had a counter argument.

It started to rain, so we found shelter between the bathroom and the office, on a bench in a covered alley. I mentioned Stefan Molyneux's aversion to child abuse, and how his main point was that spanking is what messes up humanity. He asked me if I had been spanked, noting that I did not have to answer if I was not comfortable. I told him I was, from about 3 years old to 7. "What do you think about corporal punishment now?" I froze for a minute, trying to regather my thoughts. I said that Stefan's arguments were good, but not solid. I wasn't sure either way, but to avoid the possibility of hurting a child, I decided to just find other ways. He asked about the reasons why I became a Christian. It was hard for me to remember, because of how far back. But I was a rebel. When I became a Christian, I changed. I saw the behavior of my family compared to mine. I saw God and the others as the good guys and me as the bad guy, and I didn't want to be that way anymore. He became quiet. I asked him if he was reflecting on what I had said. He said he had thoughts, but he had held them back, saying he could tell me if I wanted. I nodded. He said he thought what had happened to me was wrong. He thought the timing of when I was abused and when I was saved was interesting. He didn't think four year olds could think clearly about these things. They were too vulnerable, easily manipulated, and connected to and dependent on the parents. It was a coercive environment. I said that I saw spanking in my childhood as supplemental. My parents never spanked me out of the blue, it was only if I did something intentionally wrong. And they always explained their reasons. And if I objected to something they did, after I obeyed, I could go to them and explain that. And when I did, they would listen, and sometimes they even apologized and changed. There was respect and trust. And I thought I had a great childhood. He recognized that some environments were better than others.

Our conversation became quiet, but it was a rich warm silence. I stared off into the rain. He liked the smell of the campfires. I said there was a strange smell around this place. I was concerned what it might be since I didn't know what pot smelled like. He was shocked. "Did you even go to college?" "I commuted," I told him. He asked me what I did. American Sign Language. He wondered why. I did it in high school, and was good at it, so I figured I'd do that for a living. Once I got there and really looked into the profession, I saw that it wasn't for me, and just got a certificate in American Sign Language. I liked the language and the culture, but I didn't know what I was doing for a profession so I just went home. "You are always working with your hands." I laughed. I said I wanted to become an engineer. I said that my home town was a strange backwards place. I chatted about having had my own apartment for a while, and that I thought that society might go downhill. He groaned at that, asking me in which way I thought it would be undone. I said I thought it might be economically. He didn't want to move to New Hampshire, but he currently lives in Massachusetts. I asked him why. He had been living in another country, but his dad got sick, so he stayed close by enough to be with him, but far enough away to not bother him. He was renting from someone and just ended up staying there. He liked the cold less and less though. I asked him what made him a libertarian. He said Rand's works. He asked how I could be a Christian where I have to follow rules and a libertarian at the same time. I told him the Bible was the reason I became a libertarian. *At 18, I decided I had to understand for myself the moral justification for the government that we had. I researched authority in the Bible, and ran into Hosea 8:4. I realized it wasn't a given that everyone that gets away with calling themselves a ruler is actually granted greater authority by God to take people's property or kill them. I had no way to figure out which people did have greater divine right to harm, so I realized I couldn't justify it. We are all just people. There was the institution of government, like the institution of family or church, but the government is merely to establish justice, as defined in Romans 13:10, to "do no harm to your neighbor."* I said the Bible controlled those things that were morally significant. And it made sense that we would get our understanding of how to be from the one who created us. I appreciated both the meticulous devotion to goodness and the freedom for things that were not morally significant. Everyone can create themselves, and can have a voice. It is like a relationship. If one were to completely define the other and smother them, it would not be a relationship anymore. It would just be a person and a puppet. So I would be depriving God of me if I practiced self-erasure. The idea that I could go to another planet and do whatever I wanted was thrilling. And giving that to other people, having infinite possibilities and variety made me happy.

It was bed time. Brian volunteered to walk me to my tent. This made me nervous, but at a certain point we said good night. He hugged me, said it felt good, and went in for another hug. "No thanks." I ducked and gently diverted him. He laughed and asked if he would see me tomorrow. "Possibly, or absolutely." I nervously confirmed, said good night, and we parted. It was incredibly easy to open up to him. It made me feel all warm and cozy. But just in case, I did not go directly to my tent.

Saturday

The next morning as I ate applesauce from my car, I was approached by a bald white man who called himself Smith. He came directly to me. He seemed on edge. His body language said he was ready to pounce, but his eyes said he was afraid. He asked me if I was here all alone, and said his campsite was a swamp, but mine was dry. He asked a few questions about where I was from, and what I was doing here. I told him I used to do sheet metal. He said he was an engineer. When I asked him what he built, he hesitated and shrugged, and said lathes and mills and things. *Liar, but an interesting choice for a lie when I had just told Brian I wanted to become an engineer.* Then he said he made the equipment that made drills for oil drilling. He said a lot of the money went to managers and not the engineers, so he quit his job and started a grass mowing company. I said some people do both engineering and managing. He told me he was concerned about the collapse of the dollar. I asked him what his politics were, and he said he didn't have any, but maybe anarchy. I told him about the Alt Expo, which I thought might suit him. He asked with striking curiosity if I was a programmer. "No, I wish." He asked if I had looked at the sheet metal facilities in the area, and I said I love sheet metal but I would love to do other things as well. He asked me where I was moving to. "Southern New Hampshire." "What town?" "Mmmm..." I didn't tell him the town. As I locked up and started to walk away, he asked me if I was open to new things. *The way he asked that sounded suggestive. -2/13/20* "Some things." I replied disdainfully. That guy gave me the creeps. He feels like a predator, and thinking about what he said, he knew a lot about my conversation with Brian. I wondered if people were hacking into my phone, or had overheard the tail end of our talk last night. But if he just overheard, how did he know where my tent was? This bothered me.

As the day went by, I didn't see Brian. I wondered if I had upset or embarrassed him, and if he would not be back. The festival seemed strangely empty without him. It was later in the afternoon that I saw him. He was in the Agora at the Bitcoin wallet site, talking with another man I recognized as a doctor. He waved and called out to me, as if no worries were on his mind. I came over. I felt off. I wasn't sure where this was going. I stood by as the man at the booth tried to draw me in, not knowing what to do with myself as Brian and the doctor kept talking. "You can take her with you!" The doctor told Brian. "She can do whatever she wants," Brian responded. The doctor was showing him an app using Bitcoin. After Brian wrapped up his conversation, he went to buy food at an adjacent vendor. He asked if I wanted anything. I wasn't hungry. We started to walk, and he asked me in a rushed tone what I did today. I told him the first class I went to, Mental Health Crisis Response. He looked up in shock. "What made you want to go to that?" I told him when I used to read the news, one common problem was cops killing mentally ill people. They would corner them, trap them, threaten them, and demand things from them, and the people in crisis would be so overwhelmed they would not be able to comply, and the cops are basically out murdering people. Brian turned away when I said "corner them" and groaned. He asked if they said what to do if the person had a weapon. I said that was more Dale Brown's territory of the Threat Management Center. He asked what techniques were discussed in the lecture, and I listed listening, validating their feelings, asking permission to do things for them, reducing sensory input, and calming techniques. He told me he had heard Dale Brown say that when cops start out, they don't know anything. They don't even understand their own guns, how they work, or their capabilities. He said he had been meditating for an hour every day for the past four years. He wondered if cops were racist or not, if they acted with malicious intent. It was like he wondered what I thought about it. *The way he spoke, it was like he was personally affected by the idea of shooting someone, defensive by explaining a new police officer's inexperience, and sympathetic towards his own trauma by explaining the lengths he went to to care for his mental health. He also seemed sensitive to the image of police, and wanted me to approve. He was not direct in his language, but couched his meaning in contextually acceptable and relevant topics. -2/13/20* I didn't say whether I thought cops were racist, but it isn't as big a deal as cops actually killing people. He said he heard Dale Brown say that cops who are good have a hard time. I mentioned I had heard how good cops were terrorized for turning in the bad ones. Later I thought we were both thinking different things about what "good cop" meant.

He asked about the next class. I didn't memorize the itinerary. But I had gone to two Threat Management classes. Dale Brown was doing a franchise soon, and I was really looking forward to it. I recounted to him when Dale was speaking in the tent and a woman told him he was too loud and shouldn't use his microphone anymore. He got down into the crowd, and only seemed more excited to share with us what he had to say. Brian looked back at me with a grin. "He clearly isn't doing this for the ego," I added. "It's a balance." Brian shot back, sounding a little hurt. *He identifies strongly with ego. Characteristic of narcissism.*

I told him I went to a Health Freedom lecture at lunch, which was put on by the Alt Expo, but I said I was generally disappointed with them. They have a better strategy, but the people actually implementing their strategy well are out here with the rest of us. I told him about Swarm City, Bitcoin, and the Silk Road, a website to buy and sell anonymously that used to be on the dark web. The central point in the Silk Road constituted a weakness, because it relied on a person. Bitcoin will always be there. You cannot eradicate it. Ethereum allows contract via code, which can be self-enforcing rather than enforced through violent third parties. Brian said if he were starting over, be would learn code, because that is where it is at. I told him about mesh networks, and how the data is dispersed so there is no one place with all the data in the Internet to surveil. He got worried about that. *Who would be worried about that?* He wondered if it could be stopped before it got off the ground, if these things could be seen from satellites, or if cops could go door to door to stop them. I told him it would not be cost effective to do that. He wondered what would happen if it became illegal. I thought the nature of the thing would make it hard for cops to take it away, because people could warn each other. I said I knew the government would want to stop it, but that is because they want the power imbalance. He seemed concerned. "You are going to do this?" I nodded. He paused for a moment. "You and I both know, we know, that they do very bad things to people who do this sort of thing." "That's okay." I responded. Another pause. "Alright." *He seemed disappointed but resigned at that. Of course it isn't okay to do bad things to people. But you have to do right and risk the consequences. Mesh networks are legal, which by definition should mean you are allowed to do them. Taking away free speech and privacy is tyranny.*

When this happened, I was thinking that what I was doing was legal. It wasn't hurting anyone. And as far as the threat to their illegal and harmful surveillance grid mesh networks would be, I wasn't even a programmer. I was a supporter, not a mastermind. I assumed they'd watch and see that I was harmless and leave me alone. I had no idea what was really going on. But I had stumbled upon a chink in the armor of a monster.

I told him one reason I felt safe about this decentralized strategy was that it was creating the alternative to the current government problem. As people chose it, the government would become smaller by attrition. I gave the example of taking down big agro by growing food in your yard. When you grow it, you exempt yourself. You can get your neighbors involved. The more people do it, the weaker the big organization becomes. Just as in any business, when one fails, there is a short term problem for the people in the company, but the whole economy is better off, and those people in that position can get similar jobs in the new environment. He smiled at me, a gleam in his eye. *If he thought I was appealing to his particular circumstance, that if the government shrunk he could still find a job, it would fit his knowing glance perfectly.* It is not that when we see problems with big agro we shut it down, and now we have no food and everybody starves. The way out is building the alternative. He smiled. “I’m in,” he said reassuringly. He said he was really excited about Bitcoin when it first came out. If only he had invested a little more in it. I didn’t think there would have been any way to predict the current prices. He noted the recent talk saying it could all collapse come August. I said it was a good thing Bitcoin was going through all of this early on. We wouldn’t want to all get enthralled with this new technology, get dependent on it, and then all suffer the problems or collapse together. We needed to give it harsh treatment in the beginning to work out all the bugs. If it doesn't work, maybe some other crypto currency will.

He insisted on buying me food, despite the fact I repeatedly declined. I sat there and didn’t eat. *First attempt at collecting biometrics.* I was trying to understand why he was so afraid of mesh networks. Is he a cop? I just sat there. He asked me a few questions, like if I had considered living in Boston. I had not, since after searching I found Bensonwood. It was too perfect, so I had to try it. He said I was still young, and thought, I suppose, that I’m just all kinds of malleable. I said I had always lived in small towns, so I didn’t think of living in a big city. Perhaps if I made enough money. He asked if I had any. He ate quietly for a moment, and then told me personal things about his life--his mother dying of cancer and working on her estate. I ate nothing, but he still had me carry the bowl. The unschooling class was coming up. I told him a little about where I used to work, and why I left. “Sounds like the last straw.” He sounded uninterested.

The lecture was very good, but I felt stressed. I wasn’t sure of him. I took only a few notes. Then I resolved to ask him directly about his attitudes. After the lecture, he was about to head away. I asked him, and he said he was just being very pessimistic about the possible success. He seemed bothered. Concerned. *I think there were moments he wasn't happy he turned me in. I don't think he would have if he thought it was his choice. He seemed to see me as a possible serious girlfriend. -2/13/20* I told him about Elon Musk's "anti-motivational" video that I love, about how even if the odds of success are very low, if it is important, you still have to try, and that fatalism can be helpful. He told me Elon Musk took a bunch of money from the government. *He seemed eager to try to discourage me. His method was to smear the character of the person I admired. -2/13/20* I said Musk wasn't an anarchist, just an environmentalist. "It's worth trying." I encouraged. He still didn't seem to like the idea. We went for a walk and talked more. I had wanted to hear the next lecture, but it wasn't a big deal.

This may have been when we went to a certain table. I don't remember if this was Friday or Saturday, but as it was getting dark, I was walking with Brian, and he said there was a table he wanted to check out that had beer. We looked for the number. It was the table of a group I knew. As we approached, a leader stepped away in some sort of turmoil, sipping his beer. Brian started acting like a car salesman, telling me about their organization's new vision and what they are doing, and directing the man sitting at the picnic table to tell me more about it. He complied. I listened and then walked away with Brian. Apparently, this organization was taken over and is now a trap for activists. The leader's expression suggested to me he was horrified at someone being led to his table. I remember the organization was good and effective, and then I heard about them less, and now apparently, they have changed their tactics. I shouldn't have to point out what an anathema to America it would be for the FBI or other agency to be running a political organization. -2/13/20

At the main pavilion, the bald man I had spoken to this morning who called himself Smith was sitting behind me. We were towards the back. Brian had his arms crossed, and his sock-covered feet propped up on the chair in front of him. *This was a dramatically different demeanor. He was putting on swagger.* There was a man there who took my picture against my will. *Redacted* I later learned was his name. I held my notebook up over my face, but he insisted I put it down and look forward so he could get a "profile shot." His words. I said no thanks, but he insisted. Brian reassured me it was okay, and that this was the guy who gave the talk he liked. I still didn't comply and tucked my head down. He just ducked his camera and took the picture anyway, and said he wouldn't bother me anymore, showing the disgusting picture he took. "That's horrible!" I told him. *The cameraman did something harassing although he clearly did not want to. He appeared to be a coerced informant. Considering he had been a Playboy photographer, it fits perfectly with the sexual predator nature of narcissists. This is another attempt at getting my biometrics.* Brian mocked, "Aw, do you feel like your privacy was invaded?" *He acted like he was trying to gin up sadistic excitement, being deliberately malicious. It was totally out of character from the sensitive thoughtful person I had been speaking with. -2/13/20* I told him I had seen that people who don't respect boundaries are not real libertarians, and it is telling of what kind of person they are. I told him I was irritated. That was disrespectful. And I know the way libertarians think. Privacy is very important to us. A guy came up to me afterward to say he saw what happened to me and thought it was terrible, and the worst thing he'd seen at Porcfest. I agreed emphatically. *Brian was scanning the environment as we spoke.*

I continued explaining to Brian as we walked away that I had received a lot of unwanted attention, and that there are many creeps who will take what they can get. As a girl, I have to be especially careful. I do that on purpose. He said some guys were just desperate to get a girlfriend. *Sympathetic with creeps?* We talked about loving dogs, and what it was like for me to lose them. Several times I had seen Brian walk up to some dog to pet it, even if it was out of the way. *I had been friendly with a dog at a neighboring tent early in Porcfest. Brian could have been associating himself with something I like to make himself more appealing to me. He also said something about kissing dogs on the mouth as we walked... -2/13/20* He said he was a vegan, and made me wait as he remembered some joke he heard about it. I ranted about how horrible the condition of narcissistic psychopath was, and how tragic abusive relationships were. He had some staple response about childhood trauma. His voice was flat and numb. *Perhaps he identified with my description.*

He asked if he could hold my hand, and then reached and grabbed it. I did not protest. I told him I liked him, that as my father would say, "gentleness is power under perfect control." He shot back with "nobody's perfect." *He admitted he was not characterized by gentility. If he was defensive, perhaps it is because his brutality is not well under his control.* I let him know I wasn't looking for a relationship. Christians were not allowed to have binding relationships with non-believers, because it would pull us in different directions. And if we had kids, I would not want them to go to hell, and he would not want to abuse them by telling them there was a hell. I joked we might as well start naming them. He thought it was a little premature, since we were just hand holding. "You can never start too early."

He noted I was guarded. I told him I know that about myself. He would be surprised to see me in other contexts. I find him really easy to talk to. I told him the story of two boys who came to my church asking hard questions to cause trouble, and how I had so much fun answering them. But other people in the church became contentious with each other and debate was banned. I felt I was not allowed to voice dissent, and became afraid of offending.

Later in the conversation, he made a statement about cops, and I responded with "Protect and serve themselves." He turned away upset. We chatted about the corrupt prison system. I said with how many people were in prison it was like a gulag. He brushed it off, saying it wasn't as bad as Hitler. *Libertarians don't approve of jailing people for as many things as the government does. His dismissal of that is jarringly callous.* He said he had a friend who was a prosecutor, and he was wondering if he should even be friends with people who do such terrible things. I brought up an article I had read where someone had a job as a prosecutor, defense attorney, and judge, and in each job, he was so convinced that if only his profession had more power, everything would be better. *Once again, he is not directly saying what he is really saying. He seemed to be worried that I would not be friends with him if he was a cop and does so many terrible things, but said it in such a way he did not admit to being a cop.*

After that it was the Soap Box Auditions. He handed me his notebook and headed to the bathroom. When he came back he was worried as he took his notebook and studied my face. *It was an opportunity to collect my fingerprints.* Brian kept trying to force feed me all kinds of things. I told him no, but he even said, "You have to!" *DNA. Also, why else would he yell at me that I "had" to eat something he gave me unless he was getting biometrics?* He brought some almond milk, unsealed it in front of me, and poured some out for me. I later asked him why he did that and he said he just thought I should feel like I was welcome to eat something. *That's not a good enough reason to be so determined. The almond milk was vegan and non-allergenic, so I couldn't object on those grounds, and he unsealed it in front of me so I couldn't say he put something in it. He was eliminating excuses I could give for why I wouldn't want to eat or drink.* I poured it above my mouth to drink some. He later asked me which can I was eating out of, and I told him the beef ravioli.

After the festivities were over, he put the notebook in his trunk. *He paused for a moment when he turned to me, nervous, and asked me "What?"* I walked us over to a well-lit pavilion to talk more. He didn't like that. I went to sit down, and he said it was where he was sitting, so I went to the other side. I said he was trying to sit next to me. I told him about how I had early opinions on free will and culpability that I had formed myself, and how my mother had not objected. I explained that my parents were seekers too. I told him about when an elder at my church who was an FBI agent (Brian choked on a laugh) tried to get us excommunicated. *A very giant tell. FBI fits everything I had seen.* I told him I was almost excommunicated for being an open theist, which is not widely known or accepted. He was terribly uninterested. I said open theists tend to be very logical. *I was telling him this so he would know how to approach me–with reason.* My mom had said it was good that I polarized people, because it made them talk about things that were important. He smiled at that. He set his hand on the table for me to hold and I took it. I said that it was okay to do that. He put his other hand on my hand, then took it off, wondering exactly where the line was. He asked me why the Bible said it was wrong. As I began to explain the theology behind it, the Christian in charge of Liberty Ecclesia came through. Brian took his other hand off mine. "I have to answer for everything I do," I told him. "To God?" "Yes. I don't care what they think." He put his hand back.

By this time, he may have had one beer or less. -3/13/20 He wanted to go sit in the dark. I asked him what he was planning, and he said he wanted to kiss me. I said, "I love you, but I will hurt you." He insisted he wasn't going to force himself on me, and he wasn't into that sort of thing. That comment was totally void of disgust or tension. *It seemed he was totally not bothered by the thought.* I didn't want to go. I told him there was no chance that we were going to have a sexual relationship. He stood and tried to kiss me over the table, but I put my hand over his mouth. I told him he did not know me, and the farthest I had gone was to kiss a boy on the cheek when I was six. He was shocked and asked me how that was possible. "I was jaded and isolated as a teen, and then I was very independently minded and just didn't see myself with anyone." He said this could be special, and insisted he was not there to bed me and only wanted a kiss. *That was not at all the response I expected. He was only thinking about his own desires. Zero thought was given to my sexual life. This doesn't make sense for someone with empathy.* I asked if he only wanted a sexual relationship. I realized this was over, thanked him, and said that this had been a really good escape from "distractions." He perked up. He asked if I wanted to tell him what they were. "No, I'm going to make you wonder forever." I laughed. *I kept the mood light, but was ending the night.* He seemed terribly curious about it and I then reluctantly went to hug him goodbye. As I did, he said "Well, maybe just-" and tried to kiss my neck. I pushed him away, and wagged my finger at him jokingly, chastising him for not being in the moment and looking for the next thing. He said he'd settle for a hug now, but I was done. No more touching.

I started to walk away and he followed. He seemed upbeat and persistent. He asked to hold my hand. "We're not together." He wanted us to walk past the lit tent, and I stopped on the other side. We started to say our goodbyes. He threw in a comment about how my libertarian ideals didn't match with my religion. I gave some adequate response. "Of course it wouldn't be that easy," he said to himself. I was looking forward to reading his papers. He recommended I start thinking of names for our kids. *Given that I had just told him we were not together, it is curious he was thinking that way. It is also interesting that the fact he had just been collecting my biometrics was no impediment to him trying to kiss me.* He leaned in to whisper in my ear and I stepped back in caution. "Looks like I'm really in the dog house." He told me I looked beautiful in this light, like the actress from The Truman Show, using her name. I said goodbye, and he said that we should rather say farewell. He walked away jovially. He sent me an email afterwards:

* * *

Hi Sharon,

I wanted to apologize for being pushy last night. I hope that my behavior wasn't too uncomfortable for you. Obviously, there are a lot of differences between us (in belief, age, location) that could make a serious relationship challenging or problematic. I'm sorry I didn't have more of a friendship orientation last night, which is what I think you were asking and hoping for. Perhaps we can stay in touch as friends going forward.

I was going to apologize in person this morning. I actually came by the campground and started to walk up the hill a bit after 9 a.m. But I saw you in "The Tent" and didn't want to interrupt or create any weirdness, so I figured I'd just send you this email instead.

And as long as I'm apologizing, I'm sorry I wasn't more sensitive to how you were feeling when *redacted* (I think that's his name) was taking pictures. I guess I was trying to be playful, but he was being intrusive and it was clearly an uncomfortable situation for you, and I should have taken that more seriously. Of course, you have every right to not be photographed.

Actually~this is rather mind blowing~I just searched "*redacted*" to make sure I had his name right, and I saw some links saying he was accused of sexual assault in *redacted*. Here are the two main links that dealt with that: ... *My comment: I saw he used to be a Playboy photographer.*

I have no idea what the truth is in that situation, and I do believe it is too easy for questionable accusations to take on a life of their own, but who knows. In any case, I'm sending you these links so you can see them. I also see that *redacted* was interviewed on *redacted*, and perhaps *redacted* asked him about this issue. *A backhanded way to say I shouldn't make comments about what he did?*

I was thinking more about your comment last night that you have a lot of inner distractions from the past and present. I got the sense that you might be referring to something very troublesome and serious, something that is really weighing on you and causing you a lot of inner suffering. I may be going completely in the wrong direction with this, but just on the chance that it might possibly be helpful, I was wondering if you were referring to some kind of abuse, sexual or otherwise, which is all too common. (Out of a rather small pool of women that I've ever discussed such things with, I was amazed to learn that three were sexually abused, two of them over a period of years, by their fathers.) If anything of that nature applies, and if you're looking for reading suggestions that might be useful, I can recommend some books. I spent a lot of time reading on trauma, and I came across some that are really fine and helpful (though I'm sure there are other good things out there, too). Of course, I'm willing to talk and brainstorm, as well, if that would help you come up with approaches to whatever you might be dealing with internally.

Childhood traumas could be considered a psychological vulnerability to exploit. As should become clearer later on, a harassment or coercion campaign involves trying to get the target to admit to or show emotional distress. Distress as it relates to sexuality seems to be of particular interest to some.

At the very least, I want to say that I hope you take seriously whatever is weighing on you--that you don't just "tough it out" and accept inner turmoil as an acceptable status quo but, rather, that you seek out any help you might need. You seem like an excellent person with a lot of fine qualities and you deserve to be happy... and sometimes finding happiness, or even just a modicum of inner peace, does not come by simply or by itself. I know this is true from my own experiences. I hope you don't mind my raising all this, which obviously pertains to very personal matters.

In any case, I hope you made it back to Boston okay, and that your move to NH goes very well. It was special meeting and hanging out with you.

Brian

P.S., when I said to you last night that you looked very pretty, and a lot like a young Laura Linney, I wasn't sure if you knew who Laura Linney is. Here are some photos of her, spanning a number of years (and probably decades): *She is the actress in the movie The Truman Show, where the main character is secretly and constantly recorded, and is surrounded by actors. People under surveillance may be for years or decades.*

* * *

I posted this to select family members on Facebook in October 2020. These are some of their responses:

My mother's comment: The only reference to me that I found is this: " My mom had said it was good that I polarized people because it made them talk about things that were important." I doubt I ever used the term "polarized" as I don't really know what is meant by it. However, bringing up controversial topics is a good thing... it does make people think. So, I believe replacing "polarizing" with "controversial" would be more accurate.

My mother's comment: I hope the final paragraphs do not imply that we believed in brutal punishments... it could be taken that way. I think our discipline was fair and edifying.

My comment: You said polarized. It was after I asked the *redacted* FBI agent at our church about his theology, and almost got the family kicked out of the church over it.

My mother's comment: I don't remember any FBI agent at church. Perhaps you could inbox me with that. I still don't think I said polarizing. I don't use that term... unless you used it first. Perhaps in the context of the conversation it would have made sense to me.

My comment: Other mentions of you were that there was spanking but it was supplemental, and I described the reasonableness of the punishments. Also, I said I had formed my own theological beliefs on free will and you had permitted it, because freedom of thought was a thing in our house. That is what I remember off the top of my head from this post.

My comment: I think that was around 20 years ago you used the word polarized...

My comment: The word was impressive to me and made me think.

My mother's comment: I thought it was my views that almost got us kicked out, not yours. ;P

My mother's comment: I remember you kids were told not to speak about your beliefs in Youth Group anymore, though.

Back story–I heard the FBI agent's wife say he worked for the FBI. He was my Sunday School teacher. I asked him a question about his theology and he said it would be better for him to talk to my parents about it. After disagreeing with them, he attempted to get us kicked out of the church, but the pastor didn't go for it. I was pretty young, between 10 and 12. -5/5/21

My mother's comment: *Redacted.* I doubt we were being recorded. I have no evidence of such.

My comment: I am not aware of being recorded, besides the open recordings that daddy did, at church.

My comment: The final paragraphs of *a paper that Andrews sent me* do not *paint punishment by parents as reasonable*. They describe the unrealistically brutal way *Brian* was characterizing parents in general. The fact he does so suggests to me the papers were less of a picture of parents in general, and more of either a specific group of abusive parents, or some other dynamic that is like an abusive child-parent relationship.

My mother's comment: *Redacted.* Oh, ok.

My dad's comment: It seems to me that the guy who tried to take your picture was a predator. He might have been trying to get you to eat something in order to give you a date-rape drug. Sounds like those two guys were friends and may have been working together. I'm glad you got out of there safely!

My comment: Interesting that the predator needed my "profile shot." That is a very specific kind of photograph that he was obviously taking. Besides the man who took my photo was somewhat famous. The man with me "Brian Andrews" told me he had seen him give a talk, and in an email tells me what his name was. He is pretty famous. He was a Playboy photographer and was suspected of sexual assault a long time ago. It would be pretty sloppy for someone that famous to get up in my face if he was trying to commit crimes against me, and also sloppy of his partner in crime to tell me his real name. Profile shot has to do with biometrics, and I can't imagine why some random creeps would need it. If "Andrews" was trying to give me a date rape drug, he was picking a rather hard target as someone who was so verbally opposed to eating, and he must have been pretty talented to put it in a sealed almond milk container which he was thoughtful enough to unseal in my presence. It is also curious that he bought me food from a vendor, which would have afforded him less opportunity to slip something in the food as I could see the vendor hand it over, unless they were working together. Are you committed to any explanation other than that they were undercover police collecting my biometrics?

My dad's comment: Why is it interesting that a predator would need a photo? I'm making an observation of one possible cause based on what you presented. I didn't positively assert that it was the cause or that there could not be a different cause. If he insisted on a photo, it could have been so that he could identify you to others. Sex traffickers do this. Did you not consider this?

My dad's comment: @me, Also, I didn't say that he did give you a drug or that the almond milk was drugged. Rather, that his efforts to get you to eat what he offers you might have been motivated by wanting to create opportunities to drug you. Just a speculation of a possible motive for being so insistent.

My mother's comment: Right. Lowering her resistance for future opportunities. Photos of headshots could also be photoshopped later onto someone else's body, for pornography, then used as blackmail. Of course, that is really assuming the very worst of someone I don't know, but he sounded quite suspicious.

My comment: "Brian Andrews" provided me with his name [pretty sure it is real] and the name of the photographer. It is still strange he needed a profile shot specifically, and strange he made such a scene. You would think that sex traffickers would pick easier targets in less visible places. I told "Andrews" I had been a manager. I wasn't acting like some lost needy vulnerable sexually available victim. I was independently minded, had strong family relationships, had a track record of success, and asserted boundaries. While their behavior is not totally dissimilar to sex traffickers in so far as they seem personally bent on sexual exploitation, their behavior is not consistent with criminals hiding and seeking vulnerable people. It is also strange that sex traffickers would be very afraid of the idea of Mesh Networks, and wonder how the cops could stop them, and warn me that they do very bad things to people who do that sort of thing.

My comment: *@mom*, The photograph he got was hideous. He showed it to me and said he wouldn't bother me anymore. If they wanted to blackmail me with porn they made off of pictures they took, it would be a lot smarter to not make it obvious they were taking those pictures, and giving me their identities. Blackmail is technically illegal, so it would have been easy for me to point my finger at the correct suspects.

My dad's comment: A few corrections: • He told me he had heard a really great talk on .... [Is that a title?] • He asked, with striking curiosity if I was a programmer. I don't him no, I wish. [??] • picnick [sp] • disguising [sp]

My comment: 1. I don't know, it was probably something like the title. 2. Why would he care if I was a programmer? I got the impression from that and later instances that they really wanted to recruit programmers, that hacking was a valuable skill. Otherwise, I'm not sure why he was so interested in that. The way he said it was kind of put on and forced.3. ...4. Thank you.

2

INFORMANTS ATTACK THE FREE STATE PROJECT?

M*y first week at work in New Hampshire.* When I got to work, a girl said she was thinking about taking a second fulltime job at Planet Fitness. I perked up and said I had just been checking them out. She also said something might "happen" to her Honda, but hey, she can always get another one, and she gave me a hateful glare. I drove a Honda at the time. She really didn't like me. Another man started working for the same company through the same staffing agency that I was, around the same time that I did. He always stood behind me during morning meetings. Everyone else was usually in a circle. He liked to suck up to the supervisor. One time he got called out for brownnosing, and he replied, "You've got to get it from somewhere." He was a bit narcissistic. After a conversation I had with someone else mentioning four Virginian cities, he came up to me and told me he travels sometimes for his work, and named the same four cities I did, although he struggled to remember the last one.

I moved to a house with other libertarians. I thought it was strange the shower had a large mirror at the top angled down. While I was there I talked to some other tenants. One of them complained about his experiences with the libertarian community. The other, when I mentioned I liked to listen to Stefan Molyneux, jumped at the chance to tell me that he had spied on his wife's therapy patients in their home by listening through the vents. He said Stefan had become something of a Nazi. And the two described a time they saw him speak, how he was so full of himself. It seemed the tenant had a smear ready for someone who was influential to me. *Dave, who I will introduce next, I believe had previously been a tenant there. When I told him that the house was a good example of Free Staters succeeding, he got angry. -2/13/20*

I liked the people and the company, but the work didn't suit me and the pay was lower than what I could get elsewhere. I was texting a guy I used to work with about some of my problems at work, and he offered me a higher paying full-time permanent job, which, after consideration, I decided to take. This took me out of New Hampshire. When I decided to leave, there was a very strong effort from many people at my company, including people I barely spoke with, to find out where I was going. The older man I liked to talk to asked me directly, and when I said I wasn't going to answer, he said he hoped I would answer before I leave.

I attended a libertarian meetup. I was nervous. Liam asked me a few questions, which made me more nervous. One guy with silver hair who seemed very interested in Bitcoin as an investment asked me what the Free State Project was. When I began to explain it, he seemed disturbed, and told me I might be wasting my life. He asked me if I had any friends up here. I said no, and he said I really seemed to care. Another guy sat next to me. Dave. I asked him a few questions. He is a Buddhist. He came to town out of interest in Bitcoin. He believes it can do some good for the world, because it can't be inflated. I agreed, and said I didn't think there had been a time in human history in which people could interact on a platform where harming each other was mathematically impossible. This was his thought as well. Then he said that phones could be hacked in fifteen seconds. Even though the platform was secure, maybe someone is waiting for enough people to buy in, and they have already hacked a bunch of phones. They are going to steal the Bitcoin all at the same time. I countered that there is a demand for privacy, so perhaps some defense would be developed. *His eyes flashed, and he seemed inwardly shocked and upset by my answer. It seemed to me he expected to dissuade me with that comment, and hoped I would be.*

Dave asked what I liked to do for work or fun. I said I was trying new things. I was here to look into the Free State Project and Bensonwood, and told him about what timber framing is. I really love timber frame, Japanese and French Tudor. He said he spent some time in a tea house doing tea ceremonies. I said how much I loved how tea houses were built. You didn't have to put decorations over crap. The construction was the decoration. It was being in a space that had purpose and intention, and that really changed the atmosphere. I said they want to prefab houses the way cars are made. He asked about the cost. I told him right now, Bensonwood is trying to make their houses cheaper to reach the masses. He asked what role I would take. I told him I did CNC. I asked about his future plans. He is considering leaving town. He might go somewhere drier, and practice being a monk-like person more seriously.

We were interrupted by others. When I was leaving, Dave asked if he could walk with me for a bit. I asked him about what the situation was with the Free State Project there. He said it is basically what I just saw. Those Bitcoin meetings are about all that happens. He said there is a bit of cop blocking. I listed some of the other activism, like robinhooding, 420, chalking the sidewalk. He said most of that has stopped. He moved to the Free State, but after that, there wasn't anything else to do. I asked about the rumors that people were not really listening to the community they were reaching out to, but beating them over the head with information. He agreed, but did note that there is better outreach with Bitcoin. I noted that the early movers were often unattached young men in jobs that were easy to transition to, like tech jobs, and tended to be the more obnoxious type. There wasn't really any way for the libertarians to police their own to control their narrative. He said he had fulfilled his duty just by moving, and I reminded him that Free Staters are supposed to expend the utmost practical effort to create a government that only protects life and property. He told me he believed freedom was really about realizing that everyone has their own morality--libertarian, statist, or whatever. That is just their subjective beliefs, and freedom was to not be influenced by things that can be changed, external states of what is happening with the government. Freedom is when you can be put in jail, and your mental state does not change. It is hard to get and maintain this stoic indifference. I said he just described Buddhism, and that it was to be without passion. He said some allow compassion, to encourage others to pursue this detachment, and they can keep being reincarnated to try to alleviate the suffering of others. In that way it allows for activism. He was walking me to a place that looked like apartments, so I changed directions.

I said I was not a Buddhist. I believed people were eternal, and had value. If there was an injustice in the temporal world, it was still wrong, because it was against someone that mattered, and I shouldn't be indifferent to it. Murder, theft, rape, and fraud will always be there to some degree, but it is a good thing to try to create conditions that don't promote those things. He asked me how justice would be enforced. I told him about how common law was created. He asked if that had to do with the Magna Carta. I told him no, I think was Charles the 1st being forced by his citizens to give them some rights. Common law was well before. When people would have disputes with each other, they would ask someone they both respected in the community to arbitrate, and they would agree to abide by this person's ruling. When that ruling was published, everyone else could decide if they liked it, and could choose to use this person's arbitration services in the future. No one could know if they might be accused or accuser, so there was a natural incentive to choose someone who would give equitable rulings. So the law that emerged was chosen by the free market, and was very equal, and that is common law. I told him about a chapter in Rothbard's book A New Liberty which explains how some other of these systems worked, like an ancient Irish one. Then I explained how the king wanted to get into the justice business, and required anyone who wanted to have a case heard to go through his courts with his judges, and pay him something. People didn't want to do that, because the king was coming in with his own interests that were not the interests of the parties involved. They tried to continue outside of it, but he enforced it. He set up Reeves of the Shire, which became the Sheriffs. Fast forward, the Puritans were harassing people for all kinds of petty moralistic reasons. People got sick of it and disbanded the police forces and only left the Sheriffs with arresting power. If he wanted to arrest someone, he would have to find enough people in the community who thought it was important enough to get off their butts and risk their lives and go catch that person. And if he couldn't, he would have to go catch the person himself. That was the system that was brought to America. They didn't go all the way back to common law. Sheriffs are a constitutional office. We didn't have organized police forces for the first 60 years. They would have been considered a standing army in the early understanding of the constitution. Then you have places like Dubai which instituted common law in an area otherwise controlled by Sharia law. They have become fabulously wealthy off of that. I told Dave that this was my view, and why I am not a Buddhist. He smiled brightly and said it was a good view.

He thought it would not be scalable. I suggested maybe as Ethereum brings contracts into their exchanges, maybe there would be some fuzzy areas in those contracts and people would like an arbiter to review them. And people could use Cell 411 if they know someone they trust who knows them, their house, and their dog, to come clear their house if they were worried. Dave said he doesn't use Cell 411 for anything. I said neither do I, but it is just a way to pre-record an alert and send it out to a predetermined group. So you have to find the people you want to organize that with. He said he would still rather call the police if his house was broken into. I said then he has a community problem. He mused to himself that it wasn't a technology problem, it was a people problem. He said he doesn't get out and meet people. He stays by himself. He likes to fly under the radar. People don't even know where he lives. *He may have been describing me to some extent.* He supposed he would still need people. I said you always need people unless you can go out in the woods and build a mud hut and start a fire.

I told him what I would do if I were him is I would sell consultations to people to teach them how to use Bitcoin. You have all these people who are techies and all these people who

don't know anything about it. I suggested going to the library and teaching workshops to the community. I explained that the people who were effective and staying were renting rooms or running a vending machine. They were making money off of what they do, so if you want to spread the knowledge of Bitcoin, it should be profitable. One person could teach twenty people what it is, how to download a wallet, and how to get started. You could make $200 that hour, and then there are twenty people walking around who use it. The merchants who use Bitcoin would want to encourage this as well. He said his outreach has been mostly to the vendors, but I said it needs to be both, because you've got to have people who would like to use Bitcoin at these places. I get up to leave, and ask him if he has any more questions or curiosities. He says he is wondering where I am going. I say it is a secret. "A secret place." "No, it's not a secret place." He asks if it is Washington DC, but then says he could ask all day but won't. *Before we parted ways, he blurted something out, which seemed to be pressing on him. He said "Just don't care about anything." Looking back, it is clear what he meant. In a harassment campaign, stress responses you give are used like official permission to continue hitting that nerve. This means you are threatened in apparently any way possible, even ways that fall under the legal definition of torture. This is why people practice indifference. But the effect is they are psychologically reconditioning themselves into blank slates. -2/14/20*
He said our paths may cross again. Life takes many turns. I shook his hand and he thanked me.

Once again, I came 10 minutes fashionably late. I don't know when I got to be so fashionable. Dave waved to me. The Libertarian Party president looked very nervous to see me. I sat across from him. He said I looked familiar, and I told him I had been to Porcfest and attended his panel. He and his wife told me silly stories of their move and asked me the basics, where I worked, what my plans were. They had to leave. Next to them were Liam and his friend Jay. They both deliberately and abruptly got up and sat one chair over to be across from me. Liam asked me pointed questions about what sort of work I did. He said that there weren't a lot of people at Porcfest, and like any movement, it seemed to have peaked. There wasn't as much attention on it. He mentioned considering going to a civil disobedience rally, talked to Jay about his upcoming hearing where he faces a year in jail for contempt of cop, basically nothing, and the Free Stater who was just killed in a car accident. His conversation was intentional, but directed to what end? Was he trying to scare me away? Was he testing my resolve? Seeing what kind of trouble I would be? He asked me what kind of activism I was interested in. I told him I was interested in something like Agorism, but not the civil disobedience that these guys did. Jay got very defensive at that. His accusations were unfounded I added. I explained how I was interested in developing alternatives to government in the way that homeschooling is an alternative to public school, but as I was in manufacturing and construction that is where I would be focusing. He asked me if I was planning on building a tiny home in New Hampshire. I said I might, a little surprised, and asked how it was around here building tiny homes. He said he didn't know, but that he knew many people were interested, including one name he gave me. Liam had to run. He seemed like a curious figure to me. Calm in the face of calamity to the point it made me wonder if he was suspiciously immune or just realistic and determined. I have heard he didn't do a good job of listening to the other side. I saw no evidence of that in this conversation. He later messaged me on the forum letting me know of local manufacturing companies that are hiring. His quick response made me think he would welcome my involvement.

After he and a few others left I sat next to Dave, who was conversing with a computer geek named Don. Don is the most classically geek person you could meet. He clammed up when I came over, perhaps shy around girls? I asked encouraging questions on his recommendations of android operating systems and good privacy apps. Jay seemed reluctant to help me when I asked him. He mocked Dave when he didn't know that IRC stood for Internet relay chat. They didn't know anything about Ethercoin, but Dave did, and explained their strategies for dealing with scalability. Don explained to me something I didn't know, that the cell card intertwined with the CPU meant it could be tracked even without the SIM card. I asked about theoretical ways that could be changed. Jay told me about some possibilities, to which Dave goaded him, speculating he had something like that in the works. *Dave acted like he was sadistically toying with him.* This seemed to bother Jay and he took a much more defensive stance. *He looked shocked and nauseous. He crossed his arms, and didn't want to talk much afterwards. Don looked at Jay very sympathetically. I remembered after the first time I spoke with Dave, he had seemed to imply he was not welcomed here -2/13/20* The geeks were not extremely forthcoming with me anymore. "There is nothing to do here," Dave bemoaned to me as I searched out their activities. Dave watched me interact with interest. As we headed out he told me that I was a good conversationalist. "Really?" He noted how I asked questions and followed up. He said he wished there was something for the coming activists to do. "I will have to think about it and come up with some ideas." He gave me his email in case I wanted to catch up with him later. I asked if he was going to stay in town. He said his days in town were numbered. He told me he was ready for a new chapter in his life. I told him to make it a good one and perhaps I would see him again. I walked off to my car. I did not go to the meetings the next week. I was too busy preparing to move.

3

HARASSMENT AND ENTRAPMENT AT WORK

Maryland, September to December 2017. I took a few relevant snippets from my daily journal during this job. I have not added many of my own perceptions of the events. My insight grows as I look back. The flagrant and absurdly poor customer service, everything breaking, and the pressure to violate the rules are all typical forms of harassment and entrapment that occur later on in ways that are difficult to explain other than by a powerful, persistent, and widespread harassment campaign.

Friday, September 1st. Ace told me I would never be the engineer that he is, but I had some skills that would be very useful. *This is not the way he used to talk. Not that he would say that I would be his equal, but he thought I would be amazing at engineering school because I was so diligent. That was a genuine reflection of his, not trying to butter me up. -2/14/20*

Ace uninstalled the security software on my computer, telling me that these were so obviously backdoors for malware. That seemed.... Yeah. Then he wants me to print a file from my email, so he tells me to log into my email on said computer. I kind of freaked out, and tried to bring it up on my phone instead. He eventually realized what I was doing, called me weird, and told me to get it from his account...

Ace had also told me about the medical tests required, which if they are not taken you "can't keep people on." From what I can tell I don't have much of a problem with them. But he seems to be pushing at every turn. ...

I am supposed to be in charge of human resources documents, but I don't really know too much about it. 5 muchachos might be showing up tomorrow, and I have to lead them through the whole deal. ...

Ace said we were also in a target-rich environment, surrounded by all these high value government entities, and that the bridge was a strategic target. I thought it was more decorative, but he insisted it was an important artery.

Thursday, September 7th. ... At the clinic we waited for three hours. Ace texted me to make sure I was okay and to get a status update. The clinic basically told me to sign saying they could do whatever they wanted to me and tell whoever they wanted about it. I studied Spanish a little while I waited. The tests were simple and interesting. Weight, height, color, peripheral vision, blood pressure, audiogram, blowing into a tube to test the lungs, blood, physical, and drug tests. I was pretty calm and in charge throughout the whole thing. The respiratory questionnaire had a few points I didn't fully answer. That doctor was phoning it in. My co-worker came out a while later. On the drive back we spoke more comfortably in the tiny bit of Spanish I knew about how crazy and stupid it was that it took 8 hours to do that. ...

Friday, September 8th. ... I couldn't hear them at all through my MagicJack number, which is a piece of crap. ...

After that, I asked Alex about the parking permits. I didn't feel too confident in what Ace was having me do. It sounds a little sketchy, and I don't want to do anything illegal, so I thought I'd investigate while he was away. Alex didn't know. He said Ace had done all that. He called Ace to ask him, even though Ace had already told me pretty clearly that I was to wait till we got a lot of people at once before we initiated the cumbersome practice. I was cringing, wondering what I was going to do. I didn't think Ace would be too happy. When he asked if this was for my car, I told Alex I wanted to "understand the process," which is true, as it is part of the HR process I am to guide people through. Alex told me Ace would show me Monday. Right after he hangs up, I get a call. It was Ace, my boss. "How about instead of worrying about parking permits you finish the daily report?" ...

Tuesday, September 12th. ... Alex told me that we were getting a lot of employees from two particular companies. *His face was in shock as he spoke.* I wondered if they hadn't just finished a job. He said one of them was being investigated by the FBI for bribery. They were allegedly paying their inspectors to get away with shoddy work. "So we should be nice to the inspectors but not too nice." Alex said he had been told if they call, don't even talk to them. Have nothing to do with them. That is how serious it is. He was thinking of mentioning it in the meeting today. ...

Alex made small talk with me on the way back to the office, telling me he paces when he is on the phone so Ace makes him go outside. *Perhaps a way to stay away from me. ...*

So Ace emails me and points out I screwed up one of my morning emails. I attached the wrong file. And I tried so hard this morning to not screw up. It seems like every single email I send out is screwed up in some way. Labor hours are missing, or I referenced the wrong day. The same name appears twice on the daily sign in sheet. I gave a co-worker my two hours I worked on Saturday. The file was not attached. Etc., etc., etc. And these are not hard tasks. (It may or may not have really been my fault.) Javier texted me a 'gracias' for helping him with the clinic. He kept texting, getting more flirtatious. Invasive even, trying to find out where I live. I was trying to look through the papers he returned. I was noticing errors. Many. Then I saw his Permanent Residency card had been expired. I texted this to Ace. He said we would talk in the morning. I was done for the day. I texted Javier "La officina no esta abra." He sent me kissing emojis. ...

Wednesday, September 13th. Fortunately, I was so worried about other things, I didn't really care that I had to deal with Javier alone in the office. ...

Thursday, September 14th. ... Ace even mentioned that when we set up a company it would be in my name so it would be woman owned and get the minority benefit. This was after saying he would never go into business with his wife. ...

I got a phone call today asking for donations to breast cancer research. I just gave two dollars to a lady at the store for something like that. Cash. I didn't tell anyone. How the heck did they know?

Monday, September 18th. ... Carson said they might tow your vehicle if you didn't have a hanger for parking. I thought I might get a temporary one, but Ace yelled at me to just use the other one...

Monday, September 25th. Upon entering, Ace asked me how my home town was... After they left Ace decided he wanted to talk about Trump and how people hate him and were outright saying some brutal things you don't usually hear hurled towards the president... He joked that I might assassinate president Trump. That was in bad taste. *While visiting my parents over the weekend, I had been talking with my sister using very cutting political language about Trump. Ace was acting shocked and trying to appeal to me. It was pretty clear he had heard or at least heard of my conversation.*

Tuesday, September 26th. ... It seems like most of the time I've been here I've been alone. Are they avoiding me? Did Ace give me these impossible tasks because he needed to start creating reasons to fire me? ...

What was not easy, and turned out to be impossible for me, were the constraints on a computer software program called AutoCAD. I spent hours trying things, watching tutorial videos. I just had a slew of pieces hanging in random places that I couldn't put in a line. *Ace had asked me to use the software. Since then, I literally took a college and online course to learn it. It isn't something that can be done without training. ...*

Ace showed up around lunch time, gently showing me how to get dimensions off of drawings, telling me he feels he left me out to swim with these projects. He just assumed I knew how to do these things like he does. *Alex had come by briefly to see what I was doing earlier in the yard, but Ace seemed to be aware of my frustration with AutoCAD. I remember Ace saying "You've beaten me AutoCAD." It was as if he was aware of how things went in the office while I was alone, and was implying he had the same frustration, trying to make me feel better. As I recall, his laptop webcam was facing me. -2/14/20*

Wednesday, September 27th. ... He said he had told his grandmother what to get for him though. Hint hint? He has a tool in mind he wants me to ask him about? *When I was with my family a few days ago I was talking with my brother, very concerned about what I could get Ace for his gift, since he has such particular and expensive tastes -2/14/20 ...*

Ace told me about the inspectors and how we are supposed to provide things for them in the contract. Maria had emailed me asking me for some supplies for the inspectors. I wasn't sure what to say, since I didn't know if that was bribery or if it was permitted in the contract. Ace was telling me about the first project manager Reynold who was messing with Alex in the beginning, telling him he bought the inspectors the wrong things because they were not up to the specifications of the contract. Ace told me Reynold died like two weeks after he took the job. That was kind of... What happened there? *One could take this as a hint not to worry too much about following the contract or avoiding bribery.*

Friday, September 29th. ... *That evening I was in my parent's house talking to my father.* I said Ace isn't patient with people's faults. He doesn't work through things with people. So it has put me in a position of not being well equipped for what I am doing. And the people in my company don't know my qualities, so they were looking at me like, "Why are you ruining everything?"

Monday, October 2nd. ... This morning Ace didn't run away. He walked me through the daily report, even taking me outside to look at the equipment to make sure our information was updated, and explained some car terms to me. He pointed out I ordered the wrong type of lanyard and started explaining lanyards to me. He showed me a booklet he printed out from the manufacturer of cable and said reading these things is what puts him ahead of everyone else. *I was just talking to my father about how Ace wasn't patient with faults. His demeanor changed dramatically to accommodate my concern to my father. He did not keep up the change for long.*

... But Ace chided her again, and when I smiled, he said he liked to go off, only to himself, but would be more diplomatic directly to her. *I was diplomatic at work, and didn't dump my concerns on them like I had at home. Ace would often mirror me to be friendly. This is another time it seemed he heard what I said at my parent's house.*

I started Jujitsu during October. John Schmitt was very fearful of me. His son left the class soon after I came on allegedly due to an injury and illness, but they later returned. -2/14/20

Tuesday, October 10th. ... Drew, Ace's superior, came in to ask about notes from a monthly meeting. He said he didn't get the email. I tried to search Ace's email. My computer was so slow it wouldn't work. I got some details from him, and he said he wanted to see it before tomorrow. Then he gave me another task. He had to log on to something and wanted me to download a ton of responses into the shared file. The problem was they wouldn't load. "See what you can do." Ok. So I search around and there is no sign of the meeting he is talking about. I text Ace. He says there wasn't any meeting at that time. Hmm... The files aren't loading. I search the Internet for answers. There are a few. They don't work. Apparently Chrome eats PDFs for breakfast. So I'll need to get Drew to log in to a different browser. I don't want to disturb him... I find the meeting referenced in some schedule notifications, but no minutes. Randy is the one who sent them. Should I email him? That would take too long. Call? I don't want to disturb Drew. I decide the best thing for me to do is go knocking on trailer doors to ask if I can have a copy of the meeting notes. I go to the trailer next to mine. It looks empty, but someone calls from a back room. When I get there it is Carson. I let him know I need the meeting minutes, and he happens to have them on his desk. ...

I got the minutes and triumphantly handed them to Drew. He said he wanted it scanned. Ok. The scanner is no longer connecting to my computer. Hmm... I'll just... scan it to a USB stick and move it over. Perfect. And I'll email a copy to Drew. Funny, that's an awfully short document. Looks like it is actually two pages. So I scan each page individually on both sides and then combine them online.

Wednesday, October 11th. ... After that, everything broke. The printer broke, the toilet ran out of water. I was in a bit of a panic. Ace asked me if I found those d-rings, and I told him no. I hope it wasn't obvious to him and everyone how stressed I was. ...

A UPS man stopped by and told me he had given me nine packages. "It says ten packages." "Yeah, ten." I signed, as I was in the middle of a forklift operation. When I did get to the office, it was nine. ...

I believe it was the evening of October 11th or 12th that I did an online search for Brian Andrews. I had just agreed to meet with Ace socially. Even though there was no "romantic expectation" in that agreement, that flipped a switch in me. There was a finality that I was choosing one and losing the other. It had been hard for me to not contact Brian again, and I very much missed him at that point. I searched online, and then I cried. On October 13th, the next morning, Javier continued his strange habit of asking me if I was okay when he clocked in, but this time it was totally different. His voice was tender, sorrowful, and compassionate. During work, Ace deliberately and delicately brought up the subject of health insurance. He gently asked me if I had any, and said I didn't have to answer. He talked about when open enrollment was, and what sort of thoughts on it I had, and said his sister would be researching it. This seemed not like Ace to prioritize pushing me to get health insurance, although I had twice talked about health insurance with Ace before. He had recommended I get it from our previous company, and had asked a follow up question if I would. This was not totally out of character for him, but I got the sense he was not bringing me his own concern. This at the time seemed to be Brian Andrews's first wish he wanted to express to me, as we will see again with the HONYs. Given that I had been crying after doing a search for Brian, it may very well have been that he got the impression there was something here for him, and decided to pursue it. -2/14/20

Thursday, October 12th. ... So I go back, and Ace comes in and tells me he tried to call me again and texted me and I didn't answer, and that is like the third time this has happened. My phone is rather flaky for some reason. ...

Ace mentioned he wanted to hire someone who was smart and knew how to build things, like this guy who used to work for him. At the moment he was using me as an engineering assistant.

Friday, October 13th. ... I created a separate daily report for something ridiculous that happened and told them I wasn't putting it on the shared file. Ace told me I was writing it for my soap opera. *I had said a number of things in my journal Ace would have not been happy with in the last few days. He seemed happy with his comment. -2/15/20* ...

During my get-together with Ace, he asked about me. I said my life was complicated and there was a lot of conflict. I asked him if he wanted to walk. He did not. I said it helps me to work out the stress, if he hadn't noticed. He said maybe what I need is not what I think I need. Maybe instead of giving in to those feelings, when I'm wired to move quickly, maybe I need to unwind. I didn't know. *Also, there was some guy sitting on the bench across from us who seemed to be listening...* He wondered what I had been doing between the ages of 20 and 25. I told him raising my niece... so I was her main caregiver. He asked if this was my brother's child, and where she lives now. *I used to be very low key, and there isn't much of a paper trail of my life. The way Ace asked about it, and about my niece, it was like it could be confirmed with her what I had done during those years.* ... He asked me about my personal goals, like where to live? I told him about how I wanted to simplify my living, to make it as adaptable as possible, and to make it cost as little as possible so I could stop working. He asked if I wanted to stop working. No, but I want to work to build what I want, not to eat. I briefly explained food, shelter, energy, and all these things should be simplified and made lean. I said like a tiny house. ... He wondered how long that would take me and what concrete action steps I had. I shook my head like I had none. ...

Wednesday, October 18th. Our two new guys showed up... They both had confident professional demeanors. Ace and others questioned them for some time about their experience. *They seemed to have a lot of experience. I asked them if they had their own fall protection. Enrique looked worried for a moment. Ace spoke up and smoothed things over. ...*

Ace had texted me something and told me I hadn't responded. We compared phones. I never got those messages.

Thursday, October 19th. I had another nightmare. It woke me up around 4:30. I don't usually have nightmares, but now I've had two in a row, and it has me wondering what is going on. The last one I was at my parents' house, and I was looking outside to the back yard, and it was crawling with mice and rats and all kinds of creatures that usually hide underneath. The basement level was fractured, windows broken, doors open. It was like the earth underneath us was being torn apart. I saw my dogs in my dream. Sandy could tell I was sad so she came and laid on me. I looked into Lady's face and thought to myself how sweet these dogs were, and how I should appreciate them while they are alive. Then I woke up and remembered they were gone. There was a strange sense of foreboding. Last night, we were out on the bay and someone had fallen in the water. A rescue helicopter was coming and lost control. The pilot fell into the bay, and the helicopter came crashing after him. The blades caught the back of his neck up into his skull and froze for a moment. He hung above the water for a moment, and then they started again and decapitated him. It was very violent and I had to look away. I almost never have nightmares. I wondered what was going on. Was I being affected by studying all of these safety emergencies? Was someone in danger? What was going to happen? ...

I wondered about the problems with the union, and suggested getting Legal Shield so we could get these questions answered. Ace knew what that was, but forbade me from getting it, saying he was my legal zoom and he knew everything. ...

Alex took it upon himself to help direct me and sort things out. He seemed shocked and frustrated to hear about a co-worker and Rodrigo and *redacted* and the union. Rodrigo, by the way, did not bring his documents again. I wondered how we were going to avoid pouring more money into someone who might not be legal. I suggested we send him to the union, since he lives close by and can pick up his ID there and we would know that he had it because he wouldn't be able to get through the union appointment without it. Alex and I pieced together what needed to be done, talked to *redacted*, and sent Rodrigo and Enrique to the union office. He sent me as well to take another...

Also, Rodrigo and Enrique never showed up. It was 1:30 pm when we left the union office, and I had told them that Santana would be out of the office at 2:30. ... Ace did seem shocked and puzzled that the two responsible boys we sent never showed up. ...

The two boys came back and said they had been to the union, but still did not have their documents. This is getting absurd. I ran through the paperwork with them. *I did not sign Rodrigo's I-9.* ...

Ace told Alex that it was strange how "correct" I had to be considering I was an anarchist. It was as if I acted like I liked the government.

Friday, October 20th. ... I tried to schedule an appointment for *redacted*, as he had to get that done pronto. The online portal for the health service I had set up wouldn't work. I tried to call Jeannie, and she wouldn't answer. I tried to call Molly, and she said she would forward my information to Jeannie and she had a conference call in ten minutes. So, after some time with no response, I looked up their customer service on their website, and was told there was no clinic in the city I had set it up for. The closest one is in DC. I said that can't be right. The lady thought it was. I was pretty shocked. How could there be no clinic? I searched the contract and my email for an address. Molly had told me verbally, and I had no record of it. I was getting a bit upset. Had she just cheated me and made a fool out of me to get my company to sign that contract? Where had the money really gone? I tried calling her back repeatedly, but she wouldn't answer. Her office number didn't even have an answering machine. ...

Ace comes back, surprised to see me still there. "You really are scared of the little green men going to jump out of the I-9 form and get you if you make a mistake." ...

Rodrigo and Sergio both allegedly presented valid IDs to someone.

Tuesday, October 24th. ... Marshal, the co-worker in charge of payroll, didn't even know who Enrique was, and I was asking him to pay the guy. I apologized, and decided to get on

Alex's case about getting it together. He was running everywhere, and thought maybe I should just fill out the I-9 form, like it was no big deal. ...

Ace said things worked better for him, because he goes with the flow. He doesn't resist so much and always fight things. (Unlike some people. Unlike me.) Alex had asked if I couldn't just fill out the I-9 form. Ace had explained to me directly but gently that this was one of those things where we had each other's backs, and if things ever went south between them, he wasn't going to worry about it. Yes, going against the flow does make things harder on me. But it is not a question of choosing the easy path, and I have long since learned that the flow of the universe is wrong sometimes, and that it is those who can see through the mass delusion and risk themselves are what define nobility. I could see that Ace was irritated too. He told me he hated it when people like Marshal made excuses why they couldn't get things done.

Wednesday, October 25th. ... But there is something off. When Ace explained to me today how to fix the thermostat, he said, "no one is going to trick you with this." Who would trick me with this? Why?

Friday, October 27th. ...Enrique came in to ask about the 401k. Crap. I told him I had called but would call our 401k liaison again. I pulled out the note and wrote notes based on what he said. He kind of smiled and told me no rush. ...

Ace comes back and tells me Javier has a bad attitude and isn't getting along with everyone in the crew. He tells me these local boys who aren't part of the main group are disposable to him. I don't look thrilled, but I don't say anything to him about it. He says he wasn't able to listen to me, but asks me if I was able to use any Spanish to get my points across, and whether they understood me, and if they were coming back here after going to *redacted*. These were all things I admitted I hadn't done very well. He asked me if any of them had started to flirt with me. I asked, "From today's crew?" "Anyone from the rigging crew?" I said I wasn't sure if I should tell him because I didn't want him to discriminate. He said he just thought it was funny. I showed him my conversation with Javier. He didn't really read it, but was shocked to see who it was, and just said that was a part of being in a male dominated workplace. Then he left again. ... He said he talked to Alex and Alex didn't want to work with Javier. And it had nothing to do with me, that it was just a random happenstance, so that's that. What's that? I looked at Ace as though he were transparent. Is he saying he fired Javier, or is going to? He was kind of laughing at the thought that he fired him because of me. Yeah, maybe that is laughable. But here and there he does seem to poke into who is flirting with me and how interested I am in response. Maybe I should just not tell him anymore. If he fired Javier I think I won't.

Sunday, October 29th. Ace wants to go have brunch. He wants me to drive to his place and drive together in his car. Hmm.... Alone together? Leave my car? After some thought I decide to go ahead. When I get there it is raining. I see Ace outside in his raincoat. He runs up to my car and gets in. "Are we taking my car?" "Yeah, I didn't feel like driving today. Plus I love these old Hondas." *My flash drive with I think my journal was on my keychain at the time. ...*

Ace is curious to know what I think about homeschooling since we've never talked about it. I tell him that the reason why people think public school is important is because of the academics, but homeschoolers outperform them by 30%. That is untrained laymen doing a better job. ... I explain that public schoolers are more cruel and shallow. Ace says that this helps to prepare them for the real world which can be cruel. But I think it causes some of the cruelty. I thought the kids got used to being controlled and institutionalized. Like ducklings following the wrong thing around, they get imprinted with the government, and think that this is where security and food comes from. ... Ace gently objected to homeschooling, pointing out life needs structure and kids should get used to that sort of thing. We got back in my car and headed back. I asked him if he wanted to know about something. *I told him a story from my childhood when I was told the FBI had been contacted.* Ace wondered when this was. *He seemed particularly curious, as though it may have relevance.* I had to think. How old was I? A young teenager? ... "Ok, so not recently." "Right."

Wednesday, November 1st. ... Ace actually called me again today to ask if I'd gotten paid correctly and if I'd gotten reimbursements. It is like he thinks my money is coming his way.

Thursday, November 2nd. ...I also complained about the non-response we were getting from our 401k provider. It was like a 'forget about it.' ...

When I mentioned legal services again, he had an interesting thought. He said if you resorted to that sort of thing, legal protection, you were inclined to bring that trouble on yourself, like bad karma. He suspects people who are obsessed with legalese of being litigious themselves. This is why he doesn't stay attached to his possessions and doesn't protect them. If someone steals it, maybe he should have given it away. Easy come, easy go. *It is as though he is repeating Dave's advice. It seemed to me Ace was trying to influence me so I would not act bothered and would accumulate money. As I have indicated before, he had a thought that I would go into business with him, and perhaps saw this as seed money. ...*

Tuesday, November 7th. ... Enrique asked me about the progress for the 401k paperwork. Great. I explained that they may be changing their plan soon so they didn't have an exact recommendation... but I do know we match 3%. I could see it on his face. He was incredulous. "I'm sorry." "It's no big deal," he told me. I couldn't look at him. I stood there silently, angry with myself. This was not good enough. Enrique and Rodrigo were great workers, and we keep screwing them over. But at least I had the next step I could show to Enrique. I put together Enrique' paperwork again, another set with what information I suggested he fill out or ignore, our evil 401k rep's phone number, the 3% matching, and the next form he would be filling out if he kept going. *At the time I had no idea I could be doing anything wrong, but looking back, giving financial advice without a license is legally dubious. -2/6/21*

Friday, November 10th. ... The rest of the day I continued to work on mass alerts. This involved researching quotes, being told hundreds of dollars a month, researching open source alternatives, trying to implement two different options, getting one app to freak out my phone and delete all of my text messages, and not really getting anywhere with the other. ...

On Facebook, probably on the 14th, I posted a picture of a shirt I really liked. It said, "Need new haters, the old ones are starting to like me."

Wednesday, November 15th. ... A delivery man came by, who said he had a sea container to drop off. I didn't know much about this. I vaguely remember them talking about it. It is a large thing, so he needs us to decide where to put it. I text Ace. No response. That is strange. I call him. He doesn't answer. I text Alex. No response. I call. No answer. Now what? I joke with the man that I am going to decide where to put it and they are just going to have to deal with it. He says he can stay longer if needed. He tells me he used to work around here when he was in his early twenties. I don't remember the name. ... They worked as defense contractors for the government. I recognized that he must be talking about where one of the main defense contractors was. He told me he would shoot missiles under the water, and by reading the waves he could tell where the missile was going to go. He said that was a fun job. Then, I think, he ran a construction business, but then his wife paid a lot of the bills, and then his kids started to move out. He was yammering on quite a bit. I wasn't catching all that much of it. But basically, he was looking for a job for retirement and wasn't married anymore, and decided to do truck driving. They were very impressed with him because he actually gets up in the morning. A lot of people don't do that these days. I said I'd met some truck drivers and there are lots of different kinds. He said his brother or cousin or someone works for the defense contractor? and has 3 houses, so he guesses he has the better job. "Truck driving is a good job," I tell him. *It was like he was recommending I work for the government, trying to recruit me.* He asks me if I like my job, and I say yes. He says he doesn't think he'd like a job like mine since I get so cooped up. He doesn't want to stay in one place for too long. I get through to Ace and he tells me where it should go, and then Alex calls and I tell him what Ace said and that there is something to sign, and Alex tells me I can sign that, and so I walk out with the man and show him where to put it. I said the container is pretty good. He says he can't even believe they sell that junk. They are selling all kinds of them, even with windows cut out, and that the wood cabins are going to go out of business. *Possible discouragement from going into building tiny houses.* He hands me the paper to sign. It says that by signing you agree to the terms on the back. I go to look at the back, and it is crammed. I suggest the man go set the containment down and come back for the paper. It was strange. It says they are selling it to us, but the agreement is for a lease, and it is extremely stringent and confusing. I do some digging online and find out that it can be dangerous to sign your name on behalf of a company, because they can deny that they wanted you to do that on their behalf and you could get stuck with the obligation. So I followed the instructions, and signed with the company name and put my job title there, so it was clear I was signing for the company. I gave the paper back. That seemed off. Alex came in, and told me I could scan and email then throw away or recycle the invoices I got. He left. *We saved our invoices in every other case. ...*

I get a call from Santos that the clinic says they don't have the tubes to do the test, that we were supposed to send them, and that they cannot do the tests. And he is hungry and tell Alex to buy them lunch. I do some calling. I don't have Lacey's number so I call Molly and let her know. No response. I call back and get the scoop. Molly isn't too happy. The package has not arrived yet. She'll have Lacey call me ...?

Thursday, November 16th. ... Lacey contacted me telling me that they had actually managed to test five of our people, so don't go rescheduling them with someone else.

Friday, November 17th. Last night I went to jujitsu, and there are some tensions between someone else and me.

It was probably around this time I went to Jujitsu that John Schmitt's son had a promotion. He took a group photo, and also asked me to take a photo of him and his son. By doing this he could have gotten my picture and fingerprints. I was a little freaked out. He seemed terrified of me despite me not being a threat. I was only so so at jujitsu. I was a beginner and had good and bad days. He seemed afraid just when I told him about my interest in it. He used to give me looks sometimes, like devious grins. It seemed that he had some insider "information" or absurd smear on me that was causing his irrational fear, and may be why his son had to suddenly leave the class when I first started going. He was probably an agent of some kind. It was common for the area, and it would explain his insider "information." I remember I think after the promotion, I heard him talking to someone else close by. He was telling them clearly, evenly, and in a particularly slow and controlled way what his profession was. It was like he was trying to keep me from being suspicious. Several people there were open, if not way too open, about the defense work they did. - 10/2/20 ...

I was trying to listen and read up on laundering lead laced clothing. I couldn't make sense of it. All I could see is that we shouldn't have gotten rid of those old crummy washing machines. *Alex had asked me to get rid of them on Craigslist early on. I didn't suspect at the time that they might have been contaminated with lead. It was less than a month into working we got rid of them. September 29th. ...*

I showed up to a car repair place. The man recognized me, and I got the paperwork done requesting a Maryland inspection. The look in his eyes... Anger, fear, regret. Something was going on with him, and that stirred in my mind. ... I was told my car had failed the inspection. He gave me a list of things that needed to be fixed. Everything together looked like it might cost $1600. ...

I didn't have my current address on my driver's license. This prompted Ace to mention having multiple IDs, even fake ones, would be a good thing to get ahold of if you needed to get out of the country. Ok. I don't know how well that would go. "Too many rules," I said, trying to figure out the endless maze of regulations. Ace told me most people don't follow them, and I was an anarchist and shouldn't let myself be controlled by law enforcement.

Saturday, November 18th. ... I called Ace, and told him I didn't know when I would be going in to work, as this was to process Tom's documents. Ace said we couldn't hire him since he didn't have his documents. I said he did, he was mailing them. Ace joked that I was being easier on the white boys, and I "made" him sign Rodrigo's paperwork. "I didn't make you, I simply declined to participate and left a vacuum." "Touché," he admitted. ...

Monday, November 20th. ... There was some issue with the shipping container. It was delivered while I was here, and I was given this crazy agreement to sign. The driver was off too, so I did some research and made sure to sign on behalf of the company. But the agreement says we cannot move it without the written permission of the people who dropped it off, as that was a lease agreement. Then Randy comes in and says it is in a bad spot, and we need to move it ASAP. He required it. So I call Marshal and ask if it was okay for me to sign it. He doesn't know. I ask if he has paid for it. He says he has the check ready to mail out. So this is potentially in my name. Does that mean I am responsible if other people move it? I tell Ace this, and he mocks me in front of Alex, saying I'm afraid of the little green men coming out of the paperwork. ... Alex is the one who ordered it, told me to sign it, told Marshal to pay for it, then moved the thing when my name was on the agreement. ...

Monday, November 27th. ... I mentioned Alex had assigned me the task of finding a laundry facility for work clothes, and Ace immediately knew a company. I couldn't help but wonder if those washing machines and dryers were used on lead clothing. The last job they came from was not a lead job, but who knows? He thought I was thinking about this too deeply. I can imagine what a pain it would be. But what if those things are contaminated? ...

Tuesday, November 28th. ... Atticus, a supervisor, comes in, and he wants to know the test results for his people. See, I don't have them. I called Lacey nine different ways yesterday, and I couldn't get through. She hasn't responded to three emails, a text, multiple calls, a voice message, and I called them directly and they just left me on hold forever. Why? I don't know. ...

When the clock hit 8, I started calling. Back to voice mail, back to being put on hold forever. I called Molly. She didn't answer, but I left a message saying it was pretty urgent. Ace called to chat about something, but I noticed Molly calling me back, so I let him know I had to go, and Molly totally got things rolling. She said she would call Lacey for me. Then I didn't hear anything, so I called the company again, and tried to dial for Lacey, but ended up typing in the extension of some random person, who then physically went over to find Lacey. I got transferred. Finally I was talking to her. She said they had been on a skeleton crew over the holiday, but were ready to rock and roll. Ok, fine. I explained my situation. We had a meeting at 10 which included the head of the company, and I didn't have test results. I NEEDED them. She tried to look them up on my computer portal. No, they weren't there, and neither was the capability to make appointments by the way. So she went digging. ...

I tried calling Lacey back. I still don't have her extension, so I called that random guy again who was very helpful, but told me Lacey was in a meeting. What? How could she do this to me? 10:00 rolled around, and I did not have the results. At this point I was summing up my entire experience with the health company as abysmal, and thinking I should move on. I texted Atticus to apologize for not having them and phoned in to the meeting. Then I got an email from Lacey. I was opening up the encrypted message service as the meeting began. ...

Ace came back briefly to inform me that every piece of equipment he has touched today hasn't worked. His computer, his phone is dying, the forklift this morning, another wouldn't start on Monday, two crash trucks and Zoro's truck won't start, and now something else. *There were a number of things that suggested Ace was being harassed. He just listed eight things that wouldn't work in a short time span. Even for that job site, that is a lot. ... He could be seen as competition for Brian Andrews. I remember Ace saying something like he was okay with a fair competition. I also remember him trying to get me to look down on people who are old. Andrews is older. I got the sense these things may be related. -2/17/20 ...*

Friday, December 1st. Ace disputed some of Paige's arguments, like that I was an office person who did not need to be *medically* tested at all. But he said that there were no truly office people here. I was out there on the forklift unloading. ...

Wednesday, December 2nd. ... Then I tried to order things on Amazon but didn't because it told me that my network was under an attack and that the website was not secure. I'll just not put in Ace's password just yet. The attack subsided later that day. ...

I called Lacey, who didn't answer her cell phone or work phone, and hasn't responded to the latest email. I gave her a detailed message for the three things I was still waiting on a follow up for. ...

Thursday, December 7th. ... Ace said I reminded him of 1984, when they would go to their secret room and drink coffee and eat chocolate, and that I was acting like I was in a communist country. I was missing out on all the joys of life. *His voice was soft and gaze distant, like he was picturing something not presently around him. ...*

Again, Lacey didn't answer her cell. She didn't answer her work phone. I called her job again, and had someone go look for her. They said she wasn't at her desk. They asked me to leave a message and she would get back to me. I told them I had already been waiting on her, so if there was someone else there who could help me I would appreciate it. After being on hold again, I am told that Lacey has returned to her desk. When I am transferred, I hear obviously pretend loud breaths. "Let me catch my breath as I had to run back to my desk." She tells me. I tell her there are several things I need to follow up on as I have had no response on any of them, and go through the list. 1. Please send all future invoices to Marshal. This one she seemed to be able to handle. 2. Get me the contact information of the doctor who gave us the referral to a hematologist. I explained my situation, saying that my company needed to know what information the doctor made that judgment on, if it was the OSHA standard, to know if we should pay. And there were other things I needed to communicate with the doctor. She asked for this in an email so she could forward it to someone else for them to do. I told her I had already sent emails. She read a response like a triumph, and when I explained myself again, she just got all overwhelmed and read it again and said she didn't know what she needed to do. She acted like a whimpering blabbering child. I explained that I needed this information to make sure that my people were getting the medical help they needed, and that I would get this information somehow. I had already emailed them, then the clinic, then the clinic didn't respond so I was back to them. If I had to call the lab I would. She seemed to think they would just send me back to them. I told her one thing she could do is to track down the source of the referral to the hematologist. My tone with her was without frustration, but was firm and methodical. The last point was that the whole reason that I have worked with them over all these months and set up at a new clinic was to do lead testing, and that test was not a part of my procedure package, and so I could not even sign people up for it. And when we sent people there for lead testing, they didn't even do it. They just did ZPP. She seemed to have conflicting information with mine about what was available to me. I pointed out in the proposal I was given there were a number of tests not even on there. She said she would make sure it matched the contract. ...

I later get a call back from Lacey. She has the head nurse there to speak with me. I talk with him for a few minutes explaining my situation. He says that the tests are reviewed by a redacted doctor who does things long distance and is not going to be able to review the results in light of anything else like working conditions or the worker's health problems. And of course, the availability of this person is negligible. I related Paige's questions to him, and he said he would try to get an answer to me Monday, because the doctor was gone for the rest of the week. He said that if I had thought that this service was supposed to be for these sorts of consults, they wouldn't have agreed to do business with me because they don't do that. I asked who would be expected to pay, and he said us. The sense I got from him was sort of a 'forget you, not our problem, don't bother us with this stuff,' and Lacey like a naughty child who had just pinned something on the innocent sibling. She seemed pretty pleased with herself. She had gotten the unruly customer off of her back.

Alex came in. He seemed nervous. He asked if I needed anything. Nope. Not really. Ace called me to let me know that Enrique needed a ride back to his house. Ok. He gathered his bags. Ace wondered if we should just wait for Jordan to take him. Alex said not until he gets back with the tools. Ace told me to just go ahead. *Ace may have been trying to distance himself from what was about to happen.* Enrique asked me if he could put his bags in my trunk. I told him to put them in my back seat. "Are you sure?" I nodded. "Are you ready for a long drive?" Enrique asked me. "Yep." ... Then there was a strange sound. It kept going. I couldn't tell where it was coming from, but it was so constant I thought it must be my car. I pulled off to the side of the road. "You have a flat tire," Enrique told me. He said if I have a spare in my trunk he could fix it. Do I? "It's a good thing that wasn't dangerous." *We had just gotten on the highway.* I called Ace. He asked me where I was, and then as I was speaking, Tom pulls up in front of me and gestures with a thumbs up and a thumbs down. I do a thumbs up, and he drives off. I start to drive slowly on the flat to get to a gas station. Alex calls me and says he is coming to help. And Tom is coming back to take Enrique home. Ace calls again, and he tells me not to drive on the rim. It could destroy the tire. Even a mile. I stop on the side of the road. He says I need to use a spare. I turn off the emergency lights, and Enrique tells me urgently that those need to be on, so I flip them back on. Enrique looks in the trunk of my car, saying normally there is a jack with the tire, but I don't have one. I do have a spare though, and he takes that out. *Enrique glanced around my trunk a bit, and also around my tire.* Tom pulls up. "Girl, you don't have a jack? They're only $50." Then Alex pulls up. The three of them jack my car, take off the lug nuts, and replace the tire. The old one had a razor blade stuck in it. Enrique took it out with pliers and I put it in my car. I pulled out Enrique' things, and Alex told me to follow him. He said my spare tire was still low on air. When we got to the gas station, it turns out that it was completely flat. And the rest of my tires were almost flat. I couldn't understand how that could be. He said I would have to keep checking or they would keep going down. He showed me the cap to one. The top was broken off. He said that was going to cause it to leak a lot faster. One was okay. The one from the spare looked like the top had been cut off. And another one was missing a top. I showed that to him. He acted like it wasn't a big deal, but he seemed a bit nervous. I said I didn't understand how they could all be so empty. I had them checked less than a month ago. "By who?" I pointed to the car place next door. He shrugged. "Some people are lazy. People." "Yeah.. People." I said angrily, but caught myself. I told him he handled this well and thanked him. My anger seemed to make him more nervous. And it was strange the way he brushed off the tires not being checked. I know I wrote for that man to check the air, and I asked him afterwards if he had. It is like Alex knows it wasn't done. I drove back to the office. Ace poked his head in momentarily, saying he was really really leaving this time.

I don't know the date, but one day I was shopping at the Dollar Tree, and over the loudspeaker, as I recall the voice said "Attention customers, security check all aisles. Attention customers, security check all aisles." A black customer looked at me like, 'what the heck?' I asked the lady at the cash register about it and she said she didn't know what that was about and had never heard it used before.

Monday, December 11th. ... Ace said he really liked it, and he knew I was going to get sick of hearing it, but those name tags didn't stand a chance in the wind. That was true, I hadn't thought of that. Inside of there is the Spanish SDS that it seems Ace has done everything to delay since forever. *Placing obstacles in front of my goals seems to be part of the process. There were many many times this accomplishment of mine was delayed, to the point that it makes little sense. ...*

Tuesday, December 12th. ... Ace said the last three months had been the worst for him in terms of losing things that he had had for a decade. He still hadn't found his mouse. That's the second in six months that he's lost. That is unheard of. And he lost his special toboggan that Aden gave him for Christmas. ...

Wednesday, December 13th. ...I noted that Alex liked to put in all kinds of things in the report. He said that was because Alex had had it hammered into him while on the job that Frank and Drew didn't think he did anything. They constantly came at him with "What are you doing?" His reaction to that was to write minute by minute accounts of his life in order to "justify his existence." Ace said not to focus on all the particulars, but to see yourself through the macro perspective. Funny, that was just what I was thinking about yesterday. *Ace seemed a bit upset, and I got the impression he didn't always like what I wrote in my journal. ...*

Alex also made a jab at Ace, saying the reason the papers were getting all wrinkled in the printer was because the paper was already like that. He knew, he just never told us. He looked giddy. Ace laughed and admitted we'd been had. Of course that is nonsense. I loaded dozens of sets of paper, and they were all smooth and crisp going in. I loaded several different kinds of paper, and the same kinds that were crinkled before are not crinkled now, so if he actually did something to the printer he should fess up.

Thursday, December 14th. Tom asked me if I was cold. "No, I'm wearing a coat." He wondered if I kept it on all the time, just in case. *In non-verbals, he had asked that question like he was trying to catch me, perhaps as if I kept something hidden in that coat. I flinched at that and he took it like a blow when I did. I tried to act normal, but there was a realization in his eyes, and he looked at me sorrowfully.*

Tuesday, December 19th. ... Ace played with his phone. He didn't care. Or he was creating awkward silence to draw me out, which does not work, as it is all awkward to me. Maybe the silence less so. I don't know what his deal is. I asked him if he had looked up Ten Fold Engineering. He had not, and gave the excuse that he has been working and then crashing and hasn't even had the time. I could believe that. He told me how draining it was to work 20 hours straight, even just thinking about work. He said all he thinks about is posts. Then he looked it up, and started asking a few questions about it. What does it do? What is the point? Is the company actually doing anything? I explained what I had read. They were already selling licenses and getting their drawings done in compliance with US building codes. They expected to ship inside the US within the year. They said it was easy to build. It looked like something a fab shop might want to get involved in. It looked fun. He said maybe that was something he could do. I said if it didn't mess with the patents. He then goes into a tirade about this guy who invented this thing about windshield wipers, and Ford stole it, and he spent his whole life litigating and suing, and he won, but it didn't matter, because his life was wasted, his creative energies came to a halt, because someone more powerful than him decided to take the other side of a legal battle. He obviously was not trying to inspire me. ...

But as it is, I'm pretty bad at this, and as such am very disposable. And then it is mostly a question of who likes you. This is not a nice situation to be in. I don't get a job to wonder if the voice over the phone was concealing some sort of animosity and that my future is now very uncertain. It is hard to say. I could easily believe they will decide I am not a good fit. It is a hard thing to not be able to trust people. I wish they would not fake their approval of me. If I know where I stand, at least I can know where to go.

Thursday, December 21st. ... Alex walks in. Something is concerning him. He wishes there were some way to link these reports in with the equipment file. He is thinking something like a spreadsheet would be good, but it needs to have some way to attach a document to it. He complains about the sort of record-keeping we have. You can't really do that with the daily report. I cannot help but smile to myself. We look through the files to find the equipment documentation. Apparently there are some random folders, some of which have pictures. He said he really wanted some way to track vehicle maintenance so we didn't redo or miss things. And if there could be some kind of alert. "Which is why we need smart people like you in the office." I told him I had been working on something like that. "Is that why you were laughing?" I nod. I start to show him what I've put together. I give him a little tour of how Airtable works and how to link and sort, and the data I've compiled on the equipment. He is very interested in this. He tells me in the office they have pictures of all the equipment up on the board, and filing cabinets with the paper documents. That is about as advanced as it gets for them. He also wanted to keep track of vehicle registrations. I was taking notes. He asked if other people could join, and I showed him how they could comment on records and tag each other. He wanted to know if it could work with Wunderlist, which is a way to assign tasks to groups. Yep. He told me about how a whole group can simultaneously edit a document on Google Hangouts. He had some useful ideas. He even asked if my shadow board was ready to go, having seen me working on it. Yep. He'd take that too. Boy. All I have to do is silently flip out and people are all nice to me. The request Alex made was basically exactly what I had been doing with Airtable.

Thursday, December 21st. ...Then Ace prints off my roommate Vanessa's resume. Of course Vanessa put our address down ... He is beside himself. (The name of my street was comically opposed to my personality.) He starts to point to mock me, but doesn't know if he wants to. He is really shocked. "I'm surprised you didn't already know that." But he didn't. I would think being the meddling sort that he is he would have done that. *If he had hacked my phone or laptop he would have known where I lived. As was shown previously he often reacted to conversations I had at home, as though he had been listening or was told about them. If he did know of those conversations and he did not hack my phone, he was apparently working with someone who was able to listen to multiple of my private conversations.*

Friday, December 22nd. ... Paige let me know I was sending my Daily Activity Report email out multiple times. For my first DAR that day, I didn't remember to shrink the file size. But I had the same issue with other large attachments I sent. That, I think, is new for me. ...

4

I ACCUSE FAMILY OF BEING INFORMANTS AND THEY RESPOND

C*hristmas Break.* I drove down to my parents' house on Saturday. Conversation was about a number of things, like the business world of YouTube, taxes, and the futuristic Internet infrastructure that is coming up. *When I mentioned this, and I might have used the term "mesh networks," I remember my brother's eyes widened and a look of fear flashed across his face. This was the "bad" thing for which apparently I had been targeted. -2/18/20 ...*

Most people plead out before they go to trial anyway. My brother thought the Bible advocated something like that--coming to terms with your enemy. ...

My brother brought up an idea of how to protect my valuables. He said if the police had a search warrant, they could take keys or fingerprints from you, but if your property was secured with something like a password, the courts have ruled that the police couldn't compel you to give that over. He acted really excited about a safe that was password protected, and suggested several times I get one. I drove to the store, and my brother was walking back, so I picked him up, and we went together. He was telling me about places where things could be hidden, like in a shoe. We were in an aisle, and there was a guy standing there stiffly with a look of horror on his face staring in the direction of the shelf while I told my brother that the best way to hide something is for it to be something people don't know to look for, and mentioned how they used to hide gold under fence posts. He repeated what I said deliberately, "Fence posts..." (These days you have to consider drones.) *Written 10/20/20 ...*

I talked about Trump's battle with the FBI and the internal war going on. "Maybe you should write a story about it some day," my mother added, her tone jaded and sarcastic. Why? That doesn't seem to be the sort of story I would write. ...

I went out for a bit. When I came back, Mom wanted me to edit her story. There was one section she needed help with. She didn't know how to describe approaching a police station, and what the interior would be like. Like I know? ...

Then she gets really upset that I use sign language, and then decides I don't actually want to say something to her, and this means there is something that is really important for me to communicate and that I don't consider her worth it to make sure she understands. *We used to talk in sign language all the time. This obviously makes sense if there was audio but no video recording at that time. ...*

There was more distance between us, my mother and me. We were more like strangers.

* * *

I did not openly accuse my family members of being informants for a long time, until I amassed more evidence. The decision to do so was not easy. I had argued with them on the principle that it was still wrong to do wrong even though the government ordered it, but I did not persuade them to stop and come clean. I did not expect their cooperation if I accused them explicitly, and did expect opposition. But I decided it was better to be real with people, and not have to pretend or hide the situation. I sent messages with my accusations and why I believed they made the wrong choice, then allowed them to defend themselves and give their side as I presented my journal. I afforded them this opportunity, because by telling my story with my name, I was also by extension publicly exposing them. This part was posted to them in October 2020. Here are their responses to this post:

My comment: This is short and about family. I strongly recommend you all *family* read it.

My father's comment: I'm working on a response.

My father's comment: You wrote "I might have used the term mesh networks, I remember your brother's eyes widen and a look of fear. This was the 'bad' thing for which apparently I could be targeted for. -2/18/20]," ... "Most people plea out before they go to trial anyway. **** thought the Bible advocated something like that--coming to terms with your enemy." So you remember *my brother's* eyes widen and you assume he was afraid of the subject of mesh networks? You take any simple expression as confirmation of you theories. That is extreme Confirmation Bias.

You also wrote about your mother: "She said something and I reacted like I was pulling back, like I had recognized that she was an informant." Again. You imagined some comment or way of acting as confirming your theory that your mother was an informant.

You are believing your imaginations and taking your impressions of other's expressions as truth. I have first-hand knowledge of this: You asked about our Roku as if I was clueless of the invasion of privacy issues. I explained that I bought the one without a voice-command microphone. You stated in your Journal that we were "nervous" and imagined that we were "tasked" with informing on ourselves. So it doesn't matter what the facts are, you assume that you have great skill at interpreting facial expressions and pauses in conversations and your interpretations always confirm your assumption that others are informants.

Your tests for verifying your theory (that certain people are informants) are not good. You have stated that informants will call you crazy when they are accused. So if you walk up to a random person and tell them "Informants will call you crazy if you accuse them. You are an informant!" And they reply "You're crazy!" what have you proven or disproved? I'm not saying that there aren't any valid concerns about the possibility of informants and surveillance, but we should think soberly and with proper perspectives.

All of your book is demonstrating your belief (without solid evidence) that the government is doing all these things to you. It is orchestrating all these events in your life. That they are the reason for cars breaking down, your computers not working, making you ill by poisoning the air conditioners and foods, people harassing you, having everyone inform on you, etc...

It is true that the political environment was anti-America, anti-freedom, anti-Christian and hostile from 2009 through 2016. Obama politicized the government agencies. See: "Government Hostility Toward the Right Wing" http://www.akdart.com/obama147.html There was a lot of talk about our loss of freedoms at that time. Edward Snowden warned of mass surveillance programs. This seems to have had an extreme effect on you. While its good to be observant of potential threats, to take prudent measures concerning privacy and security, and to advocate for our freedoms, becoming obsessively concerned and fearful is not ok. "The fear of man brings a snare, But whoever trusts in the LORD shall be safe." - Pro 29:25. Jesus said "I have told you these things, so that in me you may have peace. In this world you will have trouble. But take heart! I have overcome the world." John 16:33.

You have not judged others or events rightly. The Lord says "A matter must be established by the testimony of two or three witnesses" Deut 19:15. You need solid evidence and sound reasoning.

While you have had to deal with some bad characters, allowing your bad experiences to cloud your judgment about everyone else is not right. "Let none of you think evil in your heart against your neighbor;" Zech 8:17. "There is only one lawgiver and judge, he who is able to save and to destroy. But who are you to judge your "neighbor?" James 4:12. And "Do not say, 'A conspiracy,' Concerning all that this people call a conspiracy, Nor be afraid of their threats, nor be troubled. The LORD of hosts, Him you shall hallow; Let Him be your fear, And let Him be your dread. He will be as a sanctuary," - Isaiah 8:12-14a.

Thank you for allowing us to review your journal entries and respond before posting.

My comment: @*my father*, Thank you for your response. You state that I provide thin evidence. I am not suggesting that every example is in itself rock solid proof that someone is acting maliciously on behalf of the government. Some things are merely consistent with it, or are more consistent with it than not, and so as a person observing these crimes, I include these cases as well.

I was surprised by Zech 8:17 and I looked it up. It is underlined in my Bible, and my translation says "do not devise evil in your hearts against one another." (ESV) Also note Jeremiah 9:4, Romans 3:10, and John 2:24. The reality is that people are naturally malicious and hide their evil deeds (John 3:19). This is the way of the world. It isn't just the era of Obama in which there were systematic attempts to covertly damage political adversaries. I certainly do not need to be obsessed with looking for evil to find it. There is an avalanche. "They do not rest until they have caused someone to stumble." Psychopaths tire themselves trying to destroy innocent people. There are plenty of them. If you hear someone saying they are a victim and they describe the behavior of a psychopath, and you assume they are making it up, you are possibly dismissing an actual victim.

I am not a judge in a court of law. Due process, and establishing every accusation, is necessary before punishing someone for their crimes. It is also important to be considerate of not falsely accusing people. I can help to avoid that by redacting names, being careful of what I am actually asserting, and showing the facts. That is something I am trying to be conscious of in this process. But we are not obligated towards an irrational bias that people are basically good. We shouldn't wait while people are being threatened and harmed by criminals who aren't confessing to their crimes and ignore what reasons for suspicion may be available.

My mother's comment: My perspective on these times - it did seem like you didn't trust or even like me anymore. You treated me as an enemy and would not confide in me or even have normal conversation about your life or interests. Of course this put up walls (to emotionally protect myself). When I tried to find out what was wrong so I could apologize and we could be close again, you stonewalled me. You would not say what I had done to offend you. At that point, relationship wasn't really possible. I could not reasonably continue to be vulnerable and open to someone who was rejecting me (I had enough rejection in my life and cannot handle it well). So yes, I closed off to you. I was glad when you were gone from the house again, so I could breathe. I could have peace.

I did not understand for a long time why you treated me that way. Not until I read your journal. It shocks me less to see it the second time, but you have successfully created that emotional wall between us. Your life is your own, and I won't tell you what to say in your book. It is your perception and you are free to write it. But I would prefer that you make it clear that it was your perception.

As I said to you before, I have never spied on you. I respect your privacy. I only wanted to find out what was wrong between us to see if it could be remedied.

My mother's comment: I have not shared any confidence about your life with others. When things would appear to be a negative report (such as how you were treating me), I also did not relay that. I still believe in hope of restoration, but will not hang my heart on it. Some in the household were aware of it, because they were present.

My mother's comment: *This refers to a conversation I have since removed from this chapter.* - I tend not to remember specific conversations, so can't address intelligently what we were talking about or give it context. For me, when something is past, it's really gone. I prefer to forget than keep a record of wrongs.

All I can say is that for a while, we have been strangers more than family.

My mother's comment: I do not give permission to post misinformation about me on my page OR to my friends. Even with libertarian freedom, I cannot condone you bearing false witness and dishonoring your parents.

My mother's comment: So many assumptions are made here that are untrue.

My comment: This is a problem and I'm not completely sure what the right answer is. I am required to honor my parents. Telling people you are an informant would likely be thought of as dishonoring. What then of children who know of their parents' crimes? Especially when others could be or are hurt? But the bigger issue is the pressure that must be applied to you to make you an informant, as of course you could not do so willingly. If you are under serious threat or torment, then it would be much more dishonoring of me to leave you in that position. By telling people you are a victim, likely of things like what I have experienced, I'm making it possible for them to help you without you risking yourself in asking for help. Also, I am making you less useful as an informant. If everyone knows you could be spying on them, people could withhold that information that could put them in jeopardy with your overlords. So it is more likely you won't be worth coercing to be an informant. Given these options, it seems honoring you most requires me to expose what abuse you must be suffering. As for the truth of claim, people will have to reason for themselves as the evidence unfolds.

My mother's comment: I don't know how to convince you of my sincerity. I have not lied to you. I am not under any threat, unless you consider being falsely accused of being an informant by my own daughter - a threat.

My brother's comment: I concur with dad's assessment here. I see plenty of Confirmation Bias both here and in your previous writings.

I had wanted to speak to recommend against posting an earlier writing but have seen that you've clearly formed a worldview that those who ask/suggest others to keep quite about any vile things are categorically along the lines of psychopath/narcissist/informant oppressors of those who've been treated unfairly... whereas it would seem that you haven't left any room for other possibilities of healthy-minded and loving individuals cautioning against such an action; for even a good reason. Like you can't have a healthy reason to suggest not to share such info and anyone who does is categorically one of these bad people described above... and I would espouse that this is not the case at all. A valid reason one may suggest not to share is because; like in a school-like environment bullies typically find those they perceive as weak and then proceed to bully that individual; so the idea of a "victim mentality" or the likeness to it may open you up to such characters and attacks and a person who cares for you may wish that no such bullies would find there way to you. As this is the case, a loving friend may caution one against using such language to avoid such characters — and this is not an oppressor but a friend.

I once heard an accusation against me back at youth group and I spoke to *our youth pastor* about going before the youth group to deny that claim. He advised me against doing that as I would "put that image into their mind and they would associate that idea with me" and so I saw the wisdom in what he said and never spoke of it again.

The last time you were with us all I remember you sharing and explaining the "Narcissist mentality." I have not yet grown accustomed to thinking in terms of Narcissist, Informants, or Psychopaths as terms for profiling in the way that you do. It seems strange and foreign to me, but I see that you have a developed worldview on these subjects. So whenever I hear these words from you I try to stretch my brain to grasp your worldview to try and better understand your statements and claims. And since I'm not accustomed to this way of thinking those terms are not something I'm led to to describe people. If I were to try to find the closest Biblical matching description a Narcissist, as I understand it, would be a lover of self. The other two I don't have a Biblical similarity to assign to. Though your description of a Narcissist does not match the Biblical one I would associate it to.

When I first saw you use "informant" language towards me I was puzzled at this bizarre statement and at first thought someone may have hacked your account here. As I read on I began to realize much else of the writing seemed to fit with the way you speak so my mind searched for where in the world this was coming from. After reading your first paper and seeing many heavy implications and things said in such a way that, what the reader likely sees are circumstantial, you have spoken as though there was indeed great intentional wrong done. This "way of seeing the world" and everything wrong in it, and dwelling on it, and reading into most everything, is a very unhealthy way to think and a much worse way to foster a way of thinking.

To my recollection your name has only come up in conversation a handful of times over the past 15 years or so and I've always simply said that you were the smartest one among us siblings. And with only those "closest of friends" I've shared no more than you're left handed and I think people who are left handed are talented, you know sign language, and approximately however far away you were may have come up. Beyond this I have had no reason to speak to others and I have not offered any more details. I care for you, I believe I would fight for you if need be and defend you wherever it is right to do so.

The Bible has a way of speaking about how our mindset ought to be, like in John 15:11 "These things I have spoken to you, that My joy may remain in you, and that your joy may be full," in John 15:13, 17 "But now I come to You and these things I speak in the world, that they may have My joy fulfilled in themselves. ... Sanctify them by Your truth. Your word is truth.", and in Philippians 4:8 "Finally, brethren, whatever things are true, whatever things are noble, whatever things are just, whatever things are pure, whatever things are lovely, whatever things are of good report, if there is any virtue and if there is anything praiseworthy—meditate on these things." Since it is known that our own hearts are "deceitful above all else and desperately wicked, who can know it" in Jeremiah 17:9 and "for the flesh doth desire contrary to the Spirit" in Galatians 5:17 going on to verse 22-25 speaks of the fruit of the Spirit and walking in the Spirit. The first verse mentioned in this paragraph about God's joy remaining in us, (John 15:11) in context, speaks of "if we keep His commandments" and then states "a new commandment I give to you ... to love." And this joy we have in Him by love also has some aspects of love we can see in 1 Corinthians 13 where it describes love as "thinks no evil," "bears all things, believes all things, hopes all things, endures all things" which speaks to the mindset of how we who are in Christ are to be... and by love alone, which we are called to, we are not to presume or assume wickedness or ill intent from any persons where their may be doubt, but the scripture would seem to imply that loving your neighbor would be assuming the best about their intent in general when intent is unknown. As Philippians 2:1-3 says "Therefore if there is any consolation in Christ, if any comfort of love, if any fellowship of the Spirit, if any affection and mercy, fulfill my joy by being like-minded, having the same love, being of one accord, of one mind. Let nothing be done through selfish ambition or conceit, but in lowliness of mind let each esteem others better than himself."

Part 1/2

My brother's comment: In those who are Christ's, do you not believe that God is able to perfect the work He started in us, and those you accuse, to bring about His good work to completion? Does God not indeed bring those who search Him out and meditate on His word to maturity in Christ? Would you then assume the worst about those in whom God has done a great work, without proof? There are even those in the world who are not of God who have a "law unto themselves" who live by a high standard towards good character (see Romans 2:14). We believers have Philippians 2:13-15 "for it is God who works in you both to will and to do for His good pleasure. Do all things without complaining and disputing, that you may become blameless and harmless, children of God without fault in the midst of a crooked and perverse generation, among whom you shine as lights in the world," which clearly shows blameless and harmless as attributes of which Christ continues in working in us. And even before God gave us His Holy Spirit to indwell us, before Cain slew Abel, "So the Lord said to Cain, 'Why are you angry? And why has your countenance fallen? If you do well, will you not be accepted? And if you do not do well, sin lies at the door. And its desire is for you, but you should rule over it.'" ... why would the God who created us say to Cain "but you should rule over it"? Is this not in the same spirit as the Gentiles who by nature do the things of the law are a law to themselves (Romans 2:14)? And lastly on presuming the worst about others we have Romans 14:10-13 "But why do you judge your brother? Or why do you show contempt for your brother? For we shall all stand before the judgment seat of Christ. For it is written: 'As I live, says the Lord, Every knee shall bow to Me, And every tongue shall confess to God.' So then each of us shall give account of himself to God. Therefore let us not judge one another anymore, but rather resolve this, not to put a stumbling block or a cause to fall in our brother's way."

I mentioned earlier how worshiping God can be healing. I have no way of knowing yet if this has registered with you. Even people who are not of Christ have seen the evidence of this as it is stated in the book "The Power of Habit" that when a bad habit is developed the pathways exist within the brain for it as it was created by the habit in the first place. When the habit is ceased those neural pathways remain but are merely dormant. If these pathways are not overwritten or a new stronger habit replaces it then it takes about 9 years before they're gone. Although in the instance of people addicted to pornography it has been shown that those neural pathways get completely overwritten by practicing worship. This is what I remember hearing in the audio book many years ago and was surprised that a secular book would publish something like this. Yet we who have God's holy word have many testimonies that when an individual humbles themselves before God and repents and turns fully to obeying and worshiping God that God delivers them from their enemies. And again "we do not wrestle against flesh and blood".

As to your writings here... as I read about mesh networks and you wrote "[My brother's] eyes widen and a look of fear" I was assuming you were talking about some one I don't know. But then you wrote that this was about family. I have no idea what look you perceived at the time. I have absolutely no reason to fear mesh networking, nor have I ever, as I love the idea and am actively still pursuing the idea... even now towards becoming a HAM radio operator. The technology absolutely fascinates me. If you didn't know this about me I don't live in fear, not in fear of anything. I'm in God's hands. I also resolved many years ago never to make a decision based on baseless fears. Fear is not something I'm really familiar with. The closest I come is a natural healthy skeptical fear when doing parkour and looking at a jump beyond what I'm accustomed to... and that's not a baseless fear but a fear based in reason and rational thought – also known as a healthy fear.

As to "Most people plea out before they go to trial anyway. [My brother] thought the Bible advocated something like that–coming to terms with your enemy," you seem to be bending my understanding of Matthew 5:25 "Agree with your adversary quickly, while you are on the way with him, lest your adversary deliver you to the judge, the judge hand you over to the officer, and you be thrown into prison." You say "coming to terms with your enemy," the word enemy seems a bit inaccurate with scripture, as it implies more than an adversary, as an enemy is hostile and desires to harm. But an adversary going to court is simply pursuing the laws for legal terms for which you have not held up your end on. I happen to dislike many past "Republicans" because they've been "sell outs" on important moral principles and I hope they would never "come to terms" with the immoral changes others are trying to put into law. So your depiction of my stance here is inaccurate.

Part 2/2

My comment: *@my brother*, I wrote about narcissists and psychopaths in the Bible in this blog post: https://wordpress.com/post/saclark411.wordpress.com/518 I believe they are called "scoffers" in the Bible, among other things.

You are assuming that I am committing the fallacy of Affirming the Consequent.

~

Affirming the Consequent:
If P therefore Q
Q
Therefore P

~

If Person is an informant then the person does not want me to speak out
The person does not want me to speak out
Therefore person must be an informant
This is a fallacy because there may be more ways to get to Q besides P.

I am not reasoning in this way. However, I do recognize if people ask me not to speak out, it is consistent with them being an informant, although it does not necessarily follow from this information that they are.

As for your three arguments against speaking out:

1. I would identify as a victim and attract more bullies.

Victims need to be protected from harm, and the abusers need to be brought to justice. If someone is stabbing me, there is a real and objective wrong that exists that needs to be dealt with. As for other possible good or bad things that can come afterwards, we can look at the pragmatics:

Pros:
-Victim may be able to discourage attacks and recruit aid
-Victim may be able to bring assailant to justice
-Other victims may be encouraged to not stay with their abusers and live needless lives of hell, and to speak out (it is all to common for victims to just stay with their abusers, and tragic)
-Awareness can be raised about the nature of the crimes that can occur, and it will be harder for this or any other assailant to continue perpetrating this type of crime undiscovered
-A culture of justice will be bolstered for everyone, including children yet to be born
-The victim will not have to live a false life and can have genuine relationships
-People will have a more realistic view of human nature and may be able to come to grips with the reality of their own depravity, and to repent

Cons
-Sadists will be inspired
-If no one comes to the victim's aid, predators will be emboldened to hurt this and similar

victims
-The victim will likely be retaliated against by the assailant
-The victim will be a less desirable companion as people may not want to associate with the victim's assailant

In many of these cons, I am only risking myself, which is my right to do. However if I do not speak out, the culture of oppression that is not only harming me but others will go unchecked and unchallenged. Unacceptable. Regardless, injustice isn't something we can just wink at. These are serious crimes.

Your second argument:

2. Love thinks no evil.

In this case, I would like to take a look at examples of how Love was exemplified for us. Does God think no evil when he looks at humanity? Did Jesus think no evil of others as he walked on this earth? When I am not sure about how to apply a general principle like this, I can look to the example of Christ. Matthew 23 suggests that Love does in fact recognize the sins in others.

Your third argument:

3. Do not judge a brother.

As we both know, the Bible has a lot to say on this slightly complicated topic. For example, Matthew 7:1 says do not judge, but we see in verse 5 that you may judge once you take the plank out of your own eye, and in fact it was a prohibition against judging in a hypocritical fashion, similar to Romans 2:1-5.

In 1 Corinthians 5:12 we see Paul has nothing to do with "judging" those who are outside, but in context we are to understand this as a judgment in exerting church discipline. We do in fact see that judging fellow believers is a requirement in some cases, the purpose being to restore them to healthy fellowship. (James 5:19-20, Matthew 18:15-19, 1 Corinthians 6:5) This is an organized rebuke that would result in an official sanction of removing the believer from fellowship.

As far as the Romans 14 passage you brought up, the "sin" in question was not actually a sin. A person believed something was a sin when it wasn't, and they were being encouraged to act in a way they thought was sinful, though it was of no moral consequence, and that attitude of rebellion towards God was what was in itself a wrong. There is a lot of allowing God to do His work as people follow him.

For the world, the law is a schoolmaster that brings us to Christ (Galatians 3:24), and under it every mouth will be stopped (Romans 3:19). If we were to not follow the example of the prophets, apostles, and Jesus, and command all men everywhere to repent (Acts 17:30), we would be failing as God's ambassadors to the world.

However, as it relates to my situation, we are provided with many examples and commands to speak out against injustice, to warn and protect.

2 Timothy 4:14-15
"Alexander the coppersmith did me much harm. May the Lord repay him according to his works. You also must beware of him, for he has greatly resisted our words."

Isaiah 1:17
"Learn to do good;
Seek justice,
Rebuke the oppressor;
Defend the fatherless,
Plead for the widow."

Ephesians 5:11
"And have no fellowship with the unfruitful works of darkness, but rather expose them."

My brother's comment: On the last verse you shared here where it speaks to exposing the unfruitful works of darkness you must have this verse in the context it is meant. Both before and immediately after it talks about not speaking of such things:

Ephesians 5:3,4 "But fornication and all uncleanness or covetousness, let it not even be named among you, as is fitting for saints; neither filthiness, nor foolish talking, nor course jesting, which are not fitting, but rather giving of thanks."

Ephesians 5:12 "For it is shameful even to speak of those things which are done in secret."

So then what is verse 11 talking about when it says "expose them" if we are not to speak of such things? Verse 13 explains "But all things that are exposed are made manifest by the light, for whatever makes manifest is light." So it is not "exposing" that brings them to light, but the "manifest by the light" implies the light itself is what exposes them. So use the light to expose what is in darkness, and do not use speaking of what is shameful to bring darkness to people's attention. The light makes manifest, so speak of the light and that should be the tool the Holy Spirit uses to pierce the soul and expose the darkness.

My comment: Thank you for the thoughtful response. As for verses 3 and 4, I do not believe Paul is saying don't name uncleanness that is among you. Rather he is saying don't commit the sins at all. It isn't like he meant if you are committing them, just make sure not to get caught.

It is shameful to even speak of the sick crimes committed. And this is the reason given why we are to have nothing to do with them.

What does expose mean? What is the alternative interpretation you are defending here? Let's say there is a man who is committing some crime against one of his dependents, and a Christian knows about it. It sounds like by your interpretation of this verse, "bringing light" would be for the Christian to hold up the standard of God's word that such a thing is sin, which is certainly a good and necessary thing to do, but to go no farther in actually exposing the crimes themselves, considering it "shameful" and allowing a helpless person to go on being abused. That doesn't sound like exposing the works of darkness to me.

Here is the word expose in the Greek, its definition, and all of the cases it has been used: https://www.blueletterbible.org/lang/lexicon/lexicon.cfm...

My brother's comment: Alternative interpretation? I'm speaking to the context of the scripture. We can go back even further in the passage in verse 4:29 "Let no corrupt word proceed out of your mouth," verse 4:31 "Let all ... evil speaking be put away from you." And before that verse 4:23 "be renewed in the spirit of your mind." All of this leading up to verse 5:3 "let it not even be named among you" and the thought of verse 11 again followed immediately with the emphasis that it is "shameful even to speak of those things."

And again verse 13 being the clarification of what "exposed" is to mean 'in this context' is even further clarified by verse 14:

"Therefore He says:
'Awake, you who sleep.
Arise from the dead,
And Christ will give you light.'"

Here verses 13 and 14 clearly show the light causes one who is asleep to awake and the dead to arise which clearly indicates the work of salvation being done in those who "shall be saved."

If I then use exposing the ugliness of abortion as if that were the same context of this Bible passage to shine light, how them does this produce the work of salvation in a person? That in and of itself will not produce a change in a person to awake or arise to the light Christ gives. Only the light of God, whom Jesus is, and who we are to be to the world can do this.

Same passage explains it: Ephesians 5:8-10 "For you were once darkness, but now you are light in the Lord. Walk as children of light (for the fruit of the Spirit is in all goodness, righteousness, and truth), finding out what is acceptable to the Lord."

My comment: More context for Ephesians:

Eph 4:14-15 - that we should no longer be children, tossed to and fro and carried about with every wind of doctrine, by the trickery of men, in the cunning craftiness of deceitful plotting, but, speaking the truth in love, may grow up in all things into Him who is the head—Christ—

Eph 4:25 - Therefore, putting away lying, "Let each one of you speak truth with his neighbor," for we are members of one another.

Eph 4:29 – "Let no corrupt word proceed out of your mouth, but what is good for necessary edification, that it may impart grace to the hearers." The word "corrupt" here means not useful: https://www.blueletterbible.org/lang/lexicon/lexicon.cfm...

Eph 4:31 - "Let all bitterness, wrath, anger, clamor, and evil speaking be put away from you, with all malice." The word for evil speaking can mean to damage someone's good name. Interestingly it is also used translated blasphemy in Revelation 2:9 - "I know your works, tribulation, and poverty (but you are rich); and I know the blasphemy of those who say they are Jews and are not, but are a synagogue of Satan."

As already explained, "not be named among you" wouldn't mean don't call each other out on your sins, but rather don't commit them. We already know about the requirement to call out believers who are sinning. "Shameful to speak of" is given as a reason to not commit the acts. It does not appear to be a reason to cover them up.

The context of "light," starting in verse 8, is having been redeemed by Christ we now walk in light, truth, and wisdom. Light is a generic term. It can mean:-of truth and its knowledge, together with the spiritual purity associated with it-that which is exposed to the view of all, openly, publicly

https://wwwblueletterbible.org/lang/lexicon/lexicon.cfm...cont...

My comment: I think some examples of how light was applied to the corrupt works of darkness would be useful:

Matthew 22:16-18
"And they sent to Him their disciples with the Herodians, saying, "Teacher, we know that You are true, and teach the way of God in truth; nor do You care about anyone, for You do not

regard the person of men. Tell us, therefore, what do You think? Is it lawful to pay taxes to Caesar, or not?"
But Jesus perceived their wickedness, and said, "Why do you test Me, you hypocrites?"

Jesus is accusing them of having malicious intent.

John 13:21-26 - When Jesus had said these things, He was troubled in spirit, and testified and said, "Most assuredly, I say to you, one of you will betray Me." Then the disciples looked at one another, perplexed about whom He spoke.
Now there was leaning on Jesus' bosom one of His disciples, whom Jesus loved. Simon Peter therefore motioned to him to ask who it was of whom He spoke.
Then, leaning back on Jesus' breast, he said to Him, "Lord, who is it?"
Jesus answered, "It is he to whom I shall give a piece of bread when I have dipped it." And having dipped the bread, He gave it to Judas Iscariot, the son of Simon.

2 Timothy 4:14-15 - Alexander the coppersmith did me much harm. May the Lord repay him according to his works. You also must beware of him, for he has greatly resisted our words.

My brother's comment: *@me*, Digging deeper in to the context of Ephesians 4:17-5:21 it does seem that the majority of the context is speaking as to actions of putting off the old man and putting on the new. The central verse then that would either affirm my assessment of this passage or disprove it is Ephesians 5:3 where it says "let it not even be named among you." If that verse is as you say then you might dismiss the idea of not speaking of such evil things. Going through some studies on YouTube (which is unusual for me) I found a pastor who was curious at this exact phrase and looked it up. Start at 13:28 into the video https://youtu(dot)be/O16TzQBs1M0?t=808 "the word in Greek literally means that these things shouldn't be given a name" ... "Paul's basically saying that they shouldn't even be spoken." And this was the point I was making by this passage of scripture.

I noticed you didn't address Ephesians 5:12 which speaks very plainly: "For it is shameful even to speak of those things which are done in secret." Do you have an alternative interpretation of this?

Ephesians 5 (Part 2) :3-21 • Living as Children of the Light

My comment: As I have argued, "not even named among you" cannot mean "don't point out people's sins" because we are required to rebuke and are given many examples of it.

I have addressed "shameful to speak of" in two of my previous posts.

My mother's comment: *@me* Right. "Not even named among you" - means none of you should be accused of those things.

My mother's comment: Rebuke comes in private for private things - and public for public things (as Paul to Peter or the prophets to the kings of Israel) ... but if someone is unrepentant and practicing sin or criminal behavior, it is a sin to remain silent about it. The means for exposing darkness must be godly too. Gossip would be an example of shameful speech.

5

MORE HARASSMENT AND ENTRAPMENT AT WORK

T*uesday, January 2nd*. I emailed Ace yesterday asking about buying that nut splitter. I know he told me to buy it, but then I was thinking they said Drew said not to. Alex was even saying he would pay out of his own money. It really wasn't our place to spend it, so I held back. I had emailed Paige before I left for vacation telling her about buying hot chocolate, coffee and water, asking her if that was okay. She said water was a must, hot chocolate was no way, and coffee was a maybe. Today I get the statement, and she says any unauthorized purchases are going to come out of our pay checks. ...

Apparently Enrique says he didn't get paid properly. I texted him, and he keeps his own log of his hours. It contradicted my spreadsheet so I did more looking. Turns out the spreadsheet had yet another glitch in its logic. Probably a bunch of people didn't get paid for part of Monday. I would love to blame it on the stupid spreadsheet which seems to have an error at least every other week. ...

Saturday, January 6th. ... Ace called me while I was out and about. He seemed deliberately happy. He asked me what was up. "Getting my car inspected." "How's that going?" "It's going, so that's good."...

I told him the result of my inspection, and I wasn't too happy. It had failed again. This time there was an entirely new list of things that needed to be fixed. I had gone to one place to get the inspection done and was given an enormous list of things to fix, some of which were absurd, at drastically marked up prices. I went to a more reasonable and reputable place to fix it up, which cost me what I had originally paid for the car, and then had them check it out again to make sure it was good for another inspection. Then I had gotten my car inspected at this one, and it was painfully obvious by the shrill gleam in his eye, the nonsense of the items to be fixed, and this context that he has just taken $80 from me for nothing but to try to force so much out of me I could hardly believe it. I ranted to Ace, I had worked a month just to get the car as fixed up as it was, and if I was to do these fixes, it would mean I would work another whole month. ... He said let him call his girl Darline... Ace called me back to tell me he had hired someone he used to work with. He told me a little about him. Smart, technical, reserved, like me. He could read Alex, but Reid and me he didn't know sometimes.

Monday, January 8th. ... Ace asked me what I meant with the car mechanic I had been to, when I said they were "bad." I had said that in a creepy way. I told him how when I got a flat tire Alex checked the air in all my tires and they were flat. I had been to the mechanic a few weeks before, specifically wrote for him to check the tires, specifically asked him if he had checked them and he said he had. I was driving flat bald tires in the middle of winter with a bad suspension and alignment. And he just lied to me and let me walk out of there like that, when it would have been so easy to just check them. That was dangerous for me, and this was on top of everything else he did. Ace repeated that this was a common thing among mechanics, but then said it wasn't that big of a deal. ...

He was very excited to hire Reid. It meant a lot that leadership was accepting people he recommended. "But it is a lot of pressure." Of course this same pressure applies to me. He wanted me to send an email back to Reid, the engineer he had hired, and to make it as professional as I could. This was important to him~that I put a very good foot forward here. I was hiring a real professional. ...

There was something we had to get to. My car had to be taken over for an inspection. He called up Darline and explained some other guys had been giving me a bunch of nonsense to fix, and asked if she could help me out. "All we can do is try." He said. I drove Ace in my messy dirty little car. ...

I arrived and we went out to meet Darline. She is a strong and fresh woman, who seemed to embrace us with a little love and mischief. She and Ace got along very well, and joked about the porta-potties. He paid an enormous sum for another company truck, I left my beloved car behind, and we went to drive the repaired company vehicle away together. He said I didn't need to stay and wait for it to be inspected. ...

We sat down, Ace on the opposite corner from me. He didn't look at me much or say much. He seemed pensive and sad. I simply waited for him. Given everything that had happened, I wondered if this might be the gracious way he had chosen to say goodbye. "Tell me about Reid." He told me about Reid's family. A wife and a son, maybe two or three. He said he had an associates degree in engineering. He was at least as good--no, better than Ace in AutoCAD drafting. He had worked at the same company Ace had, and that is where he is coming from, so he has stayed there a long time. He has a history in auto mechanics. "Sounds perfect for you." I really meant it too. It sounds like he is going to be a very capable help. I couldn't help but tear up listening to Ace. I tried to look away or drink something. The food took too long to get here. I just wanted to be put out of my misery. But then, I don't know how to describe what I felt. It wasn't bad. It wasn't good either. It's like closing a good book. You have come to the end, and in that you are losing so much, but at the same time, you are at no better place to appreciate the whole of what you have. As we stayed and ate together, we didn't say much. I just listened. I'm honestly not sure what else he talked about. I guess that wasn't what I was listening to. But he had finished, and I held my last bite. "Are you waiting for me?" "No rush." I snatched the whole thing away, and it was over. We walked back to his car, and he stopped at the gas station. "Today will not be the day that we test how long this truck can go on empty." Indeed not. ...

We stopped back at the office so I could drive his new truck over to the .... office. It is very much like his other one, except bigger. The thing ticked and hummed, although I wish I knew how to adjust the seat forward. ...

Ace also told me that his truck was hit. He said it must have happened at the restaurant. "So soon after you got it?" Then I realized I had just driven it. "I didn't do it. I would have noticed it crash." "Guilty conscience?" "No!" He said there were light scratches, high up. I went outside to see this thing. I searched around the car, and there it was. A large dent in the back, with small white scratches. The way it was, I did not see how it could have been me. I would have had to back up into something at a weird angle, and I only backed up by the office. Ace said it was clearly a car's bumper, and asked me who had been on my side of the car. "It's only things." Ace brushed it off and walked away. *Having experienced a few minor car dents, it is extremely unlikely I would not have noticed. Given that I could have been given some blame, this could be harassment of me or Ace or both. ...*

When Ace came back, he said he cannot believe his car got hit. "And only three days after I got it." Yeah, that is pretty unbelievable. He was ready to wrap this up and go home. "What am I going to do with you?" Fire me? No... just give me a ride back to the auto shop so I could pick up my car. "Darline hasn't called yet?" I called her up, and she said they were just finishing up the inspection and she would call me in a few minutes. Ace found it strange it had taken so long and she hadn't called. ...

As I clocked out, I made an odd discovery. My green tag worked, my red tag did not. I tried it on two clocks. *I had complained about money, and now threats and opportunities were springing up around the topic. ...*

Ace asked me if I had gone back to martial arts and if I was still keeping that up. I said I had, and they wanted to promote me again. I liked the class. It was fun and useful, but it was not as systematic and rigorous as I was used to. I wished I could have the good qualities of both. It *was after this that another black belt taught class who was much more rigorous. ...*

He was still worried that Darline had not called back. "It isn't even your car and you're worried." ...

It was a short trip from here to there. Darline called me as we pulled in, asking for my email. I told her I would be right in, and when I arrived, she said it was hard to hear me with Ace being so loud right next to me. She seemed a little upset, and made nervous jokes about my street address. I waited for them to finish the paperwork. "You passed."

Tuesday, January 9th. ... The printer was in error. I cleared it, and tried printing off a USB. That glitched so I restarted the printer. It needed more paper. It took a little while, and I delayed Alex a little, but I printed off everything he needed. ...

Liev came in and told me they needed paper towels, and that the printer needed to be fixed today. He said this in a very demanding tone. I couldn't believe it had not been fixed yet. I went back to my other tasks. Alex came in and said he couldn't stand listening to Liev anymore, and I had to do something about it. I said the last thing I heard was that the copy guy ordered a part, but I'd make something happen. I called the copy guy and left a message. I emailed him. And then I called him again. He picks up and tells me that he fixed it the last time he was out here. He also told me that Marshal had yet to pay his invoice. "I'll call Marshal and tell him how important it is to us that we pay you." He said that he was doing a job in the middle of freezing rain and had to focus, so he hung up. I went over to the inspector's trailer to investigate. The printer was on, and I tried to copy something. The man in the corner office said it worked now. He had been printing things off this morning and showed me. Everything we tried worked. I wondered if Liev had not been told. I also noted the notes to the Traffic Manager course sitting there on the table in the hall. *This was a course I was going to be taking. It was a day of training with a test at the end. The notes would have come in handy, and could have been pressure for me to cozy up to the inspector.* I called Liev, but he said there was a different problem. There were lines being printed off on the pages. He told me he would show me. I called Marshal, but he was not in the office, nor would he be in tomorrow, Melissa informed me. Ace passed through the office at this time. There was much bustling going on outside. Alex tells me the *redacted* is not doing so well, and he had to go pick up some diesel for it as it was out. Ace tells me the thing is literally sinking. But he does give me a piece of advice. If I can't get Marshal to pay promptly, offer to pay with a credit card. That will break up the log jam. I call Rob the copy guy back and tell him I did look at the printer and it seems to work well, one inspector is very happy, but the other inspector is choosing to show his frustration about other things by putting pressure on us about this. He says when he came the last time they were fighting with each other. "It's always something, but we got to try to be team players." And I offered to pay with a credit card. He tells me I can with the link he sent Marshal. I asked him to send it to me, and he suggests he just send all future invoices to me, "Because apparently Marshal doesn't have time." I say I would be happy for him to copy me in those emails and I could get that moving for him. He tells me he has some deliveries, but can be around here about 4 pm. He seems much nicer now. And so I get that invoice paid before he has time to arrive. *There had been issues with authorizing payments, as well as confusion over what was authorized and who could approve. I had been putting my foot down more and showing concern, so this may have been an attempt to push me into a gray area with a purchase, including Marshal's unavailability and the pressing demand. I may have done something wrong either in terms of HQ or in terms of my local group. Also, Liev's demand for paper towels was not in our contract with them as I will later discover, and could be construed as bribery. ...*

But then he told me he wanted someone else's information, but he wouldn't tell me who. He said this person was tested in December, and then brought another co-worker over, and they tried to remember the date, and showed me the clinic address. "If you could tell me the name that would help a lot." It finally came. I told them I'd get his latest results to him as soon as possible. *I'm pretty sure it would not be right to give out someone's private medical information to someone else without their permission. The sorts of traps range from illegal, to things that could disrupt my relationship with my support network, to reputation damage.*

Monday, January 15th. ... Then I am told that Drew's email is being spammed with like 20 emails. Oh glorious, Outlook is being its special self. I tried to go back to diagnosing that problem, glancing longingly at my task list for the day. I did manage to determine it was not my send/receive cycle. 5-10 minutes is considered about right, mine is 30. A virus scanner? I doubt it. I didn't use to have this problem, and I didn't download or activate any scanners when the change happened. Unfortunately, it is probably my slow Internet connection, and there may not be much I can do about that. If there were, that would be amazing. ...

Ace noted that I had been speaking a lot more, and Alex noticed it too. "She talks now?"

they said. Ace tried to think back to when this transformation happened. "It was after your week of working here alone. Maybe you are making up for being so quiet that week. What happened? What changed?" He seemed genuinely curious. I didn't answer, and he started to joke that pretty soon I was going to be out drinking. "I'm just joking, you know that right? You have this impenetrable fortress of integrity, and it is like throwing little rocks at it, which I think is fun to do sometimes."

Tuesday, January 16th. ... I got the confirmation back from the company, but it was not for the double cutter we had agreed on, and there was no power assembly. I had to ask them for yet another correction, and this time I got an email from the president of the company. So first they give us this awesome quote that we want boiled down to two items and updated, then I say go ahead with the purchase, then I call it in to purchase the thing, verifying the part numbers and price, and the quote number I was going off of, then I receive no confirmation (apparently because their server crashed or something like that) so I ask for one, then it is the wrong thing, and now I have spoken to the president of the company and hopefully it is right now. He was out of the office though, because there in the deep south everything is frozen. He is hoping it will ship tomorrow, no guarantees. But I'm going to have to watch this whole transaction very carefully. *This was a very expensive thing. ...*

Tuesday, January 23rd. ... Ace called me to tell me that my email was repeatedly sending my message again. I had sent that email to ...., Randy, Carson, Drew, and Ace, and they were all getting spammed. I shut down my computer. I drove myself to the post office to overnight two receipts which would have cost $25, but I just sent them priority instead. When I turned my computer back on, my zombie Outlook continued doing that no matter how many times I told it to stop sending things, so I just had to leave it off and use Gmail. ...

Wednesday, January 24th. ... I started up Outlook, and it immediately shot out that same email to our esteemed colleagues. My heart sank. When was this going to end? I tried to tell it to cancel, but it was determined to send this email. ...

Then Ace wanted me to look up Enrique's time card info, because he was wondering how they clocked in 1/2 hr ahead of time before I was even here. He got very upset at Rodrigo and Enrique for taking advantage of the company, saying it was disrespectful to him. And I mean very upset. He was talking about going off on them. It was like they were taking advantage of the situation, and he felt like firing them for it. "Do they think I'm stupid? I'm smarter than they are. And I've got all these other boys eager to work." Of course, this wasn't about Enrique and Rodrigo. Ace headed out and asked me to talk to them when they clocked out and innocently ask them why they clocked in a half an hour early. He said the way they answered would affect how he felt about it. I saw Rodrigo, and I do not think I was nearly as nice as Ace wanted me to be. I asked him why he clocked in so early. He said if we wanted he wouldn't do it, but I pressed why. He explained they had to drive from some distance, so they had to come early to make sure they were here on time. I asked him where they clocked in. The Box truck. "But isn't it locked?" "Yeah, but--" I wasn't trying to be mean, but I was still a little angry from talking to Ace, and I kind of made it look like Rodrigo was up here breaking into cars so he could clock in on unauthorized time. Anyway, I just said it wasn't up to me to set policy about when he could clock in, and we were talking about it, so that's why I asked. I called Ace after they left, saying they sounded like if we even implied we didn't want them to they would stop. Ace was sure that the behavior could be corrected, but that didn't mean that it didn't demonstrate the type of people that they are to have done it in the first place. And he said he doesn't forget that sort of thing. Neither do I.

Monday, January 29th. I went in early. I figured Reid would come early, so I wanted to have a moment to get everything settled before meeting him. I arrived around 7:30 AM. I could see many cars already there, and people moving about in the office. When I entered, I saw a new face, and presumed it must be him. He has focused eyes, but his demeanor was that of someone from the back country, casual, unassuming. He was quiet but not unsure of himself or his place here it seemed. I gave him a big smile and shook his hand introducing myself. I was excited and jittery. Ace told me he was going to take Reid out and show him around, and let me get settled. There was a weariness in his eyes. I let them go and went to my desk. ...

Reid and Ace came back in, and Ace released Reid to me. He told me one thing he could already tell, Reid would not need the job clock keys I was carrying as he was salaried. "Good catch." "You know I'm always watching." I sat across the table from Reid and asked him how his drive was. His eyes flashed. He answered agreeably, but did not say much. ... It was almost strange having someone fill out a form without much difficulty. ...

He completed his tax forms, and the I-9, apologizing for the rough state of his driver's license. His picture was hardly visible. It had been badly scratched up, though the rest was ok. It seemed to work fine. ... I was very curious to see these two together, however Ace was very nervous introducing his friend. He got through the basics, and let me get back to my task. ... The high expectations and the general lack of feedback I got from Reid gave an edge to the situation. He asked me if I had any recommendations for a doctor. That was his one introductory question to me. He said he wanted to go get regular checkups, and wondered if I could refer anyone. *This is another example of one of the first questions being about my medical access. As I pointed out around Oct 13th, this seemed to me to be the first thing Brian Andrews wanted to bring up with me. We will see it again in the HONYs. My guess is Reid was an undercover FBI agent they had taken pains to place.* I didn't have any recommendations for him, but did tell him I found a local clinic to be a good location. He said he would look around and let us know if he found any good ones. I left him with the basic information for the company's clinic, said it was very nice to meet him, and I expected to hear lots of good stories about Ace. He said he had a few, but not too crazy, and after a false start or two he headed out. ...

Ace tells Reid about how we are such different sorts of people. How I don't drink or cuss, how I love the Lord, and pray for them all the time. ... That I do what everyone else hopes to do, and thinks they can too if they just tried.

Wednesday, January 31st. ... Reid was in the other room, but he was keeping one ear bud out, and seemed to be listening with interest, trying to gauge what environment he found himself in. After this conversation he stood amongst us with a bright smile. ...

Reid came in with his completed tests. This was strange. The first test came out perfect. I almost never see a perfect test, and I don't think ever on the one I was grading. Then the next one. Out of seven tests, he got four perfect, and two with one mistake, and one with two mistakes. Even for people who are well versed and experienced in the field, that is absurdly good. Either he is really capable of absorbing large amounts of information, or he cheated, or I know not what. He worried that he didn't do well, and insisted he would retrain on anything he missed. I told him we always work with people on the things they are not sure about. This is definitely anomalous. Two of the questions I didn't know in depth well enough to educate him, so I looked them up. "I did that bad that you have to do all that?" ... He asked me for a three-hole punch, some tape, a binder, etc. I helped him out, and he was courteous, and had a gleam in his eye. When I went over his results with him, I explained that the four perfect tests were very rare. And he said one of the ones he got wrong, that there were over 100,000 injuries from falls each year, was not in the video. He suggested putting it on to check. I said I was indeed curious... And then we watched the video. He was right. As far as I could tell, that information wasn't in there. It was lunch time. I had brought a lot of food, and offered him a taco-like substance. He declined, and said he didn't know what he was going to do for lunch. We didn't talk much. I was intensely focused on my work, and it was actually rather enjoyable. He would whistle every once in a while, and joke about something. ... He seemed pretty focused and diligent himself. He found very useful work to do right on his first day. When he headed out, he thanked me on our first full day together of lending him various office supplies and offering lunch. It was nice to work with another person that I could totally ignore. He was wondering if he had to work tonight, looking over the weather. He said that might be the hardest thing about this job, waiting until 4:30 pm to know if you need to go to sleep or to get back up and go to work. Ace came back, and wasn't super happy. He didn't think we were going to work tonight. The weather was crap. ...

I noticed on the time sheet Rodrigo hadn't signed in again. "Rodrigo still hasn't been back." Ace reassured me it was fine. I think it was since I had spoken to him. "I wonder if I upset him when I spoke to him." "We never talked about that. After they spoke to you they came directly to me. I played good cop-bad cop with them, and basically blamed you because you were paying them for unauthorized time. They were getting you in trouble. Although I did know about it. But they said that they didn't know they were getting paid for that time." ... Ace tells me that not everyone is frugal like me, and sometimes they just need the money. They are not bad people, they just have expenses. "Yeah, Sharon," a sarcastic Reid interjected. Ace said this goes to show you that sometimes bad behavior needs to be corralled. ...

Ace apologized for knocking me on the shoulder this morning, saying it wasn't meant to be anything abusive. "Me too," Reid added. *His voice was high pitched and mocking.* That struck me as a reference to the #MeToo movement. Let's say for argument's sake that that was his thought. Then he would be injecting himself into an argument he has no concept of, picking a side, and attacking by mocking victims of sexual assault in the work place. Have you not heard the saying "don't grab a dog by the ears"? Reid, Reid, Reid. Child. Let Ace and me work this out. You are not a party to this, and you don't know what the heck is going on.

Thursday, February 1st. ...This morning was snooper training. ... The technical problems persisted. The projector failed, and they turned to the TV, but there was no cable. I eventually took one from Ace's extra screen, and that worked, but it didn't matter because no remote meant we could not change the input. This is such a small office, where could the remote have gone? They went back and forth to a few things, and it took probably a half an hour for them to get started. ... I had never used a snooper or seen one work up close, so it was hard at first to picture what they were talking about. After their lecture they took us outside. Enrique asked me if I could get him some more wool gloves, and I ran back to get a set, checking carefully to make sure I had one for each hand. I gave them to him, but then he calls me back and says I gave him two of the same side. He also asks for a pair for Reid. I grab that and return. There were 5 gloves left in the bin. I gave one to Enrique. I gave a pair to Reid. And then I had two of the same side left. ...

I did however realize that employee pay was in the cost estimation, and I know Paige would spaz out if I gave unauthorized people access, so I just deleted that for now. Normally it is Ace and Alex and I in the office, and we are all authorized to everything that I am, but with Reid it is different. ...

But this looks more like someone who is a good fit for their job. Reid asked a question about the 401K, and I explained he did not need to sign another direct deposit form. I also warned him of what my experience with this process has been like so far. They seem to make it hard on you. I said I wasn't going to say they did that on purpose, but that had been my experience with people I'd tried to work through it before. He asked me if I had it and I said no. He asked me why, and I told him, I just didn't want it. ...

Friday, February 2nd. ... Before I got there, I was pulled over, and criminally charged with having a sticker in the wrong location. When I got back I clocked out for a few minutes and switched my plates around and did some legal crap. Reid was still sitting there quietly by himself. ... *Shortly afterwards, Alex called me and told me he needed some information from our other location. This would mean I would have to drive past the same spot the cop had just pulled me over. ...*

Monday, February 5th. ... Reid asked me what I did over the weekend. I told him the normal chores and reading. He asked me if I did jujitsu. I said no, it is hard to practice without a partner. He joked about asking people to volunteer to be thrown. I said that is one great thing about this class, you can show up as a white belt, and you are handed a black belt who shows you how to throw her on the first day. That will sell a class. I asked him if he had done any martial arts. He said he did Tae Kwon Do in middle school. He was really small as a child and got picked on a lot, with his brother too. There was one kid who would always flick his ear. He spoke to him about it one day and the guy got enraged and grabbed him. He defended himself using Tae Kwon Do, but then his sensei heard about it and kicked him out of the dojo. Because self defense is not what that is for. *There were things about his story that are similar to my personal experience.* I was sweeping the floor when Reid came in and started coughing. "Just kidding with you," he said. Reid makes a variety of strange and disarming noises throughout the day. He has a light and friendly, yet cynical sense of humor. He makes an effort to be friendly with people. ...

Ace talked about a boat that he wanted. He talked about a girl he has dated a few times, a medical doctor. She didn't want to come to our city, but he thought she might if there was a boat to go to. *After this the tone in the air shifted. I was soft and subdued, like I had been hurt. Ace was putting on an air of confidence, but wasn't vicious towards me. ...* Ace headed out for the day, thanking me. Reid tried to ask me more personal questions about my schedule, like how often I did jujitsu. ...

When I went home, while alone in my room, I ate the lunch I had forgotten that day which may have gone bad.

Tuesday, February 6th. ... Reid asked me if I did jujitsu last night. "No," I said flatly. Why does he keep asking me about my schedule? Does he want to come? Maybe I should invite him. There was more awkward silence. I found Alex to be more relaxed than I've seen him. But there didn't seem to be the same sort of rapport, or attempt to come up with one, between Reid and Alex. Alex told me that I got the same grade as him on the traffic manager course. I was shocked and elated. I got a 90. Not bad for a topic that was unfamiliar to me. I laminated our certificates. I seem to be developing a little stack of these things. *Often people who claim they are victims of intelligence agencies spying on them will be accused of being delusional, or paranoid schizophrenic. Reid was someone who was extremely smart, educated, and dedicated. Working at this job was a time in my life when my "mental health" or positivity and clarity was lower than usual. However, I was still functioning well enough to take tests alongside someone like Reid and get the same score. Disorganized thinking and speech are a warning signs of schizophrenia, so taking this and the other tests should have been more difficult for me if I suffered from schizophrenia. ...*

Reid asked if anyone had any fingernail clippers. I said I did. He asked if I had any rubbing alcohol for it. I said I wasn't aware of any diseases that could be spread by fingernail clipping. He said Hepatitis C could actually be spread that way. Ace laughed at my expression, saying that I didn't know that but now I was going to look it up. I got him the fingernail clippers and the alcohol. *The evening before, I had acted hurt when Ace talked about going out with other girls. Then I go home and go ahead and eat some food which may have gone bad. I was clearly upset and did something suggesting I wasn't taking very careful care of myself. The question is how aware was I about the health risks? Reid gave me a test of my general awareness shortly after it. Ace was afraid and insisting I was the sort of person who would be very careful. It appeared to me Brian Andrews may have thought that Ace had done something to cause me to endanger my health, and was angry with him, as he was "competing" with Ace.*

Friday, February 9th. ... I forwarded Randy's email to Rob, and as expected I received no response. I texted him that the cyan was out. His response: "I just put a blue one in" Okay... were we supposed to ration ourselves? I went to the printer and took pictures of its status, and sent him many more messages explaining what it was, and asking him when he would be by. I got no response. I called him. He did not answer. I called and left a message. He called again later on, and told me that he just changed the blue one, and there must be an issue with the sensor, but it should work fine. I ran over to the printer and pulled out the cartridge as he asked. He said I could tell if it was empty by the weight. I compared it to the black and could not tell any difference. Then I put them in. It still said there was no ink. I tried printing something in color, and it told me there was no cyan. I asked him when he could bring more and he told me he would "order" them, and they would be here Monday, maybe Tuesday. "Ok, that's what I will tell them." Then he acts like I am imposing on his valuable time. He says he just walked away from a customer and is getting paid $150 an hour and he has to go. I look up the service agreement I paid for him. I only paid up through November. Maybe Marshal didn't pay any more after that. Either this man got paid and is resolutely useless, which would be irritating because I would have to double pay to get another service started, or he did not get paid, and is wasting my time being passive aggressive rather than just telling me. ...

Reid stopped in to ask about the work orders, and I walked him through a few things. He seemed to be getting worn at this point. He wondered about working nights when you know you're coming in the next day, and flipping back and forth. "I don't know how Ace does it." I said. But Reid said he still wanted to still be involved in the day shift, because the one sets things up for the other. He also didn't have many critiques of my job description for the job listing. He only asked that people know how to use basic hand tools. I don't know Reid, that is asking a lot. When I was updating my post status table to match his notes, I told him when he selected the start and finish times for a night shift, they should be on separate days, so as to not get -16 hours worked. "Ok Sharon, I was tired!"

One afternoon I went out after dark and took an impromptu walk around the neighborhood. The next time I went to work, Reid asked me if anything exciting happened last night, and watched me for a minute. Then at my Jujitsu class, there was loud conversation between others that I overheard. Drake was telling someone else a story. Someone had an emotional outburst, and they were threatened that if they left the house, they were going to be committed.

Monday, February 12th. ... Reid popped in to say good morning... Reid asked how my weekend was, if there was anything exciting. No, not really. Ace told me he didn't want to pick a fight with me on this, but he heard on the radio some lady taking his side with the whole "Me Too" thing. The woman argued that the newer generation was more sensitive to normal human interaction, and were taking away the human experience, equating serious with trivial. This was due to the fact that they are raised by helicopter parents and are scared of everything, and they are 'getting their fix' through technology, AKA porn. Rather than face the rejection and complications of real human interaction, the younger generation is less promiscuous, has less sex, fewer marriages, relationships, or children, and therefore is more freaked out when they see these things. He mentioned Japan. Japan, Russia, really actually the US and the developed world are not procreating at the same rate they are dying off in their native populations. ...

I wrote this next part in my journal, but did not say it to anyone. But anyway, here goes Ace trying to get a rise out of me, and telling me he doesn't even want me to respond. He did of course admit that not all cases of women objecting to sexual harassment were over-reactions. I think it makes total sense to say that populations who are less exposed to sex will be more sensitive to it. Of course. Does that mean that sensitivity is a bad thing? After all, people can be acclimated to pretty much anything. The Spartans used to leave their weak infants outside the city gates to starve to death. The Indians used to burn widows alive with the corpse of their husbands. Cannibalism has from time to time and place to place been totally normal. So the ability to 'get used' to an action isn't proof that it is okay. What could be wrong with getting used to sexual behavior? I have seen a lot of unwanted sexual advances in the form of jokes wrapped up in the sexual revolution. I do not believe for a moment that Abu Graib would have been received the same way in the America of the 1950s. The public had maintained such a level of respect for each other that such a thing would have been beyond unthinkable, exactly where it should be. How have people allowed themselves to let that standard slide? What normalized that? It is entirely possible that you are more okay with some spontaneous displays of affection than other people. That is why choice has to be involved. You may be out of touch with someone else's "sensitivities," but that doesn't make them wrong. How should I say this? When in doubt, don't rape people. Also, don't rape people. Having said all this, I will grant that there are degrees of crime. Making a joke is not the same thing as a sexual assault. But what about this: if Al Franken had made a joke about lynching black people, of course that would not be on the same level as lynching black people, but it would nevertheless make him a piece of trash unworthy of our esteem or tax dollars. People who relish the idea of rape suck. On the other hand, society as it is is a sick and scary place with its hysterics and venom spewed in all directions of confusion and discomfort. It is an unfortunate thing that mature topics are in the hands of these children. I would also imagine that innocent or at least well meaning men and women are at risk of being badgered and harassed by it. Anyway, back to the day's agenda. I received another slew of emails from Reid. ...

Tuesday, February 13th. ... Reid did a beautiful job of giving me requested updates in anticipation of the daytime closures for Airtable, and a detailed report of his progress on the posts last night. He was not coming in today. Unlike everyone else, he gets to sleep some regular hours. ...

I got a response back from Paige about Javier's pay stub. She had mailed it. I notified him, and he starts getting into all kinds of flirtation. He sends me two pictures that never load. I ask what they are and he starts sending me kissy emojis, telling me I'm beautiful. I explain I am only interested in a professional relationship. I do not want any romantic attention. I have already told him this before. He asks me how I would like him to be professional. Is he stupid? I wondered how that isn't just him toying with me, trying to look like he is complying while getting some terms to wriggle out of "just professional." He laughs. "Tratemos... kieres?" "Do you want to try?" is what he asked. "Let's try a professional relationship please." I respond. He tells me he is professional. I say thank you, and then he sends me another kissy emoji. He obviously thinks I'm a joke he can toy with how ever he likes. At this point I can't interpret his actions as in good faith. I'm done with him. And his conduct is inappropriate in the workplace. I tell Ace that Javier is being obnoxious, giving me sexual advances after I made it very clear

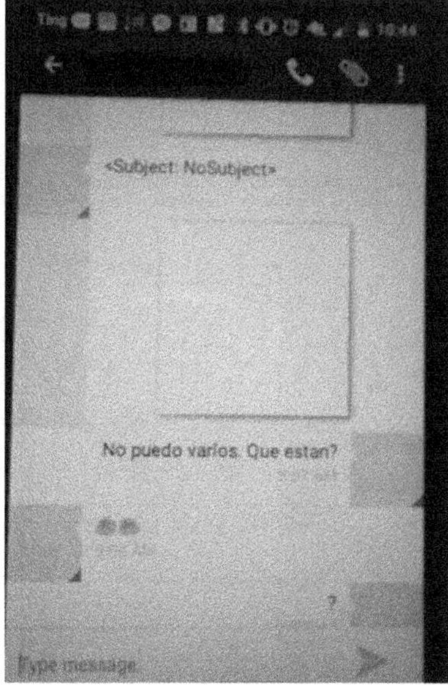

for him to stop. Ace tells me to keep records of the conversation. ...

If he keeps going like this, we may have to do something unfortunate. He says Javier probably is doing this because he doesn't expect to come back. I said I wanted to just tell him that he is a jerk and he can talk to someone else, because I don't want to deal with him anymore. Ace thinks he has taken me out from under a rock and has shown me what the world is really like. Not everyone reads their Bibles and treats people with respect. It's okay, we take new admissions. ...

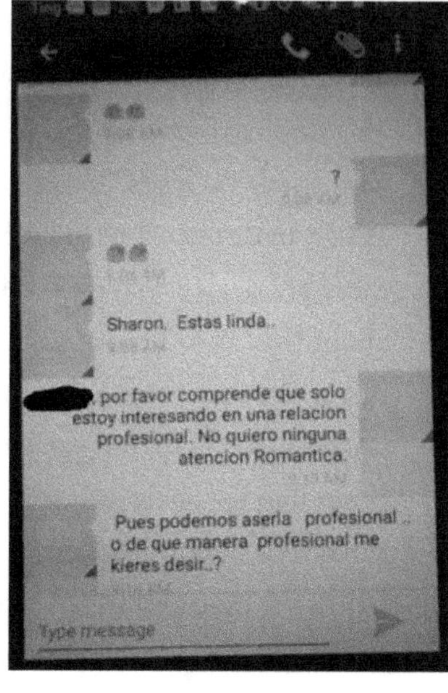

Liev stopped by to tell me that the printer wasn't working. Now I feel horrible for him. It has been days on this volley of complaints since it has worked. But Liev would not say a cross word about it. I texted Rob, who amazingly responded telling me his part was bad and he ordered another one. It would be a while. ...

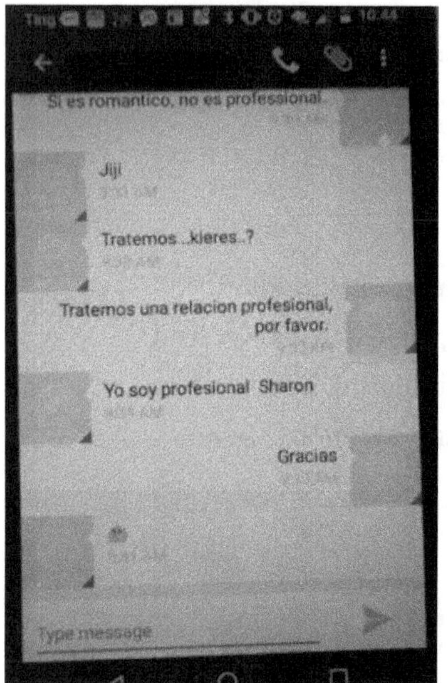

Wednesday, February 14th. ... However, for a first, nothing from Reid. Reid did ask me to print out some work orders he had prepared for today's lane closure. ...

Reid called me to tell me he would be late. He was driving back from *redacted* dropping his wife and kid off at the train station. He asked me to give the work orders to another co-worker and he would call him and tell him what to do. I went about distractedly, telling Alex what was going on. People were coming in to clock in and prepping to go. A co-worker wished me a happy Valentine's Day, apologizing for not bringing chocolate. I hadn't even realized what day it was. I never really think about this holiday. ...

Reid had come in by this time. He looked like he had been run over by a train. He asked for the credit card and said he needed to go buy a wrench because they broke one.

Thursday, February 15th. ... A delivery man from YRC came. It was a teeny tiny little pallet of rubber bumpers. I got to ride the forklift for the first time in forever since I was the only one there. He backed his truck so far back he covered a lot of the area I could have put the skid. I set the forks up, and he mostly pushed it on. I put it in its place. As I was backing up to put the forklift in its spot, some guy wearing no safety vest walked in a straight line right where I was backing up. He didn't even look at me. I had to stop for maybe a good 30 seconds waiting for this guy to get out of my way. He disappeared into the porta john, and I looked all around to make sure the area was clear before parking in my spot. The truck driver was just standing there watching. *He had this demeanor like he was watching an execution. ...*

Reid had not done a work order or submitted a daily report. ...

Reid called in the guy early since he was just sitting out there. ... But during the interview, he basically just explained what the work would be like. He seemed very uninterested in Jake (who I think ended up being a great employee). ... Jake wanted an answer, but Reid told him we would do a lot of interviews and decide in a couple of weeks. Reid didn't really have any other questions and dismissed him. I was waiting to hear Reid's impression, but it was not terribly robust. He didn't seem either excited or put off by Jake. ... I logged back in to my computer, and Reid made a comment that that was the longest password he had ever seen. He joked that I would say it was my shortest one, and the others were like a paragraph. I suggested Reid look through the rest of the applicants. We talked through them. He said one person had said he was great with interpersonal relationships but broke the golden rule, which is where he referred to a general group of people as male, rather than saying he or she. "Because we are all equal. #MeToo." *He seemed enraged. ...*

I don't know why Reid thought that was a point of controversy. He didn't like one of the guys, because he had been in the military in 1980. So he would be in his 60s. It is probably less likely that he is going to be able to handle the physical aspects of this job, which are the primary aspects, but that isn't a given. I've worked with a few that would do better than most. But this was something that Reid fixated on. When I would talk about someone, he would ask me, "How old is he?" He pushed the topic. It is illegal to ask applicants about that, and I don't think we are supposed to discriminate for that reason. Reid also asked questions about the pay rates, and then asked me what a co-worker made. I told him in general, and I don't think I should have. We are deciding on the pay of people we are hiring, but at the same time, people who are already in the company tend to keep that hush hush. I thought better of it and made a note to myself. "Oh, this one's going in the pocket," he said of me. *As if where I put notes is a matter of significance.* "And this one is going behind the monitor," I mocked. He said that someone knew what someone else in the company made, and that he was mad about it and might just quit because of it. That made no sense with what I know about these people. It sounded like he is just making stuff up. He was pushing for information he shouldn't have. He was pushing to discriminate against people. In general, he is acting with flagrant disregard for me and for the other workers. He reviewed the resumes, and picked things out of them I might have overlooked because I was distracted by the presentation. He said he would pick two from the "white kid" pile, and fill the rest of the positions with a Hispanic co-worker's friends. He asked me what I thought about that. I said if it were me, I would want to talk to co-worker's friends too and see if they were any good. I love the guy, but it would be good to know their qualifications. I left not too long after that. There is something grisly about Reid. Snide. Underhanded. Like he enjoys watching people fall. I don't think I want to work with him. I don't think he is pulling quite in the same direction. I told him his daily reports were good, but lagging behind the past two days. He said I needed to tell him things like that because he didn't know there was a time requirement. But from when he first came, he seems to not have the same work ethic. He seems eager to let shifts be canceled or report less or less frequently. He is different than he was.

Not too long after Reid was obviously trying to get me to break the law and I was acting coldly towards him, as I recall it was a Friday morning. I sat up during the night and acted like I was terrified, or in a lot of pain. When I went upstairs not long after that, the youngest boy who lived in the house acted terrified of me. It may have appeared that I had become aware that I was under surveillance, and was acting upset by that. The son's reaction to me makes sense as many informants, especially those families I stayed with, could feel especially frightened of retribution. -2/14/20

6

LEAVING MY JOB

F*riday, February 16th*. ... Reid came in and asked me how I was. "Good." "Good?!" He seemed surprised and shaken. I asked him if he still had the resumes. He got them for me. It was another thing I had been thinking about after I had left. There were applications with social security numbers on them. I had redacted them in a different version. I swapped them out for him. I told him I had been talking to Paige and some information was supposed to be kept confidential. It was her understanding that everything on the job site could be shared with Ace, myself, and Alex, but he was not to be included in some things, such as payroll. I said it would be messy trying to include him on everything, but I asked that he understand it is the expectation of the company that our co-worker's pay be kept confidential. He seemed eager enough to respect that. He brought his laptop into my office. He was printing things off, asking me for the three-hole punch. Honestly, I was still upset with him. He was deliberately trying to get me to slip up yesterday and tell him things I shouldn't. I met many of his playful comments with silence. I'd rather not have spoken to him at all. He hung around, lingering over my shoulder. I had to keep thinking through what messages I was sending, what I was bringing up on the screen, how far I stepped away from the safe when it was open. But he hung around like he was desperately trying to read where I was with him. I'm sure he could tell I was angry with him. He asked me for some pins. I asked how many. He thought fourteen. I went to Alex's office to get them. "Ah, that's where they are. Now I'm starting to get to know the office. Soon I won't have to ask you anymore~" I walked off, ignoring him. ...

Reid asked for the three-hole punch again, and then asked for my permission to have access to that drawer, so he could get it himself in the future. "Yes," I said flatly. "Thank you for the access." ...

Reid was called into the main room of our trailer by Frank, the company's president. Frank told him he had been here long enough and knew what was going on. He was to go to the white board and demonstrate. One of the first questions Frank asked him ironically was about the pay rates of the employees doing post replacement. He asked about fringe, and I stepped in for a second to tell Frank what I knew. Reid, from what I heard, gave a thorough description of the work process and progress. It didn't sound like Frank had too much to complain about. When he was done Reid and I were back in the office. Frank and the others went out for a few minutes, and Ace came in. "Ace, buddy." Reid called out to him sounding desperate for support. ... Reid told Ace yesterday he had tears coming out of my eyes when he was joking about using Ace's chair with all of the levers as an intelligence test for the job applicants. ...

Reid came right back in, a pep in his step. He asked what the WIFI password was again and I gave it to him. His skidmore had arrived. He came back into my office. I was having a hard time just dealing with doing my job, and I certainly didn't want to deal with him. He sat in Ace's office chair. I managed a scowl at him. He was holding his phone, looking at me with this gleam in his eye, his hands in front, fingertips touching, his chin down, looking up at me with a devious grin, then left singing, "I'm so excited." ...

This is a problem. I do a job to make money. If people are putting me at risk with my coworkers, let alone legal risk, it is no longer worth it to stay at that job. Legal risk entails losing said money, as well as job continuity, relationships, freedom, safety, health, pretty much anything. Reid doesn't seem to care. He is rubbing it in my face that he can get in my space and ask for my participation. What good is that? If he means to create a harassing environment, besides his temporal sadistic satisfaction, what good outcome is going to come from this? I wonder if he doesn't know what to make of me, or how to work with me. He has just shown himself to be reckless with my life. He needs to give me space until he can demonstrate that he is aware, by some miracle, of the error of his ways and that he has become more dependable. Of course, this world is a rather ruthless place and I have no reason to expect that of him.

Monday, February 19th. ... I spoke to Reid here and there. He kept coming into my room again, and I would have to turn over papers with social security numbers on them. I closed the door, but he just burst through it to ask me more questions. There wasn't really anyone in charge, and lots of people drifting in and out. Reid asked me if I had anything for them, because today would be the day to do it. Esteban was in the room, and I told him he and Pedro had to do training, but who knows where Pedro was. Reid took it upon himself to go find him and get them going. I was about to step out the door again when there was a grinning Reid in my face about to open it. I asked him nicely to please knock when he sees the door closed. He agreed to this, and the hectic disruptions stopped. He wouldn't even open the door when I called. I had to open it myself. I found this very nice. As they were busy in the other room doing training, I kept my door closed much of the day.

Tuesday, February 20th. ... Ace sat in our office and handed me an application Javier had brought him. "He's here. What do you want to do about this situation?" "We can do two things. Either we just keep going, and let it escalate, and I keep records, until it gets to a point where we have to do something that isn't good for me, or Javier, or the company. Or he can not deal with me anymore." Ace asked me if he had my permission to speak to Javier about his behavior with me. I told him in my opinion Javier's behavior was inappropriate. Ace asked me if he should be fired. I said I wasn't advocating that. He wondered if they should do a verbal warning. I said he could be talked to first without anything going in his record, but that Ace should keep records so that he could show he was doing everything he could and wasn't liable. Ace recommended Javier and I not be alone together, and I thought that was a wise precaution. He said this was sort of my job, as an HR assistant. I said I hadn't told Paige, and wondered if I should recuse myself. Ace said that wouldn't be necessary. I was being objective enough. "Maybe too objective." He said Zoro would have to be brought in on it, since he would have to translate. He asked me if he could speak with Javier, and I told him I was okay with that. Reid asked me cautiously how I was, and told me he had bought me a box of Swiss Miss to replace the two packs that I gave him. I told him he didn't need to do that. ...

Zoro came in, and Ace talked to him about what was going on between Javier and me. He asked Zoro to speak to him. I was already blue, and I wasn't sure if I liked this. After Zoro left, I asked Ace how Zoro did the last time he spoke to Javier. This topic can go a lot of ways, and it is important to try to give an appropriate response. In the past, guys have retaliated or pre-emptively attacked, just in case I don't want to put up with any crap. And Zoro was told no details about what was actually done. Ace was very confident in Zoro's abilities as a leader. I have never seen reason to believe otherwise, but since it is my decision and is about me, I would like to know this is going to be done properly. At least I have a better idea of how Ace addresses misbehavior. ...

Reid came to my office for a moment, and knocked on the open door, just to appease me....

Wednesday, February 21st. ... I got an email from Melissa asking if my vehicle sticker application project had gone well. She must have heard one didn't have one. It's good of her to check. I told her as far as I knew, but that I didn't have a list to compare the results to. She sent me this, and I went outside in the beautiful day to look through documents in vehicles. It seemed like a mess to me. The first truck had an expired inspection and a document for *redacted* in it. I went through each vehicle I had access to, and the end result was that I had failed to put on two inspection stickers, one needed an inspection, two vehicles have yet to be accounted for, and the process is still too chaotic. I wasn't happy with myself for missing those stickers.

Thursday, February 22nd. I got there a little early. No lane closure today. When I got there, there was a box of Swiss Miss on my desk. Reid came to my office, and told me, holding up his arm in front of him impulsively and defensively, that when I was ready he had two questions for me.

Friday, February 23rd. ... Alex was speaking with someone in his office about someone named Darius? He said he found this person crying on the job site. He asked him what was going on and Darius said he needed to talk to him. He said his wife? was poisoning him with cyanide. She was having an affair, and they were putting things in his food and everything. Alex said that is way too much for him to handle. He told Darius he needed to go home and sort all of that out, and Darius left and never came back. *The message seemed more like any complaints or suspicions I would have against harassment would not be welcomed if I voiced them, and I may lose my job. ...*

An applicant who had canceled his interviews showed up unexpectedly. I told him the project superintendent had just left and the Forman was across the bridge. He and Alex chatted for a minute while I called Reid and asked if he could swing back over for an interview. A few minutes later Reid arrived and asked me if I had given him an application to fill out. I had neglected to do so. Reid seemed to improve his interviewing technique since the last time. The applicant spoke with Alex and me. He seemed a decent and steady guy, but when he spoke with Reid he was nervous and unsure. He gave brief, even one word responses to questions about his work experience, seeming unsure of what to say. He seemed to want the job well enough. He thought being a manager might be somewhere in his future, although not necessarily at this job. After the interview, Reid came into my office and told me that he thought the applicant would make a "formidable" employee, and that we could depend on him for leadership roles. "Thank you for calling me." I think that comment had less to do with him and more to do with me. Reid left again, and I got my medical done. The whole ordeal took an hour plus driving time.

Monday, February 26th. ... Ace was picking over something I had done, and I heard Reid behind me tell him not to trash me. *This was shortly after I had praised Zoro for coming to my defense for speaking to Javier about me. The way Reid stood up for me was very awkward and halting, like it was the sort of thing he thought he should say, not that he felt he should say. -2/19/20 ...*

Reid brought his work into my office so he wouldn't have to listen to training. He asked to enter my office bubble to access the copier, saying he knew there was all manner of confidentiality going on over here. He said he was happy I was doing the paperwork, and that at his last job, he would get 30-70 emails a day. Now he gets maybe two. He asked me if I ever felt like I could never get the sleep out of my eyes, because that is how he felt today. Ace called me to go over a few things, and asked where Reid was, and why he wasn't answering his phone. I repeated Reid's comment that he was ready to talk now. "Don't get Sharon in the middle of our fight." Reid said to himself speaking of him and Ace. *Reid is mirroring the thing I was upset with before, namely that Reid was intruding in a fight between Ace and me. Echoing a person's feelings is a tactic used by narcissists to create the conditions for friendship and gain trust. I had written those feelings in my journal and not told them to anyone. -2/19/20 ...*

No one had given me anything for Friday. Reid apologized for his oversight. A different applicant called back to ask if he had gotten the job. I told him he did not. He seemed genuinely shocked and upset, and asked when there might be an opening for him. I said I didn't see one coming. He asked why he was being refused. I told him that I would send him some explanation. Reid said something like, "Look who's angry..." like he was gleeful he had caught someone showing anger. I shot back with, "He's upset." *That seemed very strange to me. Why would he be happy he got someone he isn't hiring angry? This appears to be totally normal in the culture of a harassment campaign. -2/19/20* ... He was going to go home and try to get some sleep, and he can get Sunny, the boat captain, by if he does not.

Wednesday, February 28th. ... Ace was ready for a break. He asked me after I kept saying during the winter that there was nothing to do how I felt now. "I'm ready for a break." He burst out laughing. *There had been a lot of talk recently about how tired everyone was. The way he laughed it was like he had tricked me. -2/19/20*

Thursday, March 1st. ... Reid came in, and was thrilled to see Jake studying. ... Reid had said if he failed the test again, he was going to watch the video with him. I graded it right then, and found out he did fail it again. I wondered if Reid really was going to do that. I started to look over what he got wrong, and explained two of them to him, but Reid came back and said he would have to watch the video again. He got a test for himself as well, and they sat down together in the conference room. *I had recently expressed dissatisfaction with an attempt to pencil whip employees through a test. Reid was once again reflecting characteristics I had recently approved of. -2/19/20 ...*

Jake found it hard to watch the video and read the test at the same time. "The nice thing about the video, is you have a remote, so we can pause and rewind." Umm... When it got to a point Reid wanted to pause, the remote wasn't working so well. "This is getting frustrating.

Is everything we have around here broken?" Oh crap. He tried to mess with the TV controls, but got the blue screen of death, and didn't know how to get it out. He asked me, and I explained how we pick up the TV and throw it to the floor. I messed with the controls for a while. I couldn't find an option in the menu. Then probably after like seven minutes of me not figuring it out, Reid pulls the TV aside, presses a few buttons, and gets it. ...

When I came back, Reid was telling them over the course of our contract, two, maybe three people would jump off the bridge and kill themselves. *The next morning, he seemed ashamed and deeply apologetic towards me. I don't think Andrews wanted me to kill myself.*

Friday, March 2nd. ... Reid went to make some coffee. "This may be the last cup I ever drink." I got a call back from Maria, anxiety in her voice. She wanted to know which people would be going out by boat. "In case anything were to happen, the rescuers need to know which bodies to look for." She seemed serious, and she would know more than us the severity of the situation. I made a few revisions and spoke to Alex. We were getting three guys from a towing company coming down. I had a list of Sam, Dean, and Bill. I asked Alex if these were the three, and he said they were. For one guy, I didn't have his phone number. I remembered they wrote those on the temporary parking pass sheet and went to check. I managed to match one to one of the numbers, and asked Alex to verify the other. I was waiting for an answer when I realized the obvious thing to do was to just call it. It was out of service. Reid came in and asked about my list. I read through it, and he said that sounded right. The three boys showed up, and I went out to physically meet these people and verify their information. Turns out, they were none of the three on my list. ...

The power kept going out, which meant I had to turn my computer back on, and restart it to be able to send Maria a finalized version of the sign-in sheet. When I came back to give the sign-in sheet to Reid, I couldn't see anyone at the dock. Then Alex came and called them up. "Sunny needs to come back and get me. Randy and Barry are pissed," he said. Apparently he goes to get something for ten minutes, and they all left without him. I followed him as he paced, listening in. So, the guy who I would guess is in charge of the job site in the middle of an operation of questionable safety wasn't even informed that everyone left without him. And obviously my sign-in sheet was wrong again. I called Reid. No response. I called Zoro. No response. I texted Zoro asking him to confirm the list, since he is usually very good with this. No response. I texted Reid, then I texted Alex, and got a list. Then I got that same text verbatim from Reid, including spelling Atticus like Atticus0. The difference was that in Alex's text, he added "and Reid" to the list, and then the "me" referred to him. Reid told me ten people were on the list, but in Alex's list there were 11 including Alex. I asked him if he was on the boat and he said no. Ok. Now I have something. Normally, people don't respond to me, and it's really okay, because what I do is less important than what they do, but in this case, this wasn't good enough. I asked Reid and Zoro to keep me updated. I figured if I kept getting information from two independent sources, maybe I could check the one against the other in case there were any mistakes. Or someone didn't bother to respond. Reid gave me a heads up that everyone except for the three guys were headed back. ...

I heard Reid saying yesterday that he got two hours of sleep and woke up in someone else's bed. A new employee only got two hours the night before last. And then there was another new employee who wasn't faring too well a few days ago after doing a night shift after a full day's work.

Monday, March 5th. ... Reid asked me if I did anything exciting over the weekend. He asked me if I went to DC and got crazy. He also said he didn't want to be looking through my stuff, so he let me fetch the *redacted* for him. Reid also told me that an employee had not been correctly paid last week. He was missing his hours on his trip south. Reid knew he went on that trip, and what day and for how long. ... I spoke to the employee and Reid about his hours. Reid saw my phone with the tape over the camera and asked if I was afraid of spies. I asked Paige when she was going to send the statement. Turns out she already had, but someone else said they hadn't gotten it too, so she sent it again. And then I spent a few more hours fighting through disparate receipts. Reid, Greg, and Randy came back. *I acted like Reid hit a nerve when he asked about spies. I also acted nervous afterwards. This may have been when I searched the bathroom for cameras. I had been suspicious of Randy. There was a moment before I left for the day that I seemed to reflect on something and freak out at the thought. That was in view of Ace's web cam I believe. I was alone. The next time I saw Reid, he continued to be polite, but he was containing a raging excitement. One of the first ways I was harassed after leaving the company was my food somehow went bad and I got an upset stomach. -2/20/20*

Wednesday, March 7th. Reid was in his office when I got there. It is snowing today. Mucky really. Enrique was there as well. Reid was in and out of my office copying and printing things. "What's new in the world of Sharon?" I smiled at him, but didn't tell him. He laughed. He went outside for a moment and started coughing badly. When he came back, he said he felt like he had been run over by a truck. I heard he has the flu again, this time not as bad as the last. Derrin and Jake are both home sick with it as well. I got him a vitamin pack. "Do I put this on the desk and snort it?" He asked. We had no water. We also have no cups. We had a good 20-30 or so a few days ago, but they disappeared. Reid was sick, and was asking about the water, so I went to the conex box to grab some bottled water, but that is basically gone as well. Also, the water in the tank outside is empty. ...

At one point I heard a crash, and Greg, the company's mechanic, asked Reid if everything was broken around here. "You should know that by now. If it catches on fire immediately after starting, you know you're working on the redacted." ...

An inspector came in to ask us to hook up their printer. He laughed, saying he understood my weirdness about it as it was always something they used to do for themselves, but Ace would always bring a thumb drive and do it. ...

Thursday, March 8th. Tom and Greg were at their laptops in the conference room. "What's going on today?" "Just staying positive. If you stay positive, good things come your way," Tom tells me. I gel well with Tom. ...

I hung up and asked Reid if he had anything for the daily report yesterday. "I just sent it!" He yelled. I had just checked that. Turns out he sent it five minutes before Ace called. A co-worker brings me his DOT card to laminate. I never got around to it last time. I went straight to it, getting the laminator from Reid's desk. It went in, but it didn't come out, and then it started smoking. Reid came in at that moment and used his knife to get a piece to grab from the other end. I managed to get out the crumpled DOT card, and the rest of the laminate sheet was a solid/gooey mess. Reid started to joke and I walked out of the room, trying to straighten and salvage the card. I couldn't get a good copy of it now. I had a full sized one in his DOT folder, but when I scaled it down it was fuzzy, and when I tried to laminate that, the laminator started smoking again. ...

Friday, March 9th. ... Derrin came in with doughnuts. Two boxes, and two pints of orange juice. Ace was happy to see Derrin. ... "Where did these come from?" I asked. "Derrin brought them," is all Ace would tell me. *Ace seemed a little evasive and nervous about the question. -10/13/20 Derrin brought doughnuts. I later learned Reid had authorized it. Reid had seen me bring my own a while before and noted I had a bit of a sweet tooth. -2/20/20* ...

I also got the inspector's plastic cups in, but after reviewing the contract, I could find nothing in it that suggested we should provide the inspectors with cups. I pointed this out to Ace. "It says computers, software, printers, and camera. It says nothing about cups or paper towels." Ace didn't think those little things were a big deal. I wondered if it wasn't bribery to give the inspectors things. Ace wondered if a judge would seriously rule that giving them plastic cups constituted bribery. I said that is assuming that people are reasonable. Which they aren't necessarily. *At some point shortly after this, Reid came in and asked me if we fill out any kind of paperwork when we give things or do things for the inspectors.* ...

Reid came in all happy. Like, reeeally happy. "Sharon, we have a skid of water!" *I had just reacted well to Tom telling me to be positive. Reid's over the top behavior seemed put on. Given that it was the next day, this seems to be another case of mirroring, or parroting back to me my likes so as to fabricate trust. -2/19/20*

Saturday, March 10th. Ace texted me after 9 pm on Friday letting me know Saturday would be a good night to work. ...

I heard a worker apologizing to Reid, saying the painkillers and sleeping pills were a bad mix and that is why he had to go home early. "Painkillers and sleep medication would make you feel out there." Reid didn't seem too upset or concerned. ...

Ace asked me to ride with Reid. He would be driving the forklift. We stopped at the exit through the black fence. I said I had never gone that way before. Reid asked me several personal questions. I asked him if he liked his job and he did, except the crazy schedule, although that is one thing that made it interesting. He asked me if I liked mine. I said it was getting better compared to the beginning. He asked me how long I have worked with the company I think it is 6 months now. He asked me if I do Facebook. I said I do some things. He said in 2004 he vowed he was never going to do Facebook. ...

He said the first time he came up, he was nervous when he passed the police officer because he was driving the wrong way. Reid thought it was so cool that we were driving a forklift onto the bridge to work. We were driving Ace's truck, but the windshield was getting foggy. I asked if he used the Rainex for fog, but then remembered it was Ace's truck anyway. *Why I would say something that stupid?* I love that stuff. *I kept some in my car. My instinct was to reach for it. This was one example of me not being mentally clear that evening.* Reid said he didn't know what Ace used on his windshield. He asked me to grab his laptop because he didn't remember the exact location they were going to. I searched around in the back and pulled it out. There was a paper stuck in there with the post number. He told me it was the same password. I typed in Ace's. He said of course I would remember, it is the one I gave him. He told me it again. ... I typed this in probably a good ten times, with and without caps lock, and it didn't work. I was never able to unlock it. "Thanks Sharon." Reid said as we arrived. Thanks for what? *I basically never have that kind of trouble putting in passwords. I was feeling rather vague and alarmed. -2/20/20*

And here we were. After being stuck in a box for six months, I was in a real world with three dimensional objects that were moving around. It was like work or something. There were snoopers on either side of the bridge, bright work lights punctuating the spaces, workers in safety vests grabbing tools. Enrique and Jake said “Hi” again. I could see Ace approaching in the distance. He welcomed me to the jobsite. ... As I was standing around in the commotion, Ace called me to step back, and told me to stay alert, or at least look like it, as he motioned for a vehicle to back up. ...

Ace discovered he needed paint, and asked me if I knew where it was in the office. I remembered the one gallon jug in the conference room, and he asked me to take his truck and get it. "Are you able to get back here from what you've seen?" I wasn't paying enough attention. I was also horrible with directions anyway. I wasn't totally sure, but I realized I didn't have my driver's license with me. Ace thought it would be okay, but left it up to me. I said I didn't think I should. Ace asked Randy to go get it, and since I had a key with me sent me along. ... I grabbed the paint and my license and we headed back, only for Ace to say that is the wrong paint. He left to get it, and brought back a bigger gray bucket with a red hazard label on it. He said it had been buried in Alex's office forever, and gave it to a worker to mix. ...

Reid was complaining that the mag drill was wanting to pick up. The magnetic force that was holding it on to the post wasn't strong enough. He wondered if we could put more ferrous material underneath to give it more hold. Ace thought the galvanized layer on top would cancel that effect. I asked Ace if just putting another magnet on the other side would work. He thought that was a good idea. I asked Reid what would happen if someone made a mistake drilling. "You don't. That would scrap a post. Everyone has to have a 100% success rate. It is not like traffic managing." Reid said with constrained anger. I watched him as he marked the next post. *Lol, Reid got a 90% on his traffic managing test like me. Reid acted like he had been emotionally burned when I suggested magnets. He was an engineer with experience and was not drugged, and yet I offered a better idea than his despite my inexperience and how I felt. This suggested he had a fair amount of ego, and irrational expectations of superiority. This fits the trend of narcissism. -2/20/20* ...

I asked how far Atticus and his guys were. Ace asked me to drive his truck over there and see. *Ace had asked me multiple times to drive his truck. Every time he did, he would flinch. Ace told me once he had a history with a drunk driving accident.* He told me 15 mph around people and 35 mph elsewhere. I honestly wasn't too sure about this. I am totally new to this worksite. I don't know the layout or the rules. I drove carefully, and came to cars parked on both sides of the bridge with flashing lights. I wondered if they meant to block the bridge, and went out to meet the people and talk to them. I met one guy, and asked if he was with the state agency. I was trying to read anything off of their vehicles. He didn't seem to expect me to be there, but admitted he was an inspector with the agency. I told him what company I was with, and that this was my first time up here. He still seemed unsure, and asked if it was a cold night. I said it was fine, and then he just left down some contraption on the bridge. I figured it was okay for me to keep going. There were a lot of other people on the bridge. I kept having to drive around them, and other passing cars. There were signs on the gantries that would tell me to stay in one lane, or green arrows, but sometimes they would be blocked. Ace called me and I stopped to pick up. Ace told me to come back. They needed something in the truck. When I got back, Reid came up and went straight for a tool in between the seats. I went to see Ace, who was on the forklift helping with the other snooper. He told me he got a call. I must have weirded someone out, because they called and said someone was wondering on the bridge. Ace told him it was cool. Gee thanks. He asked me if I made it to Atticus. I had not. He asked me if I was ready to go. I was. *I was not happy, because it made me look like I wasn't with it.* He told me to drive his truck over here and he would take me back, and waited till he could extract the post he was working on. ...

Gaslighting is used generally by psychopaths and governments infested with them to discredit victims of their crimes. It is standard practice. As I appeared to have seen through their cover, they may have started to develop a smear campaign so no one would believe me and they could surveil and abuse me without consequence.

We talked about some employees. We liked them, but Ace told me about how one had to be taken home Thursday he was so out of it. He didn't show up Friday, but called an hour in to say he had taken sleeping pills and had slept through. He wasn't happy with another, who he had told me "isn't really with it". He asked me if I had any plans this weekend, and I didn't have much to report. He thinks he will bring up his boat with Sunny and Greg. He thinks I should come more often Saturday nights to get everyone started. He told me Derrin had been pulled over and told his license was suspended. Apparently some nonsense with him not paying child support. The cop let him go because this was the first notice he had gotten. But this is a problem, given that driving equipment is a big part of his job. Ace said we'd see how things go in a month, whether it was going to work out. ...

I grabbed another doughnut. I think this is the fourth one I've had. Maybe a little greedy. I hope Reid knows he can't use the company credit card for that. *I had eaten three doughnuts on Friday. Derrin brought them in and I heard they were from Reid. I had asked Ace where they were from, and he seemed a little defensive in his answer.*

I believe it was after March 10th. Samantha and Kelly tried to deliberately hurt me at Jujitsu during sparring. I had given a snap kick to Samantha. She grabbed my leg, paused a moment, picked me up, and threw me down extremely hard on my back. I had my head tucked in, although that could have been dangerous if I didn't. I gave an over the head chop to Kelly. She got ready to throw me, paused right before she did, and gave extra emphasis to straining my wrist, which hurt some time after. I do not know why they did that. -2/14/20

Monday, March 12th. Ace was there when I came in. He was sitting in a chair in view of the door, leaning forward, shoulders hunched. He had a look of recognition and dread on his face. He held his cell phone up subtly as I came in, then let it drop. He said he had barely slept in the past three days he was working so much, although he was pretty good handling night shifts compared to some. Even so, you feel it after a shorter period of time. In a worker, you can really see him tiring.

If Ace had read or heard of my previous journal post, and the doughnuts were spiked with something to make me drowsy, the way I had described eating so many and pointing out they were from Reid could cause Ace to fear I had figured out what was done to me. He used his camera to get a mood check to try to read me. Looking back, Reid may have changed his password and asked me to open his laptop so that I would think of myself as not with it. Then he suggests being nervous driving past police, maybe so I would be when I did in my condition. Ace suggested that people who were not with it were undesirable employees, and talked about being pulled over and having your licence suspended. He had asked me to drive a route I was unfamiliar with in front of police officers. He kept flinching when he did. All of this may be intended to have the effect of making me feel weak and more in need of his approval and help. It is possible that I may have been pulled over that evening. I could have gotten a DUI if I had been drugged, lost my license, and been left with a record. I had recently gotten my Maryland license. But they seemed to be satisfied with others thinking I was strange and confused, given that is when I was called back. Though Ace broached these topics later on. -2/20/20 Reid is away for a few days. *Perhaps to protect him in case I wanted revenge. ...*

Ace and Alex left in his boat to bring it over, and he asked me to pick them up in his truck. He told me he would call me, and texted me while I was finishing up payroll that there was no rush but that I should head over. This would mean I would be driving the same truck across the same spot I had last Saturday. When I got to the restaurant Ace said they would buy me lunch. It was an upscale establishment, and they were sitting at the bar, discussing work planning strategies. I declined lunch and got my own. Ace insisted I at least drink some water, and when I didn't, he sighed and shifted uncomfortably. When I got back, they had already finished their meal and seemed to be waiting. They did not seem upset with me. Ace drove back, and told Alex about Derrin being pulled over with a suspended license, and said leadership gains a lot of respect by not freaking out at things like this. The child support scam punishes you by taking away your means to get to work. ...

One of the things Derrin was cited for was not having a medical card with him. We had no idea one was required. I looked up the rule and found it was. This is the first we had heard of it, and considering Paige's questions when another employee went for his test, she didn't know either. Ace wanted me to figure it out and resolve it. *Derrin had been given a $1000 ticket while working with a company vehicle. Not all of the charges seemed reasonable to hold him responsible for and not the company, such as this one. Several leaders in the company seemed to not like him. ... Ace alleged the leadership was racist, and one reason Derrin was disliked was because he was black. I argued to a higher boss Derrin should not be held responsible for the lack of medical card, and the response was to* *command we fire him. They punished him because I stood up for him.*

Ace asked me if I am such an anarchist, why do I try so hard to conform. Why don't I break more rules? Why not drive without a license, or avoid paying taxes? It is fun. I should try it. He asked, isn't anarchy refusing to obey the government? I told him it was not. He asked what it was. I explained it is the idea that each person has the greatest claim to themselves and their own lives, and to the extent that we organize as a community, we do so by mutual consent. Whereas the government forces the will of some on others, and is for the most part, an unjust act of threat and violence. Ace thought I should stop calling myself an anarchist. He wondered that I get much of this from my Christian faith, but that would seem to say that I ought to follow the rules. I explained that the government is not authorized to execute injustice, but as for us, "as much as is possible with you brethren, be at peace with all men." Ace wondered if my anarchy was purely ideological then. "In what way do you live out your anarchy?" I did not answer him. He said “Good talk.” And promptly walked out of the trailer. *It was as if he knew he had been unmasked, and was asking more directly why the government might have a problem with me. He also encouraged me to break the law, which is more entrapment. It sounded like he was saying things would be better for me if I didn't call myself an anarchist. If my political views are a reason why I am being targeted, that would be anathema to what the American system is said to be.*

At Jujitsu around this time, several people told a horror story of an employee stealing from the company they were leaving.

Tuesday, March 13th. ... Drew was now very alarmed at how we must get this material storage payment that I had reminded him of a few days ago. *If I was angry with the company and wanted to retaliate by way of theft, this would not likely be something I would have taken the initiative to remind them of. If they had let it slide I believe they would not have gotten around $200,000. ...*

Ace said he was getting more and more tired of the codependent Mexicans who can't drive themselves, the more he hired English speaking people who had driver's licenses. ...

He asked if I was getting bored or didn't have enough to do. "I have a lot to do, it's just that it isn't here." Ace said he had been meeting this girl, and said how she can't believe what a thing tiny houses are. Ace said I would be the one to talk to about it.

Wednesday, March 14th. ... I was attempting to complete the request for payment of stored material. This involved printing off a formal letter and signing it, but of course the printer decided to take some artistic license with the toner. I replaced the toner, and then I was getting a different problem. Now was the time to finally troubleshoot this thing. Eventually, this led me to discover how to stop the printer from crinkling the papers, but created yet another problem. There were a few tutorials and FAQ pages with software that didn't exactly match, and all kinds of recommendations. ...

Thursday, March 15th. ... Ace told the boys he got a text from a kid he used to work with in the shop. It was a picture of a part, and a message about how Ace picked him out of nowhere and taught him to weld. Eight years later his welds are consistent every time. Ace said that made him tear up a little. *Perhaps a reminder to me of the opportunities that Ace had given me. ...*

Ace wondered out loud how he gets into these situations. "Because you work for--!" I stopped myself. "Did you have a more specific question?" "Just what you were about to say." "--People who need Jesus." He laughed. "That's perfect. We all need Jesus." I laughed to myself, saying I just needed to wear a T-shirt that says 'Y'all need Jesus.' "You need that sign above your desk." "Yes!" *If I were to be accused of stealing from my employer, my anger at them could be used as motive.*

Friday, March 16th. ... As I was about to leave, I saw a credit card on the table, and put it back and texted Ace. Ace came in and said it was Zoro's.

Monday, March 19th. Change of plans. I had been doing a good amount of thinking over the weekend. I didn't feel totally confident that I was making the right choice in quitting right after taking my vacation. ... I drafted a one week notice resignation letter and went in Monday morning. In comes Ace and Reid. "You still here? Are you going to work or what?" "Hi Sharon, good to see you again." Reid stood in my doorway for a moment. "You're not very good at taking vacations." Very true. "One moment," I tell Ace. He leaves the room for a second as I print out and sign my resignation letter. *If I was trying to retaliate against the company this also would not make sense.*

Friday, March 23rd. I texted Ace, asking him when and where he would like to pick up the keys. Today and tomorrow would be good for me. He texted back, now is good, and gave me a coffee shop. 15 minutes. I drove there and found the place. Ace was at the cash register getting some coffee. I found a seat and waited for him. "Sharon, how are you?" "I am well." "So, are you staying here or going back to your home town?" "Probably not." "What are you going to be doing? Jujitsu? Tiny houses?" "I think there will be tiny houses in my future."

7

LOOKS LIKE MY STALKER VIOLATES MY PRIVACY, PROPOSITIONS ME, AND APOLOGIZES

This chapter covers my time before leaving Maryland and staying with family for a few days. It is some of the first HONYs (to be explained). I stopped my daily journal for a long time after leaving work. After quitting my job while living at the room I was renting in Maryland, I saw a very out of place news story about a cop giving a man advice about how to break up with his girlfriend. It was short and very generic, and did not have their names. It said she did not tell him how to do it, and just said it was up to him.

My food that I kept in the family's fridge began to go bad over the course of days to weeks. I asked my landlady if my chicken taco mix smelled okay, and she said it was fine, although it did smell bad. My cream of chicken and rice smelled awful. My milk went bad a few days after buying it, and I got sick from drinking it. They did not seem to have any problems with their food. The next time after I got sick from milk and went to use the bathroom, my landlady rushed to get in first, then called me so that I could go in. One possibility was there was a camera, and that they were expecting to film me sick. This was before the shower curtain slipped.

Two weeks before leaving, I thoroughly cleaned my room. Afterwards, there was one of what looked like my landlady's hairs resting across the back corner of my desk. My room was always locked.

I knew they were watching me. I heard that FBI assessments had to be reviewed every so often, so I thought it would probably end in a few years. Drugging me and ordering me to drive around construction workers at night was extremely dangerous. They were using me to endanger the public, and I couldn't accept that. I decided to go to college to study engineering. I had wanted to be an engineer. I figured as a student they would have less of an ability to order me to do dangerous things. By the time I finished college I expected the investigation to be over.

The following is the Humans of New York entries from Facebook that I saw over a period of months. I had enjoyed reading them for a long time, and at one point they went from a normal variety of experiences to almost all of the posts resonating with themes in my own life. However, they also had hundreds to thousands of comments on them relating to the content, though I didn't check every comment for authenticity. I include some speculations about what these posts may refer to or their intention. It seemed to me like the real author was Brian Andrews.

> Humans of New York - Page Liked • April 2 • Manila, Philippines
>
> "Soon after my father passed away, my mother got addicted to gambling. We began falling behind on the rent. I realized what was happening when I found a Casino Filipino membership card in her wallet. I tried confronting her, but she got furious. She told me I had no right to tell her what to do. She began to disappear for days at a time. There was no money for my thesis project at school. I'd borrow food from our relatives just to feed my younger siblings. Then a few months ago our landlord finally kicked us out and we moved into a slum. It was so noisy and dirty. But I did my best to ignore it and focus on my schoolwork. We live in an evacuation center now because the slum burned down. My friends at school have been helping me with clothes and food. And during it all, I've kept up my grades. I'm graduating on April 3rd with a degree in Secondary Education. I'm going to become a teacher. I think I've already learned a special skill that teachers have to keep their personal problems out of the classroom."

I was planning on going back to college. It seemed like many of these were an encouragement to do well.

> Humans of New York - Page Liked • April 3 • Manila, Philippines
>
> "My boyfriend left as soon as I got pregnant. I was terrified to tell my father, but he discovered my pregnancy test hidden in a drawer. He didn't speak to me for a few days.

We'd always been close, so I knew something was up. Finally he asked me if I wanted to tell him something. I began to cry. I thought he was going to kick me out of the house. But he just went to speak with my mom in the other room, and when he came back, he asked what I planned to do. I told him I wanted to keep the baby, and from that moment on he was very supportive. He cooked me all kinds of dishes whenever I had cravings. He gave me words of encouragement. He started saving money in case I needed a cesarean section. But during my seventh month he came down with a fever after wading through floodwater. The next week it turned into a cough. We took him to the hospital, went home to get clothes, but he died by the time we got back. It was so sudden. I had no idea what I was going to do. I got all my strength from my father. It seemed like keeping the baby had been a mistake. It's been a tough few years. I had to drop out of school and find a job, but my son is doing well. He's very smart. He comes home from school with stickers and stars. He's a 'Mama's boy.' It's been hard, but I've proven to myself that I didn't have to end a life just because I couldn't face it."

This has been a theme that came up a while later. It seemed that if Brian thought I was pro-life, that a child I gave birth to could be used to control me. There is a lot of discussion in his work about abandoned children as well. -2/20/20

Humans of New York - Page Liked • April 4 • Manila, Phillipines

"I work on cargo ships. I'm usually at sea for nine months at a time, but sometimes it can go past a year. My last trip was 25 months. It's tough out there. You're so far from your family. It's been easier since we got Internet last year. But before that you could only make phone calls when you got to a port. And you'd only get a letter once every two months. My mother died during a recent trip and I couldn't even go home for the funeral. She was fine when I left, but somewhere off the coast of South Africa, the captain came into the engine room and told me she'd passed away. I was so weak I couldn't work. The other guys volunteered to take over my shifts. Everyone chipped in some money and gave me a gift. We do that every time someone loses a family member. Your crew mates are all you have out there. All of us are going through the same thing. And if you don't share your problems, you'll go crazy."

It is common for a target to have various pain points presented to them to see which one they react to. Another possibility would be to get me to miss my mother and confide more to her.

Humans of New York - Page Liked • April 5 • Manila, Philippines

"I come from a village. My life would have been nothing if I'd stayed home. I'd just wake up, cook for my siblings, and clean the house. I wanted to do more with my life, so I'm working in the city to save for my education. It's been a lot lonelier than I expected. I'm so far from home. I spend my evenings alone in my room at the boarding house. I have nothing to do but think of my family. I've been here a year, but I still haven't met many people because I work so much. My coworker is my closest friend. She's like my mother away from home. She reminds me to eat, take my medicine, and get enough sleep. If she sees that I'm sad, she tells me to rest and does the work herself. It's just nice to feel cared for. I'm not sure if I could make it without her."

...

Humans of New York - Page Liked • April 9 • Manila, Philippines

"Since there are only two million Assyrians left, there's a feeling that we might not survive. So we lean on our rituals. We lean on our church. We lean on our language, which nobody else speaks. It's a 'we' culture. Everything is about the group. And if you wander too far from the group, you become a threat. Because the group can't afford to lose anyone else. Your relatives will remind you that you should be proud to be Assyrian. You'll be reminded that our people were slaughtered. So it's tough to go your own way. For the last couple months I've been traveling alone. My mother is convinced that this is my breakout plan. She's been so strict on me my entire life. But a couple days ago she sent me a text message that brought me to tears. It said: 'I know that I said you've seen enough and that you should come back, but if you want to stay longer, and you feel that it's safe, than you should definitely stay. And we'll hear from you when you come back.'"

Lots of themes of loneliness and dependence on others.

...

Humans of New York - Page Liked • April 11 • Sydney, Australia

"Both of us are very passionate about the environment. We actually met at the screening of a documentary about ocean pollution. Maybe we'll get politically involved one day, but right now we're just trying to live sustainable, happy lives without harming anything. We try to focus on the little victories. Recently we set up a triage hospital to help injured ducks during hunting season. And a few weeks ago we organized a beach clean that picked up half a ton of rubbish. It can be hard to affect change on a global scale, but we try to set an example, and it's nice to see ripples of change in the people around you. I've even got my mom teaching vegan recipes to her friends."

Brian Andrews is a vegetarian. He often seemed to try to encourage me to become one. -2/20/20

Humans of New York - Page Liked • April 12 • Sydney, Australia

"He was clean when I met him. He'd drink and use drugs a bit, but only when he partied. But he's not strong like me. He tried heroin and he liked the feeling. And he couldn't stop. It's not that he's a bad person. He has a soft heart. He smiles a lot. But he has a demon to fight and I already tried my best to help him. I tried to move him from the area. I tried to get him into rehab. I took him to parenting courses and counseling. Things got better for about six weeks. He was acting positive and he was there every day. Even if we got in a fight, he'd stick around and work things out. But then he started disappearing again. He started getting angry and violent. Then he'd come back on drugs and act like everything was fine. And I wasn't going to allow it. You can't just do anything you want and come home to my children. I hate being a single mom. It's lonely. I hate that I'm playing into an Aboriginal stereotype. But ultimately my dedication is to my kids. I haven't cut him off completely, but now he's on his own. He's got to figure it out himself. He can't visit my kids until he's 100 percent."

I believe what had just happened was that I saw through the attempt to sicken me and film me in the bathroom. I had acted anxious, then I left the house and struck up a conversation with a homeless man. After that my behavior made a substantial shift. All tension left me. This lasted for a while: I think hours. I took no drugs. The reaction was psychological. However, it may have appeared as if I had. This HONY post seems to be a reaction, depicting me as in a romantic relationship. Brian Andrews did not seem to like the idea of me getting hooked on drugs, and did seem to like giving ultimatums of "dumping me" during this period. -2/20/20

Humans of New York - Page Liked • April 14 • Sydney, Australia

"This is the first time I've travelled alone. My friend told me that you learn a lot about yourself when you travel alone. But so far, I find it the other way around. I feel like I learn more about myself when I have to relate to other people. Today I walked around Sydney. I saw everything I was supposed to see. I don't even know why I did it. It just felt like the thing I should be doing. Maybe I'm just not a contemplative person. I generally feel satisfied with my life. I don't feel like I'm missing anything. I don't have to love what I'm doing to be happy. But does that make me ignorant? Should I be searching for something?"

Humans of New York - Page Liked • April 16 • Sydney, Australia

"I moved here from Kenya with my husband. He became very abusive when we arrived. He made sure I didn't have any friends. If anyone came to visit me, he'd immediately say: 'I don't like them.' I was scared all the time. When my mother came to visit from Africa, she could tell something was going on. A mother can always tell. She saw how he spoke to me. When she left for the airport, she seemed so worried about me. It broke my heart. So the next time he hit me, I called the police. And I've never looked back. I have a great new boyfriend now. The kids are happy. I've got a job and I'm back in school. Things are really perfect. But I beat myself up a lot. I think: 'If I'd only left earlier, I'd have been here so long ago.' But I did leave. I'm here now. And that's the important thing. Sometimes I need to remember to pat myself on the back."

As if Ace was an abusive relationship and a new one is not? To be clear, I was not in a romantic relationship with Ace. We would have been considered friends and colleagues.

Humans of New York - Melbourne, Australia

"I'm not looking to set the world on fire, but I need something to challenge me. It feels like I'm reaching a critical juncture and I need to make some sort of decision. Up until now I've just been floating along. I've been at the same job for a long time. I do the same things day in and day out: smoking, drinking, things like that. It's just so easy to be a consumer. It's so easy to reach for pleasure and avoid pain, so that you never have to face the future or think about getting old. I don't have anything elaborate in mind. Maybe just get out more, or move to a new place. Maybe have my son live with me for awhile. I just want to prove that I can set a course and do the things I say I'm going to do. Or if I can't, I at least want to be honest with myself. So I can stop beating myself up about it."

Humans of New York - Sydney, Australia

"I'm studying abroad right now. I have a bit of a 'boyfriend thing' going on back home. He's a nice guy. We met at a party and twenty minutes later he held my hair while I vomited. Even though I wasn't very attracted to him, he intrigued me. I'd never met a boy who didn't just care about sex. I'd only dated football players and gross teenage boys. He was different. He genuinely cares about people. He'd bring me all kinds of presents. One time I had a bad week at school and he brought me a gift package with all my favorite things. It was nice to have that much attention. I did just enough of the girlfriend thing to keep him around. Nothing he did affected me, and everything I did affected him. It was a weird sense of power to be the one with less feelings. I'd always been in the opposite position. Even after we broke up, I still hung out with him and let him give me gifts. He even gave me this journal for my trip."

Ace technically was never a football player although he does love it. After reading this, I started copying down this and all the previous ones that I thought were meant for me. What he is describing, having a sense of power by being the one with less feelings, that describes a narcissistic relationship. It is about making people desperate for you, to need you, so you have power over them. I had been keeping a regular journal while working, but had stopped afterwards. It appears Andrews wanted me to continue writing.

Humans of New York - Melbourne, Australia

"My father had an ulcer that became infected. It was relatively simple to cure but he refused to believe the doctors. Instead he diagnosed himself with some sort of virus. He stopped taking his medicine. He created his own ointments instead. He's very intelligent so his reasoning could sound very convincing. It was hard to identify when it crossed the line into mental illness. But the infection never healed. He went from surfing and swimming every day to barely being able to walk. He aged twenty years. And still he refused to go to a doctor. He'd isolate himself from anyone who challenged him. When he finally collapsed and was admitted to a hospital, the doctors said he had the lowest red blood cell count they'd ever seen. Only then did he accept that things were out of his control. He's much healthier now. He's almost back to normal. He'll occasionally fall into the old script of defending his actions- but he manages to catch himself."

I mostly stayed away from doctors, and don't have medical insurance. I used to take essential oils. This is the other example of medical insurance being the first thing he seems to want to ask me about. My act of copying down the HONYs would have communicated to him that I knew it was him that wrote them.

> Humans of New York - Sydney, Australia
>
> "We met two years ago at the office. At the time he'd just gotten out of a really bad breakup. It started with just lunch and coffee. Then we started meeting after work. We hooked up a little– somewhere between second and third base. I told him that I liked him so if it wasn't going anywhere then we couldn't be friends. But that's exactly what ended up happening. It's excruciating. It seems like we're always on the edge of a relationship. We hang out. We go to the beach. I'll go to his place, cook dinner, watch a movie, and then leave. We get handsy. We might kiss a little. But that's it. Recently we went on a trip to New Zealand and shared a bed for four days. We spooned every night but nothing else happened. I know I'm complicit, but when I push him on it, he acts confused and says that he has a lot of friendships like this. We kissed a little on my birthday last week. The next day I texted him: 'I'm not going to pretend this isn't happening.' He wrote back: 'Let me think about it. I'm in meetings.' And he still hasn't replied."

I am usually careful about being covered up, but one time, a few hours before this, the curtain in the shower slipped. After that I acted very hurt. My mother posted a passage from Luke on Facebook about not worrying what you will wear. Also, the son of the family who lives in an adjacent room was talking it sounded like on a radio program about himself, like he was psychoanalyzing himself. I used to like to listen to psychological lectures. He was hyped up and shouting this way for hours. It should not have to be explained how wrong it is for a man who was looking for a girlfriend to then put that girl under surveillance, get to see this girl naked, and then ask her for sex when the balance of power is such that it would be no different than statutory rape. -2/20/20

I responded on Facebook: You are doing the right thing being open with him. Whether friends or more, you don't want to be in a situation where you are hurting each other. You have to be honest in your relationships or they aren't real. Even if you care deeply about someone, sometimes people have differences or are in different situations that get in the way of being close. If that is something that is going to tie you up in life and cause you pain, you need to face that and move on.

Attempt number 9,000 to say "No" and that that is absurdly inappropriate, considering the "coercive environment."

Humans of New York

"I was at a rave when I was sixteen, and my mates said 'Try this.' And it made me the opposite of who I normally am. I'd always been really shy, but suddenly I was dancing in the crowd and talking to everyone around me. Everyone else had issues too so it felt like I belonged. Soon I found a source and it became every weekend for the whole weekend. I'd be completely wiped on Monday so I started skipping school. I ended up flunking out. My depression and anxiety got really bad. I was getting in fights. I lashed out at anyone who tried to stop me. When I was seventeen I tried to run away from home but got pulled over. My mom sat me down and said: 'If you keep going down this road, you're not a son of mine.' I'm better now. I just do it once a month. I know what's at stake. My anxiety is much better now, but I think the stutter might be permanent."

Sometimes I would seem content out of the blue. It seemed to me that this person was very concerned I was going to get hooked on drugs, and tried to steer me clear of them.

I had just moved out of my in Maryland room and was staying with my family for a few days before moving to Tennessee.

Sunday, April 29th. I'm staying with my parents for two days. I arrived yesterday and greeted the animals. I saw my father first. He still hasn't gotten a job, and things are not looking good. *My father is an experienced software engineer. The job market was booming. It should have been easy for him to find work. ...*

While I was rearranging my things, my mother entered the room to talk. She wanted to know if everything was good between us as I had been quiet and staying away. ...

She asked if I had been traumatized by something during my childhood. ... *It seems childhood traumas are considered vulnerabilities or pressure points which are used as rationale to harass people. It may be difficult for the average person to wrap their head around the depravity that is status quo in a harassment campaign. A person's mother can be forced to betray her child, and get them to admit to being abused, sexually or physically, or to something that causes them unbearable pain, just so that pain can be used against the child to turn them into a puppet of their tormentors. The heartbreak of both the mother and the child is beyond what most people could imagine. ...*

We talked about the Korean drama she is watching with Daddy, where people live under cameras like Roommate and a panel of judges tries to determine who likes whom. She started to ask about my life, if I was going to move where the company put me. I just said I had no such plans. She asked me what my plans were for future living situations. Would I want to buy? "I don't plan to rent forever." "Do you like living in a room in someone's house?" "It's better than some things." "You don't have as much privacy." "It isn't mine." I was vague and changed the subject. I told her I had been listening to a guy named Jordan Peterson. She started asking more questions about my life, and I just said I didn't want to talk about it. Then she went downstairs. We watched some of that Korean drama a bit later. We started talking about how nice their police are, and this crazy video about a North Korean cop being beaten by an old lady with a purse and sulking away, and how amazing it is that the North and South are ending the war right out of the blue as it appeared to us. Then we started talking about my brother's new job. She didn't remember what the name of the company was, just that he had had a phone interview, and they wanted him to come in and meet everyone. She brought my brother out, and he told us that the company was called *redacted*. He said it was two blocks from the White House, and that they are asking him to supervise some junior developers or programmers. The location is some real estate. *That is around where FBI headquarters is located.* ... He said the guy who called him was named *redacted* and that he thought the "interactions would be better." I asked what he meant by that, and he told me that people often felt the need to fake their qualities *Narcistan! Clear narcissistic culture*, and the unrealistic requirements they place on themselves can be discouraging, so he felt as a leader, one of the most important things he could do was to cultivate an environment where people could be open with their flaws. ... Mom called it the "imposter syndrome" and said I should watch Ted talks about it. ...

Today, Mom came out while I was packing things in the car. She had some conversations she wanted to share with me that she had had with a friend. She thought I might find them interesting. Then she said she had been thinking about what I said yesterday, when I kept asking if there was anything else with someone from my childhood. She said she thought she might remember something. Normally, she just puts things behind her and forgets about it, because what good does it do to dwell on the past? She thought there might have been something about a drone or a camera, that he had a camera in my room, or was filming me when I didn't know it. She couldn't remember what she had done about it. She asked me if that had happened. ...

In response to the topic of children being bullied, I said that someone's level of development or gender doesn't mean that that isn't a person and it is okay for them to be used as a punching bag or trampled on. Just like anyone. If I had seen someone treat someone else the way that this boy treated me, I'd say that person is trash. And to the one who was abused, that I am sorry this happened to you, and we should go with better people so we don't have to be so miserable. She said her mother wanted her to talk to the boy about the way he treated someone else. I thought she should. She said she did, but that didn't matter. "Then he's going to hell. That's his choice. You've done what you should do." "But I still hope that he can be redeemed. Isn't there anything that he can do?" *This wasn't the way she normally talks, and was kind of forced. It seemed to me like perhaps she had an earpiece and I was in part carrying out that conversation with Brian Andrews. That would mean my stalker was forcing my mother to act as his mouthpiece so he could work on playing me. To think of apologizing or making amends in such a way, it is hard to imagine this person is not a malignant narcissist or psychopath.* "Of course. He can realize that there are things he has done for which he deserves to burn, and... really what we are asking is that he get right with God. He has to learn how to respect another person." I told her when she said that this is just the way things are, like I should just accept it, "It is not acceptable. I would not tell the victim to accept it." Mom thought things done in the past should be let go. "The past is relevant in so far as it is relevant to the character of the people in the present."

> Humans of New York
>
> "I was raised with that Jewish intellectual worship of knowledge. But all my professors in college were small-minded nasty little ***** getting off on their own power, wanting me to parrot them while telling me they didn't. So I decided I was a nihilist and that I was going to do as many drugs as possible. If the goal is to spend your whole life trying to get rewards to trigger chemicals in your brain, why not go straight for the chemicals? But that didn't work out very well. It quickly became less of a philosophy, and more of a massive drug addiction."

This appears to be an apology. As though he felt the way to heal the shame I might have felt was to show some of his own, so we are on the same level of ego.

* * *

Some comments from family:

My mother's comment: This is confusing, and I don't recognize the conversation.

My comment: About childhood trauma?

My mother's comment: I did not consider your childhood to be a traumatic one. And I was (as far as I knew) always fair with you.

My comment: ... I do not need to name him here, and I only included what was necessary to get my point across. I am aware there is nothing in that short statement that demonstrates that you are an informant, but I think the point I make is an important one for people to understand the nature and depravity of the program.

My mother's comment: The program...

My comment: The harassment program.

My comment: The harassment program meaning the political harassment program that began in 2017 at Porcfest.

My mother's comment: Ok, I was never part of anything like that, and to my knowledge (which is considerable), none of the family at home were.

My mother's comment: Ironic that in the place we thought you would find true libertarian freedom, you found emotional tyranny.

My mother's comment: The flow of this post is a bit confusing because you keep putting stories from Humans of New York in between personal things.

Maybe if you format it with quotes in-set from the other text, it will be more obvious.

My comment: Unfortunately, people interested in freedom seem to attract undercover police. It's like we threaten their choke hold on the country or something.

8

A HYPNOTIST MOVES IN? MY AGENT/STALKER TRIES TO RECRUIT ME

T*his is my time at my first apartment in Tennessee, May to June 2018.* It is mostly a continuation of the HONYs and my comments on them. I stayed with my family briefly, then two days were spent at an Airbnb looking at various rooms to stay in. When I got there, I wasn't receiving any cell service. On my laptop at my Airbnb, I contacted customer support through chat and told them the problem. It was fixed instantaneously.

One landlady I had contacted, Julia, wanted to think about my application and get back to me. I spent a day sleeping in my car in a parking lot. This may have been the day that the Walmart employee dropped her cellphone and it slid into my bathroom stall as I was changing, and then another very nervous employee outside of the bathroom asked if I wanted to sign up for a gift card. I would have had to show ID.

I rented the room from Julia in May and June. She knew that I was uncomfortable living with men, and told me I would be able to help choose the next roommate. About a week after I moved in, I was told the day before that a different man would be moving in with me. He was called Harold Repitanski, as he "likes to repeat himself. What was strange about him was that he almost never used the bathroom. The only shampoo in there was almost always left in the same spot at the same level, as were the rest of his toiletries placed neatly on the counter, although those were adjusted a few more times. I almost never heard him go in. He would often talk to himself loud enough for me to hear, repeating himself over and over again, saying very simple things. His name and his habit of repeating himself were rather coincidental. He may have been a linguistic programmer or hypnotist or some such person. He often tried to set me at ease around him. He installed some wiring in the house so he could work in the back and I could have the living room outside of my bedroom undisturbed. I could often hear him and Julia speak outside. One of the earlier conversations was about recycling in the laundry room not being rinsed out and attracting flies. He was very upset about it. I later asked to speak to him and we went to the living room. I told him that I could hear him outside through a single pane of glass. I told him I was the one who did that, as I didn't know anything about recycling. I said if he has a problem with me, he should speak to me about anything I do, or else it would be complaining to the landlady about me.

One day not long after I went for a hike in the park, I had been experiencing back pain under my ribs, at the location of an apparent bite. Later, when I went to take a shower, the joints in my hand hurt and I held them and bent them a bit. After this, I heard Harold talking to Julia about how Lyme disease presents with muscle and joint pain. Harold said he had been having some pain in his back, but it might have been how he was sitting. Julia talked about how bad the condition could get. When I was speaking face to face with Brian Andrews, he said Lyme disease was a concern of his. He had known friends who had had it, and didn't want to walk on the grass. I went out and got the antibiotics. This is evidence of video surveillance in the bedroom and bathroom.

A rescue cat that did not get along with people befriended me. He had been found abandoned in a cardboard box as a kitten. After that I happened to walk into the kitchen and overhear Harold talking loudly on the phone, admitting to some nervous problem that had been somewhat debilitating. This may have been to recreate my relationship with the cat with him.

I heard Julia talking about the crazy neighbors who could shoot if you came over. But she said she thought she saw someone moving out. Harold said he thought someone was living there. *It seems to be typical for FBI agents to try to live as close by as they can. They spied on MLK Jr. from the neighboring hotel room.*

Over the summer my family's dog died. The date he died was 6-25-18. That is about the one-year anniversary of Porcfest. I hadn't noticed the date.

While I was working on getting my high school equivalency test done for college, during my second meeting with the teacher, he kept asking me pressing questions in a low, controlled, urgent voice, demanding I tell him where I am taking the test, and at which location.

I found another place to stay closer to the college. When I left, I went to say goodbye to Harold, who I had stayed away from almost as much as humanly possible. He asked me if I was moving to another state, and said in a negative tone "Good luck, you never know what could happen." He may have overheard me on the phone with my legal service asking about the terms of where I was moving to next.

> Humans of New York
>
> "I want to make sure I don't miss a second of connectedness to the brands I'm representing. In the digital world, there's always this feeling that if you don't respond back—it's a lost opportunity. If someone is talking to you, you have to answer or they might think you don't care. If a client asks my opinion, and I don't reply 'I agree with that'—he might ask someone else. My paycheck depends on always being connected. So there's always a screen in front of me. I'm always responding to 'pings' and 'dings.' But it has a lot of consequences. Especially on my family. My kids are growing up, and the moments I should be focusing on are happening all around me. So that's where I am right now. I want to figure out how technology and innovation can give me more time with my family, not less."

My brother had just posted something to my Facebook page to which I did not respond. ...

> Humans of New York
>
> "Annie had a tantrum because our magazine had a Fun Zone with puzzles and I did all the puzzles. So she started stomping around but Mommy got sick of it so Annie went to time out in our room and turned out all the lights. I tried to go inside but she kicked her boots at me. I waited for ten minutes and then I went in quickly and asked her to help me on a puzzle where you had to find all the differences. And that made her happy again because Annie loves puzzles."

Annie does not participate in puzzles that involve terrorizing innocent people. -12/7/18

Note: Andrews considers torturing innocent people all day to be the Fun Zone. -3/10/20

On May 5th at around 1 am, the dogs barked, and were let loose. The next day one had a limp. ...

Humans of New York

"I'm producing a podcast right now and I keep coming home pissed off. I dread getting emails from my collaborators. I get angry every time they disagree with my approach. It's just that I want to feel proud of what I create. I want everything that I make to be a reflection of myself. And that's impossible when you're working with collaborators. So I have to get better at separating myself from my work. Every project doesn't need to represent me as a human. The reality is that the podcast is bigger than me. There's a lot of money involved. There's a lot of people involved. And for some reason I'm the only one that's pissed off. If I keep saying that the problem is everyone else, and one by one they're saying the problem is me—then it's probably me."

5-8-18

Humans of New York

"Five years ago I had a bout with breast cancer. I didn't catch it very early. I had to get chemo, radiation, and a mastectomy. I'd never felt so tired in my entire life, but it didn't just throw me off physically. It made me really, really sad. I lost all my enthusiasm. I lost my positivity. Before it happened, I had so many dreams. I had been thinking of starting a business. Or maybe writing stories again. It seemed like I could accomplish anything if only I did the things that I was supposed to do. But all that disappeared after the cancer. I got much more self-conscious. I started thinking: 'If bad things can happen at any time—why even bother?' So I've been in a bit of a rut these last few years. I've been floating along as an office manager. But I recently lost that job, and I'm thinking this might be my chance to go after my dreams again. I'd love to work with young folks. I'd love to write books and stories for children. And I know it sounds crazy, but I really want to open a bookshop."

5-9-18

Humans of New York

"We've been married for almost twenty years. We have two children. But he suffers from depression and self-medicates with alcohol. He'll quit drinking for stretches at a time, but he keeps falling back into it. So I have to support our family on a single income. And I'm just so tired of keeping him uplifted all the time. I don't feel emotionally supported. There's no physical intimacy. But I can't bring myself to leave.

> He's a great dad when he's sober. And I know that our family might be the only thing holding him together. But I can't help but wonder: 'Am I missing out on an amazing relationship?' Especially when I feel tempted at a work party. I just miss that feeling of connection. But my husband hasn't crossed any red lines. He hasn't hit me. He hasn't cheated. If I found out he cheated, it would be so easy. And it's gotten to the point where I almost hope he would."

5-10-18

My comment on Facebook: You aren't really together. I don't see any way forward with the way things are. You should find someone who can give back.

A few hours after I wrote this, my landlady gives me a clear shower curtain. She says she realized I didn't have one. The shower curtain was obviously a reference to the recent incident in Maryland where it slipped. Narcissists feel empty alone and look to others for emotional support. If they are trying to get that from someone who is blank and numb from the devastation they have wrought or for some other reason, it is highly unpalatable to them. They are constantly trying to create the right emotional energy in someone, and are willing to use threats to get it. In this case, it was more like threatening to leave the "relationship."

At the time my days were spent mostly in my room studying math. My mood was generally sullen. There were a number of things that did help my disposition. I remember I used to listen to Jordan Peterson, and one of his points that had made an impression on me was that there is good reason to be resentful, but people were meant to slay dragons. They were meant to go out into the wild and the chaos, and struggle with it to create order. He talked a lot about personal responsibility, being proactive rather than reactive. I was feeling sorry for myself, which was totally legitimate, but he made good points about making the most of the opportunities I had, no matter how slight. This was one of several things that changed my orientation from victim to fighter (peacefully) in the next several months, starting around August.

Another reason was that at first I had thought they were human beings capable of normal compassion, and if I showed them what they were doing was upsetting me, they would understand that it was wrong. If I acted "Ok," I thought it was like saying that I was okay with what they were doing, and that was a statement that I did not want to make. But I came to understand that they weren't listening like normal people. It is still hard for me to wrap my head around, but they set out to upset me. I couldn't control how other people choose to be irrational, so I decided to "let them go" in that I didn't feel I needed them to realize anything.

I used to really admire Vulcans from Star Trek. That was a good visual of how to approach problems from a productive standpoint.

Another thing that really helped was worship. Being able to meditate on real purity and goodness helped to ease the misery of the filth that I was constantly presented with, and it gave me a direction to strive for.

5-10-18

> Humans of New York
>
> "When I'm home, nobody will talk to me. It's like I am dead. I don't like quiet because then I have nothing. So I ride the train into the city. Compared to home, the city is like heaven. There are a million people you can ask for help. There are people to help you up the stairs. And there are so many smells. I love the smell of food. Right now I'm trying to memorize my way to Carnegie Hall. I like to go to theaters and museums where my mind can be nourished. Sometimes I can hear tourists talking about the exhibits. Sometimes I hear college students talking to each other and it makes me feel younger. It makes me feel like I'm still alive in this world."

5-14-18

> Humans of New York
>
> "When I went to college, I thought about joining one of those Asian student organizations. But I wasn't sure if I wanted to go 'all in' on being Asian. I had to ask myself how integral it was to my identity. I've never been very traditional. I grew up in a white town on Long Island. If I described myself in three adjectives, 'Asian' wouldn't be one of them. But on the other hand, the world is going to see race anyway. I view myself as Chinese, but Asian is the first thing people see. So if it's how everyone sees you, should you see yourself the same way?"

5-15-18

> Humans of New York
>
> "I'm from a small town in the mountains of northern Georgia. We're famous for apples. I moved here a week ago to try to be an actor. Right now I'm applying for waiter positions. I've got a little crypto currency and $5,000 saved from working at the carwash, so I figure I can make it for at least a year. I did have one major role back in

Georgia. It was the guy's first film. I had a big death scene where a ghost blew some powder on my face and melted it off. I'm really just taking all the jobs I can get right now so I can build a reel. It's mostly unpaid stuff. I booked a music video for Sunday that I found on Facebook. Don't ask me the artist or genre. All it said was: 'Have to be comfortable being painted.' Whatever that means.

There's a double meaning in "being painted." One meaning I remember hearing is to be made the target of a drone.

5-16-18

Humans of New York

"After graduating I worked as an industrial engineer. I spent five years designing presses for all kinds of factories. But it got too predictable. I was spending eight hours in front of a computer every day. It wasn't enough for me. My mind was always somewhere else. Engineering has never just been a job for me. It's what makes me feel alive. It has to be something I struggle with. If I find the answer too easily, it has no value for me. So I went back to school and got my PhD in biomechanics, and now I'm doing research in exoskeletons. My lows are now lower. I never feel smart enough. I'm constantly discovering people who are doing similar or better work. But my highs are also higher. Because every time I discover a solution, it feels like I'm bringing the future closer."

My major was engineering. Andrews has a degree in medicine.

5-17-18

Humans of New York

"I have pretty bad social anxiety. But I decided that I was going to be more outgoing when I went to college. So I joined the Facebook group for incoming freshmen, and I sent a generic 'hey' to everyone. Almost everyone gave me a generic 'hey' back, but he kept responding. Then he added me on Snapchat. He started sending me selfies and I responded with pictures of my living room. He wanted to FaceTime, but I hate seeing my own face in the corner so we just talked on the phone instead. When school finally started, we went out together with a group of people. We didn't make much eye contact but we did stand next to each other the entire time. A month later we were in class and I was making fun of him for not using soap when he washes his hands. And he said: 'If I use soap, will you date me?' And I said 'yes.' So here we are."

I am introverted. Also, I had been taking pictures of the living room or bedroom, not really selfies.

5-29-18

> Humans of New York
>
> "I worked at a make-up counter after graduating with a chemistry degree. My African mother was so mad. But I love make-up. It's like therapy. You make people feel good. You can change how they think, how they walk, how they talk. It's transformative. Even when I got a job at a tech company, I still primarily viewed myself as a make-up artist. I had my own website. On the weekends I'd work weddings. But I always wanted to do it full time. So I finally took the leap. I moved to New York. I started getting on assistant lists. I did make-up for a few web series. I networked with people on Instagram. It was scary at first, but it's been three years now and I finally feel safe. I'm getting magazine jobs. I just did a pilot for Comedy Central. Last month I paid off all my credit cards. And I think my African mother is finally coming around."

5-30-18?

> Humans of New York
>
> "We had a Native American museum today in third grade and the whole school came. I've been looking forward to it ever since second grade when I learned that third graders get to make dioramas. The museum was open from 10:15 to 10:45 or something like that. There was a cooking section where we gave out pumpkin bread. Then there was a tools and artifacts section. My table was in the games section. I put my snow snake on display. Snow snake is a very fun game in my opinion, but only four people came to my table. They said: 'What is that?' And I said: 'It's a snow snake. You can read about it on my poster.' Then they looked at my poster for two seconds and went to get some pumpkin bread."

"We had a Native American museum today in third grade and the whole school came. I've been looking forward to it ever since second grade when I learned that third graders get to make dioramas. The museum was open from 10:15 to 10:45 or something like that. There was a cooking section where we gave out pumpkin bread. Then there was a tools and artifacts section. My table was in the games section. I put my snow snake on display. Snow snake is a very fun game in my opinion, but only four people came to my table. They said: 'What is that?' And I said: 'It's a snow snake. You can read about it on my poster.' Then they looked at my poster for two seconds and went to get some pumpkin bread."

I had just gone for a walk in the park behind my neighborhood. I met a dog there. This dog was full of energy and friendly, so we made friends and scouted through the woods together, poking at things, running down paths, being perfectly natural. The park had a place to "cook" at the ovens, it had some old tools, and there is one gravel path that goes by the main building that may be a "snow snake" from above. The next morning, I went to the gravel path at around 10:45 am, and off in the distance there was a man standing at the front corner of the building who waved to me and said hello. I looked at him curiously, as I did not recognize him. "How are you?" he asked. I began to approach when another man walked up wearing the same thing. He was bald and had sunglasses. I backed off and walked around and into the building to check to see if a bug had gotten in my eye. As I walked up the steps, one of the men (they seemed to be maintenance men) had half a smile on his face while looking down. When I came out, the first man got a phone call, and then no one approached me. I waited, but they stayed away. I went back home to where Harold Repitanski was angry about something I don't know what.

On 5/30/18, my sister PMed me on Facebook "Also, have you seen the college humor video about America being like a bad boyfriend? I got a kick out of that too ... Lol, it's sad cause it's true" After that I backed off and barely spoke to her, hoping that that would protect her. I was wrong.

5-31-18

Humans of New York

"I married when I was sixteen. It was an arranged marriage. I'd never seen him before. I just came home from school one day and my dad told me that someone is coming to see you. He said: 'You're going to get married.' The man was twenty-nine. I was so upset. Nobody ever discussed it with me. I had wanted to finish my education. I had wanted to be a flight attendant. I fought so hard but the whole family turned against me. Everyone stopped talking to me. My father stopped eating. So I gave up. I married my husband and came to America. I had three kids by the time I was twenty. I've accepted it now. He's a good father to my children. He tried to tell me what to do at first but he's given up. I work at Starbucks and the bakery. They're nice people. They treat me good. But one day I'd like to maybe have a higher position so that I can work just one job. So I can spend some time on myself. And so I can maybe finally go to school."

I gave no response. This seems like a very angry reaction, like he can take me whether I like it or not and I'm just going to be miserable. It describes a romantic interest that is about using someone rather than loving them. Consistent with narcissism and stalkers. Doesn't give me the impression of safety given his position.

6-2-18

Humans of New York

"It's International Whores' Day today. It's about reclaiming the word. 'Whore' is a hateful word. There's so much stigma in that word. It can be used against any woman that you want to hurt. It's dehumanizing. And it strips sex workers of dignity. Construction workers get paid to use their bodies. Factory workers get paid to use their bodies. But if you use your genitals then suddenly you're an outcast. Sex workers are at the highest risk of sexualized violence. And it's funny that in this era where everyone is calling out workplace harassment, the most vulnerable group is being ignored. They're not seen as worthy of protection. Language matters. So we shouldn't be calling people 'whores.' We should be calling them 'people.'"

6-4-18

Humans of New York

"I turned fifty a couple weeks ago. I've lived in the same neighborhood for most of my life, which makes it more challenging because everything around me has changed so dramatically. My best friend and I got our first apartment here when we were twenty years old. We used to play this game where we'd race each other through the streets. We'd take off our shirts and run to the Hudson. First one to get there was King Of The World. There was a vibrancy back then. People would see us running but they'd be OK with it. Because we were young. We were allowed to take up space. You think you'll act young forever but the rules change. Your audience won't allow it. We're programmed to see older people a certain way. You can almost chart it on a graph. You disappear as you age and the world notices you less and less. And it makes you realize how much energy you got from being noticed."

This is obviously in reference to the fun I had "alone" running through the woods. It seems this stoked some desire in him, and the next thing he did was set up a meet where presumably I would be recruited and he could get closer to me. The failure of that attempt seems to have first created rage. Now he is taking on a more conciliatory tone, seeking to gain my understanding.

6-4-18

Humans of New York

"I felt humiliated and suicidal in college. It seemed like my personal failings were on display for everyone to see. I'm not all that attractive. I have a speech impediment. I'm not good socially. I saw other guys having romantic success and I felt a lot of envy. I concluded that women owed me something. They owed me a chance. And I was angry they weren't giving it to me. I'm ashamed of it now, but during that time I formed a lot of bad and hateful opinions. I joined 'incel' communities on 4chan and Reddit. I found a lot of men there who felt just like me. The community provided this pseudoscientific justification for hating women. It let us feel like it wasn't our fault. We stoked each other's anger. And it felt good. Honestly, anger is just very addictive. You want to feel angry when you're suffering. It gives you adrenaline. It gets your endorphins going. It's a release. It's a substitute for what you're missing."

A much stronger attempt at an apology, and asking for my understanding for his behavior. He seems to put his sense of entitlement for sexual access in a bad light here, which is encouraging.

6-5-18

Humans of New York

"I was not a tough kid growing up. I was timid. I was very sensitive to pain in other kids. I never wanted to do anything that made people feel worse than they already did. And God forbid I ever hurt somebody. That would just destroy me. I'm having to learn to dial that back as an adult. There's such a thing as being too compassionate. If you're too scared of causing pain, you can easily be manipulated. Your fear becomes a button to be pushed. In my last relationship, I was made to feel hurtful or aggressive whenever I stood up for myself. So I always backed down. I've got to learn the line between being compassionate and being a doormat."

7-21-18

My comment on Facebook: Things to appreciate in people: having sincerity, wanting the best for you, trying to empower you. Things in people to not appreciate: having a false front, attempting to put you in compromising positions, dragging you down.

-Liked by my mother

6-8-18

Humans of New York

"When you're a kid, Jesus sounds like a hippie or Bernie Sanders or something so it all sounds pretty nice. But then the rules get confusing. You go to Catholic school and some guy in a dress named Brother Roy starts beating you cause you got in a fight. It's sorta like Gitmo in there. And you start to realize that all these rules are just to keep people down. To keep women down especially because they have the ultimate power of not ****ing you. I do like the Jews because their version is less full of ****. A lot of those Talmud guys are so smart that they're practically just atheists who love fairy tales. And Buddhism is pretty cool too cause it's all in your head. No Pope. No mandatory meetings. Anyway, let me know if you figure it out. I don't know **** I just dress well."

This sounds similar to Brian Andrews' thinking.

6-9-18

Humans of New York

"I was eating, sleeping, and ****ting libraries. My life was becoming a little one note. All my friends were librarians. My social life consisted of professional development conferences. I needed another source of inspiration. So I started writing comic book reviews online. I built up a nice little portfolio. One of my reviews was actually quoted on the back of a comic book. Another one got copied and pasted into a marketing email. They spelled my name wrong but it still felt great. I haven't made any money yet, but you can't put a price tag on this. I'm writing all the time. I'm engaging a part of brain that was being ignored. Two years ago I just worked in library sales. Now I've got a press pass to Comic Con."

I was pretty much studying all day. Narcissists are thrill-seeking and get bored very easily.

6-11-18

Humans of New York

"There was never any joy in it. I practiced every day since I was four years old. I was just afraid of what would happen if I stopped. My father was a 'rageaholic.' Even our piano playing came from a place of hate. He wanted to humiliate his colleagues and prove that his children were superior. He was a hematologist. He was respected in his field. His only friends were his colleagues. Occasionally he'd have them over to dinner. Or more accurately, they'd invite him first and he'd feel the need to reciprocate. Those dinners were an escape for my sister and me. He'd never act out his worst stuff in front of other people. I think the other doctors could sense something was wrong, but nobody ever pulled me aside. It felt like I was trapped in a castle with an evil king and queen and nobody was allowed inside. People did come in, of course. But they would never meddle. They were his guests and it's not polite."

This sounds like the situation Andrews is creating for me.

6-12-18

Humans of New York

"He's had problems with speech since he was two years old. Even as a baby he would get frustrated when he couldn't express himself. He'd scream. He'd clench his fists. He still occasionally has trouble knowing what he wants. Sometimes I can calm him down with words. Other times it just makes things worse, and I'm better off doing nothing at all. It's a challenge every day. It's especially tough in public because it seems like you have no control. You can feel people looking at you. And you feel judged, judged, judged. But every child is so different. Nobody understands your situation. And they don't know your story."

He was not able to control my feelings?

6-12-18

Humans of New York

"I've known I wanted to be an actor ever since we performed Horton Hears A Who in 5th grade drama camp. I studied theater in college. But right now I'm in between roles. It's been a minute. My acting teacher told us to just focus on the callbacks. But getting callbacks is not getting a part. The last role I had was a space pirate in a Star Warsy kind of play. It was at an art gallery in Long Island City. I was fighting an evil race of aliens on a zombified planet, but I'd actually been hit by a train and was in a simulation to keep my brain active. It was every Halloween costume that I ever wanted to be, but I only made enough money to buy myself dinner. Do I choose more stability and less joy? Maybe I could find a job that has one element I enjoy, like Human Resources at Wells Fargo. Overall it would suck but at least I'd get to help people. Sure I'd spend six hours being upset, but at least I could help Jane with her issue."

Agents do a lot of acting, and try to terrorize people in all manner of ways.

When a person is going to sleep or waking up, they are in a hypnagogic state, and their dreams can be altered based on their sense perceptions. Dream modulation is something that later on would become apparent to me. Dreams would become different in tone and uncharacteristic of me. There would be a series of nightmares going through different topics, some of which were relevant to current threats being posed. There would be many attempts to judge what emotional resonance a given scenario has with my subconscious as a way to read me. Sometimes it is just another way I could be spoken to. There may be attempts to alter my feelings towards people, or to get me to do things, though I may wake up. -2/24/20

From Wikipedia: "Hypnagogic cognition, in comparison with that of normal, alert wakefulness, is characterized by heightened suggestibility, [19] illogic and a fluid association of ideas. Subjects are more receptive in the hypnagogic state to suggestion from an experimenter than at other times, and readily incorporate external stimuli into hypnagogic trains of thought and subsequent dreams. This receptivity has a physiological parallel; EEG readings show elevated responsiveness to sound around the onset of sleep. [20]"

I have just learned this is called Targeted Dream Incubation. From lifescience.com, "dream manipulation machine" -9/28/20:

"MIT scientists have figured out how to manipulate your dreams by combining an app with a sleep-tracking device called Dormio. In their new study, the researchers were able to insert certain topics into a person's dreams, with some pretty bizarre outcomes.

To do so, the researchers at MIT Media Lab's Fluid Interfaces — a group that develops wearable systems and interfaces to enhance cognitive skills — used a technique called targeted dream incubation (TDI)." ...

6-14-18

Humans of New York

"I was eleven when my mom divorced my stepdad. She had four kids at the time. I remember we were in the bedroom, and she said to me: 'You're the oldest so I'm going to need your help.' And ever since then I've been 'Mom Number Two.' I picked my little brothers up from school. I cooked for them. I made sure they did their homework. I met with their teachers. I'd be the authority figure until mom came home from work. I was always the responsible one. Nobody ever had to worry about me. But now I'm twenty and my whole life has been about my little brothers. I've never really felt the security to figure myself out. But today is orientation at my new college. I just finished meeting with my advisor. There are so many clubs and organizations that I can join. I want to meet a lot of different people. I want to be more outspoken. I feel like this is my chance to learn who I am."

6-15-18

Humans of New York

"Obama had been president for six days. The old timers in the twelve-step program tell you to associate the memory with something—so that's how I remember it. The weather was just like this, even though it was November. It was sixtyish degrees. I was sitting on a stoop, having my morning beer and cigarette, and feeling disgusted with myself. I was wheezing so bad that it felt like I'd swallowed a whistle. And I had this moment of clarity. I knew I was done. So I took a couple more swigs, threw the pack of Newports into traffic, and walked over to Project Renewal on 3rd Street. I'll be ten years sober if I can make it until November 10th. That was my day. And it still is my day. Even if I fail, I'll remember that on that day I succeeded. And if I did it then, I can do it again."

This was my birthday. I studied, bought myself a breakfast burrito, went on a walk through some woods, and spent a good amount of time crying in my room. I viewed my situation as a tragedy. ...

6-21-18

Humans of New York

"I'm writing a Grandma Noir. The premise is this: a lady comes to an old person's home, but nobody likes her. Suddenly she turns up dead and our protagonist Helen has to solve the mystery. There's a motorized wheelchair chase. There's a Viagra orgy. There's a villain who's faking Alzheimer's while masterminding a pill-trading operation. It's got everything. I sent the book to a bunch of agents. I got a nibble from one of them. She told me that she made it to page 100 before quitting, so I figure I'm on the right track."

I had confirmed that I was going to move to Raelynn's house, who uses a motorized wheelchair. She is older. I was very stressed about going there. ...

Humans of New York - Page Liked • July 2 •

"I came to it late in life. I was already in college. We were playing a dice game in the back of a bar and my character transformed into a lion. I've been hooked ever since. Now I'm part of a huge role-playing community, and next week I'm going to a three-day event in Pennsylvania. Basically it's a bunch of people getting together and pretending to be something we're not. It's the bonding that's most important. The hobby is great, but you always spend more time talking then doing the hobby itself. We're building a shared history. And each time we meet there's more to reminisce about. It can be hard to meet people when you're older, but I've made hundreds of friends in the community. When my dad got sick recently, I asked for 'spells, prayers, and cat videos.' The post had 111 comments and 94 emoticons."

One thing I heard before this was posted was Harold Repitanski on the front porch saying how much he hates recruiters, because they get into your network and then get into their network and so on. Later he was on the phone talking to someone, saying repeatedly and emphatically that there was no way, and I don't remember exactly what he said but it was sort of in code like 'Elvis has left the building.' It was apparently clear to Harold that I did not want to be recruited. He described what the FBI does to innocent communities. The way he spoke on the phone it was like he was trying to convince someone that I wasn't going to sign up. This subsequent entry is like Andrews trying to convince me I would like to be a part of the "community." He describes role playing, which is what agents do. It is pretty sad to see him characterize a machine that churns human souls and makes free people into slaves, body and soul, as something with nice perks like water cooler talk. His "not getting it" when it comes to "no" is also familiar to me with other narcissists.

9

AN OVERVIEW OF COLLEGE: BEING DRUGGED, HACKED, AND SPIED ON

T*his covers my time in college.* I did not keep a regular journal in Tennessee, but notes here and there. Much of this section is from memory and more topical. After this will be another section based on my notes which are dated, and some of that information will mirror the information in this topical section.

When I moved to Tennessee, I rented a room from Raelynns and her daughter Remi. We had agreed on a price and that I could mow the lawn to knock it down a little more. One of my first conversations with Remi was that she no longer wanted to give that option. She talked about past roommates and may have described her expectations of me by praising how everyone used to do house chores without compensation. My demeanor to her was cold and distant. I generally kept my distance from the family and did not involve myself in their affairs. One tactic I have observed is to couch harassment in layers of plausible deniability. You are presented with something that may be taken as a threat, but usually there is a non-threatening alternative explanation. Attempts are usually made at damaging your relationship with the people who have power over you, such as a roommate. If you give any reason why they could be upset with you, including that you are not happy with their unreasonable treatment of you, then that becomes a possible pretext for why they would commit crimes against you or harm you. If you were to get past the first layer of an innocent explanation, they could say their retaliation was personal and not because they are informants. In this way, innocent people around the target can be coerced into committing crimes and other slights against the target, and be forced to become a scapegoat or fall man for the crimes of the handlers. This may be an example of that.

Apparently Remi was studying for the same major I was, and was the same age. I found that a bit improbable. It is typical for informants to pretend to have things in common.

While staying there in the beginning, Remi suggested she wanted to draw me out and become friendlier, and said something like "not staying in your room all day reading like I've seen you do." Also, one day, when I was leaving through the front door with my pillow, my landlady called from her bedroom, worrying that I was moving out. She said she "saw" me, apparently with my pillows in hand.

Remi did not have a handle on her door when I first arrived. When we were talking, I was telling her about the travel lock I made, and she was on the phone with her boyfriend. She said a 2x4 propped up under the door handle could lock it, and I said excitedly that this wouldn't work because it could be knocked out from something coming in from under the door. She told him the reason she didn't have a handle was because of the time he locked himself out of his room and they had to bust the door down. This conversation made her tear up, and she left it quite upset. It seemed she wanted to encourage me to not lock my door.

Written early spring 2019. In late August, while living at Raelynn's house, I prepared burritos for myself for the week before school started. After the first one I had I slept for four hours, and did wake up briefly when the dogs barked. After I awoke, I felt shaky and strange. I tried another a week later on September 4th and only ate a half, and tried to stay awake. I felt hot and flushed, and ended up sleeping for two hours.

Warning: sexually explicit content

I was on my bed, watching videos on my phone. I watched Bill Maher, and he gave a dirty joke about Trump being full of himself. I smiled and played the video again to hear something back. Then my google news app froze. I could scroll, but I couldn't open any story. This had not happened to this app before. There were several stories about sexual assault. One was, "A turtle was found in a woman's vagina, police suspect sexual assault." I went for a walk in the park. I was catcalled two times. At no other time in Tennessee have I been catcalled. One man asked me where my man was, the other was driving by and said it was his birthday and he wanted to get wonked.

Before fall break, over a period of days, I noticed I felt unusually blank and dizzy. It got to the point that as I tried to study, all I wanted to do was lay down and let my head spin. I was not sure of the cause, so I began to make sure that everything was in order. I made sure I got enough sleep, exercise, vitamins, fresh air, and healthy food. I had up to that point regularly taken a half a pill of Melatonin to get to sleep. I cut that out of my routine and felt better quickly. The next day, the air conditioning was broken in the house. The main floor was uncomfortably hot where Raelynn stays all the time, but upstairs, my air conditioning worked. Raelynn was reasonably wealthy, older, and in poor health. The next morning, I felt dizzy again. I made sure to drink lots of water and felt better some hours later. The vents were blocked off in the other guest bedroom, and I put my foot by the bottom of Remi's door, who also lives upstairs, and did not feel any cold air. I taped up my vent and opened my windows. The air conditioning was broken for one more day. I generally didn't have any more of the same symptoms for some months afterwards.

They later returned, apparently due to a gas in my room during the night. I designed a screen clamp, so I could keep my window open at night and still not easily broken into. After I did this, Remi asked me almost desperately if I kept food in my room, and kept offering me a place downstairs to store it. There wasn't any issue with me eating in my room, so she wasn't concerned about cleanliness. Many nights I noticed Remi walk back to the adjacent room's closet which goes behind my wall before she went to bed. On those nights I would wake up with my heart pounding harder and more steadily than naturally. This disrupted my sleep, and was not good for my health.

There was a nearby park I liked to go for walks. One day, I had an upset stomach while walking. I had to stop several times on the trail and rest. When I made it to the visitor's center, there was a park ranger sitting there with a snide grin. He watched me and asked with contained glee "Hi, how are you?" I later saw that ranger driving truck #*redacted*. The next time I walked in that park, a path was blocked off and that ranger's truck was there. It was two times that he followed my car out of the park. I had not done anything improper in the park to get that kind of attention.

At college one time I walked away from my food in the microwave. A blond girl walked past me grinning, her posture rigid. I was not gone for long. After I ate, I had a seriously upset stomach. The pain and duration was more severe than my natural symptoms. It seems that drugs that cause symptoms are considered after the target has shown those symptoms without them, as a form of plausible deniability. At my home, I left my food in the microwave and briefly went upstairs for a minute. Downstairs was Raelynn in a wheelchair and the caretaker. After I ate the food I left I had a severe upset stomach. *Left in one microwave was a sweet potato, and the other time was ramen noodles so I wasn't reacting to a specific meal. -3/9/21* This and other cases suggest that informants around me were regularly carrying the drug waiting for the opportunity. When Remi got home, she asked me if I wanted some guacamole. That night she went to the closet, and I was woken and kept awake for hours with my heart painfully pounding. It was a half hour of diarrhea and I remember noting 8 hours of the effects of stimulants, and negligible sleep. When I got in my car, Remi got in the car in front of me, and seemed to watch me to see if I was going to do anything threatening. It is often the case that informants, especially the families I have lived with, are in serious fear for their own safety. The amount I appeared to be drugged that night went well beyond my normal treatment, and it makes me wonder if this was Remi trying to intimidate me into not retaliating. Informants can be forced into these dangerous positions, and so are effectively human shields for the agents. Some time later, a bookshelf collapsed in Raelyn's room and I rushed in, as my instinct was to help. After this their attitude changed towards me, and they realized I was not going to hurt them.

Many other cases appeared to be attempts to drug me. At one church around Christmas, they were passing out bags of treats. When it was almost my turn to get one, a woman tapped me on the shoulder behind me, and nervously asked me the usual small talk questions, glancing over my shoulder at the man handing out the bags. I am turned away from the man before I can get my bag, so he had an opportunity to select a particular one for me.

While I was volunteering in January at the Point-in-Time count, I ate a chocolate chip cookie. When I went to a church, there was a table of snacks, which were all one sort of cookie except a chocolate chip one. I didn't take it. After service there was only one cookie left.

At the time I was going to churches at random. I arrived at the potluck first. There was an older man who commented about the casseroles, "The thing about casseroles is you don't know what's in them." An old man, perhaps the same one, offered me a can of sweet tea at the drink table. I selected the lemonade, and he suggested it would go well with sweet tea.

One day at college there was a presentation on 3D printing. I selected a chair. The woman next to me was hunched over and turned away from me. Her body language suggested she wanted to get away from me. The treats served were from Little Debbie. One was a pie in a sealed bag. The pie had an opening in the middle. The glue on the packaging was a bit tough. After a while, the woman next to me had her cell phone in her hand on the table, directing the camera at me at an angle. After eating the pie I felt drowsy and spaced out for several hours.

There were several attempts besides drugging to disrupt my sleep. One was a strange screaming sound by my window. That sound was repeated later nights, but quieter and farther away. There was also one morning where dogs barked for 2 hours between 6 and 8. That did not repeat. Noise disruptions were rarely used at that location.

One Saturday at a club I attended at college, the president of the club said in the military they have found that you only need 4 hours of sleep to function. That is generally the amount of sleep I was allowed to have. It seemed he was probing my attitudes towards the military. I had previously politely declined to show support at a veteran's table. Another thing the president mentioned was military brainwashing. I had looked up in interest. On my drive home, as I pulled into the gas station, on the radio there was a story about a method the military uses to get to sleep in two minutes. She started describing steps to be hypnotized. I had acted very shocked to hear the story. That is the first time I inferred that my car radio was hacked. When I went into the station, the man with dark curly hair behind the counter was laughing to himself. I asked him "What?" and he shrugged as though he did not want to tell me. Then after he reflected for a moment he told me that I spaced out for a minute there, and asked if I was okay.

At college after getting only 4 hours of good sleep some nights, I felt exhausted. Sometimes I would go to a bathroom and just relax for ten minutes or so. I believe it was in the month of April, every time I would lower my head, someone would come into the bathroom and do something different to disturb me. This suggested to me that they had the ability to know my movements in the bathroom at any given location in the college, and at other locations as well. One girl came in and started loudly cussing on the phone. The way she spoke, it was as if it bothered her to cuss.

There were many things that came over my car radio that were like messages directed at me or attempting to influence me. For example, I changed my profile picture on Facebook to an inkblot. I was often misunderstood, which I usually did not correct, but there was a reason I wanted to point out that he misunderstood me. When I got in my car and turned on the radio, the song started with the line "I'm surprised how well you cut my feelings to the bone. Don't wanna leave you really I've invested too much time to give you up that easy to the doubts that complicate your mind. We belong to the light we belong to the thunder..."

In another case, after I started covering holes in my bedroom walls and more kept appearing, the woman on the radio said Megan and Harry were moving out of the house of Kate and William, and how funny it was that she didn't know this whole time they were living together. In another case, I was in my car in the park, and I put up some opaque sheets around the back seat so I could have some privacy. When I took them down, the radio announcer said "we play anything" and started a song not typical for that station, which was Love the Way You Lie, in which the man says if the girl ever leaves him, he'll tie her to the bed and burn the house down.

Warning: sexual content

In another case that I have written about elsewhere, it was after Christmas, and he had apparently broken into my room during the night and "unwrapped his present" by removing some of my clothes in my sleep. He decided he very much wanted me to look better naked as I have a skin condition. From the 12/25/18 passage: "I go to the library shortly after listening to a guy on the radio talk about the military. In the library, a girl talks about needing a wheat/sugar free diet. Back in my car, the same program has a guest speaker talking about a wheat free diet." Both a topical cream and a wheat and sugar free diet are methods to treat my skin condition.

One time I heard this song, I believe in reference to him worrying I would publish his treatment of me during Porcfest. "Do you really want to hurt me, do you really want to make me cry?"

In another case it was like the song on the radio was a message, and the next one would be a response to the expression on my face. For example: This Feeling by the Chain Smokers, the lyrics "Do you love me or not," "you should really get to know me," one about being in love with a psycho, screaming "mine mine mine," "come on over sit next to me," "I'm a' tell em all, you can either hate me or love me, but that's just the way I am," "hell no, been waiting for too long, " which is about insisting on sex, "nothing breaks like a heart," "I'm a rebel just for kicks," etc.

This is why it seemed to me that there were also cameras in my vehicle. Before I got rid of it, I went out with my tools to the driveway to look. A car pulled up with a man who apparently was some kind of pest remover. The man lingered around outside in the neighbor's yard, so I was being observed, and there seemed to be some concern I would find something. I did check in my rear view mirror which looked clean.

The man at the gas station was one example, but it seemed that some employees from the stores I frequented were also informants. For example, a cashier at the Dollar Tree picks up headphones I was buying, looks over them carefully, and comments they can be used to listen to things so no one else knows what you are listening to. The same guy sat in a chair by the exit one day and watched me check out with a gleam in his eye.

Shortly after they started drugging me, I visited a church again. A woman I had met before sat next to me. She had her leg propped up in the pew, and was holding her cell phone in her hand facing me. After service she caught me before I left, and said "I know you don't remember my name." She emphasized the word "know." How would she know that? Her name is *redacted.* It seemed as though she expected me to be out of it and to not have a good memory. That may have been a known effect of the drug. During that period, I spent most of the day studying, so it was likely intended to disrupt my ability to get an education. She encouraged me to join a Sunday School or some group where I could get personally closer to people.

The pastor of that church, introduced himself to me twice on different weeks. The first time I had told him I was a college student. The second time he first asks me "Which college do you go to?" And after that asks me "Is this your first time here?" It was like he was pretending to meet me again for the first time. He strongly encouraged me to go to the church's night meeting, which again, was as if church fellowship was seen as a good place to spy. During the beginning of his sermon he is very nervous, which was uncharacteristic from what I know of him. He said we ought to get a buddy to study the Bible with, because we don't internalize the Bible as well if we are just studying alone.

There were many cases where it seemed at least some part of a sermon included some material I was to be tested with to see how I reacted, or was an attempt to influence my decisions. This was in Maryland, but a church I went to for a while had a whole series of sermons insisting we fellowship more deeply with each other, excoriating those who cut out right after the sermon (which is what I did.) They brought in a guest speaker one week who had some history working with the government, and he gave a very well written sermon on how we don't fully know ourselves until we interact with different people, and how we as a building ought to be dependent on each other, and when one part shakes, the rest should shake. When he looked at me in the eye, it was like I had struck him. He seemed to be shaken and hesitant for some time after that. He knew I could see through him.

Many other pastors seemed to participate during a time I was picking a church at random, which speaks to the reach that a single "investigation" can have.

One of the things that was extremely common was for news sites to have some stories which were fabricated (more rare), or were relevant to something they wanted to test or say. One thing that is done almost dutifully is to mock me at every available moment. For example, I was constipated for a while, and there was a headline that said someone died of constipation. During the time I was being drugged, I saw a story about a mechanical caterpillar that crawls inside you while you sleep and drugs you. I think it was after taking a walk in a park with bees, I saw a headline that a woman had four bees under her eyelid that would damage her if she rubbed her eye. I also had pain in my eye at the time and had been rubbing it.

One time at college I had been studying outside, and ended up fighting mosquitoes. It wasn't long after, when I opened my passenger door to put my things in, a swarm of mosquitoes was released. I killed about 5 in my car. Having distractions while driving is potentially dangerous to me and the public.

One time not long after being sick I went to visit a church. I got there late, but figured I'd look around the building. I touched a handrail going to the youth room. The next week when I went there, I went to the bathroom, and some women came in and talked about how many of the kids got sick. That is often something done. If I have done something that could have gone wrong, I am made to think that it did. "Murphy's Law enforcement."

Many times people seemed concerned when I went into a bathroom. I was usually followed shortly thereafter. One week I went to a church, and saw a girl leave the sanctuary to get to the bathroom ahead of me. I decided I didn't like the sermon and went to another, which has a lobby and an adjoining single bathroom. The sermon was already going and I could hear it just fine from the lobby, so I stayed. After a few minutes, a man came out and looked at me worriedly, and then checked out the bathroom. Then there were two men talking very loudly behind the door outside, perhaps to encourage me to go in. Then a guy came in and entered the service, perhaps to show me it was okay to do. My backpack that I usually carried around with me had been knocked over in my car when I got back.

I had some additional roommates for about a month. I had been told I could help decide, but given the fact I was keeping my distance, it is understandable I was only informed after the fact. We had a Jack and Jill bathroom between our rooms, meaning the doors on each side went into our bedrooms, not the hall, so it was a little complicated figuring out which way to face the locks. I remember Remi telling me I could either have my privacy or my stuff protected. It was a girl who moved in, but apparently unexpectedly she brought her boyfriend. They made some noise and mostly I ignored them. Though we did have a rule that when the bathroom fan was on it meant it was in use. At least once they left it on for hours while they talked in the bedroom. One time they brought friends over and stayed up late talking loudly. They moved away, and for the rest of the time (besides perhaps Raelynn's sister visiting) the other room was vacant. I was strongly encouraged at one point to move to the other room. I was told if I agreed to stay for six months I could have it no extra charge. Raelynn said it had a larger closet, and just "makes sense" for some reason. The other room was towards the front of the house, and did not have an easy way to get out of the house through the windows as it was on the second story. The one I lived in at the time was towards the back yard. The two windows were a few feet over a flat roof to a deck that was easy to stand on. There was railing around the deck that made it very easy to climb down. The back yard had a large privacy fence, and beyond that was a large wooded area. Also, one screen was dented in on one side, and was small enough that it was easy to slip to one side and pull out. If I had wanted to escape out the back, that would have been a convenient way to do it. Raelynn strongly suggested I move twice or so. This suggestion was made before my room was broken in at night.

There was a neighborhood dog who had no collar. It barked at me as I first moved in. Later I made friends with the dog and thought all was well. Then one day it went back to growling for no apparent reason. Remi saw this and wondered what had changed. I believe that dog belonged to a police officer who lived in the neighborhood.

After I visited my family in October, Raelynn tells me Remi will be gone for 2 weeks, and asks me to turn the porch light off when I get home after 8 pm. She explained it was left on for me, but that she wanted it off because it made it harder for her to sleep. I did not necessarily know what time I would be coming in on a given night. I told her not to bother leaving it on for me. It was a little unusual for me to communicate and coordinate with the family, so our conversation was a little strained. After that, there were two motion detecting lights placed in the main hall and upstairs hall. It was as though if the light was bothering me, I would have lights turning on all the time. It was a message like I am not in control of my environment, and they can annoy me as they wish, and do so in a way that people are socially obligated to assume is well intended. I had read before that this is also exactly the sort of malicious control stalkers and abusive exes use against their victims.

After my car broke down, I would regularly walk to the grocery store. This was not convenient to do as there were places with no shoulder and tall grass. One day it rained. I remember Remi on the side of the road practically demanding I let her give me a ride home. Drones cannot fly in that weather, and there wasn't a convenient place to observe me along the whole route. Another time I went out to my car, the caretaker came outside and stared at me while on her cell phone for a while. It was like they were not prepared to surveil me when I went outside unexpectedly at that point.

I believe Remi told me one time she put dryer sheets in the dryer for me, but I'm not sure. My washcloths no longer absorb water well. I read more recently that dryer sheets will coat towels with a wax that ruins them.

While I went to college, I attended a club. I had looked it up online beforehand. When I arrived, I found the woman who ran it. She brought me to the room and gave me a specific computer to use, and said I was to speak to a boy named Gage. She was extremely exuberant. She repeatedly told me to sign in, and for Gage to help me. Gage was laughing, and told me it was because she was so excited. Apparently that is not how she normally acted. There were several alerts on my computer. I would close one and a different one would show up. Gage told me to ignore it. Gage was a programmer. He talked a little about Java. Quinn, the son of Professor Kimberly, was the other person in the room. I went pretty regularly to this club. One week Gage mentions I dress like a school shooter. After that I noticed a staff member in the business section ask me nervously how I was. I didn't respond, and he repeated his question almost frantically. Around this time as I walked across campus, a police officer in full uniform approached me and walked past. Campus security don't usually wear the same black uniform. This appeared to be to test if I was nervous, perhaps from carrying a gun and planning an attack. I had not intended to have my good fashion sense make such an impression. I went out and bought a fuzzy jacket with a green and black flannel pattern. After doing so, what I heard on my radio was a woman asking if you ever do something that makes people misunderstand you, and get so frustrated about it. She said not to worry, because God knows and loves you. That wasn't the only time Andrews used God as an analogy for himself.

I took four classes the first semester and dropped two. It was almost as if I was not allowed to go to college. One class, the math class, had good content but was review. The others were disorganized, painfully simple, and strongly encouraged lax behavior and cheating. Walking the halls and hearing the other professors, it seemed this was not the norm. Other teachers had good content prepared and talked about the importance of meeting standards.

In math class, the information was online. It was correct and functional. The teacher was good, although I had already taught myself the material. My advisor had insisted I retake it. In the first class, a blond girl with a British accent sat next to me and asked me if I would tell her things like when we had to be in class. She asked for my number so I could apparently answer questions she had about class. I directed her to the teacher and had no further problems. I asked for and was granted a recommendation for a scholarship from the professor. I never received any scholarships. I had brought my scholarship essay to the writing lab, and was told it was "outstanding." I did this twice, once for each semester. I had to get people to write letters of recommendation to submit as well. Each time, someone took an especially long time to send in their recommendation, as though it was contingent on something. I was very popular with the people I asked, so it is unclear why they did not get to it.

I had to take my math tests at the math lab. During the fifth test, I was given a seat right next to the tutoring section. I was the only or one of the only people taking a test out of maybe 20-30 computers. The tutoring section was mostly empty. During most of my test, a tutor loudly conversed with a student at the computer right next to mine. The girl at the welcoming counter was laughing hysterically. I got an A. There was a tutor at the math lab who had this fixed half grin around me. He would have that expression as I passed him in the hall, and his eyes were on me and followed me.

In my AC/DC class, Mr. Rasputin didn't seem to know what information he wanted to cover in a given class. He seemed to ramble a bit, and would end class early for no pressing reason. I received the answers to the test on my online portal. When I pointed them out to him, he announced to the class they could remove them "at your leisure." I did so but was still able to access them. I have written more extensively about his class under August in Chapter 11.

Christian Pastor's class was an exercise in lethargy. *That wasn't his real name, but the one he gave was about that ridiculous, and he used overly religious language in his emails.* He arrived late (15 minutes I believe) to his first class, sending us notice not long before class. It was a four hour class, but he told us to expect lectures from 45-60 minutes, as his mouth gets dry, and to expect the class to let out early. He described studying as something we unfortunately had to get through. The first week no academic material was covered. The second, he gave a short talk describing the introduction, but gave the excuse that many students didn't have the textbook, so we couldn't start studying the first chapter. Classes were very short. I had ordered a textbook which arrived with many things written in it that looked like they could be answers. I did not verify that but erased them. Christian Pastor wanted to take us on field trips. He asked us if anyone would not be able to go to one. He made the grades such that missing one would mean failing the class. He kept insisting it was important to attend these. At one point he got very aggressive in his tone. It was so spontaneous, it reminded me of an abusive husband who feels comfortable intimidating his wife in a split second. I don't often see people speak that way, comfortable to be so aggressive, especially for not attending a field trip. He described a high security location, and told us with particular pride that he got to see such places. He didn't seem like a professor to me. He would have been more interested in lectures. He didn't seem like someone who worked in the industrial field. He would have been more comfortable with working the time he was scheduled to work. His disposition struck me as a police officer. I wasn't losing much by dropping his class. I had multiple roadblocks trying to drop his class. The computer would give me different excuses why I couldn't drop it, maybe three or so different ones. I spoke to my counselor about the problem. She had some issue dropping the class as well. She ended up calling tech support. I remember she said something in reference to me to the people on the phone as if they knew, but had not discussed me in her earlier conversation. I had to drop the class by a certain date, or else I would lose a larger percentage of the refund. It was ultimately successful.

The fourth class I took was a CAD class. This seemed to have a real teacher who knew the material pretty well. During the beginning of the class, Professor Trenton said the word "mesmerize" and paused, smiling, looking at me. This was around the time I was attending the class of the apparent stage hypnotist Rasputin, which I describe later, and lends to the credibility of my assessment of him. Early in the class I was approached by the professor about a student who sat next to me. This girl was effectively ignoring him, and the professor wanted to know what I noticed. I said I didn't want to get in the middle of it, and directed the conversation back to my own studies. This could have been to "sow discord" among me and the other students.

There was another student who seemed to be an undercover cop, called Memphis. He talked about wanting to drop his Solid Works class often after I had dropped mine. I usually sat in the same place. When I moved to another chair, there was a look of dread on the face of a student next to me, as I recall on more than one occasion. There was no reason. I was helpful to other students, and asked questions in class. At one point during the semester, likely during the time I was being drugged, the professor changed his teaching style. He seemed to want to do a poor job of his lectures, and asked if it was clear as mud. Many lectures were fill-ins or repeats. At the end of the class, he said the next teacher complained that he hadn't taught them anything. The tests were open book and could be taken twice. The correct answers appeared after the first attempt. Before the final, he said we could just reference the screenshots we took of the answers, so this class was also encouraging cheating on the test. Though it was never explicitly said, the teacher suggested it seemed to him some of the CAD drawings were very similar to others, and he would hate to have to call anyone out for cheating. I was one of the better students in the class, and I kept my CAD files on my school email. It was possibly a way to frame me for giving those files to other students. The teacher often recommended his friend Christian Pastor's Autodesk Inventor class to me.

During the lecture on November 5th, the professor said "The Bible is written one way, but it is open to millions of interpretations. Don't leave your dimensions up for interpretation." This was right after I had read Romans 13, the passage about obeying the government.

During the lecture on November 12th, the professor warned us we could be legally liable for mistakes in our CAD drafts if it resulted in damages.

During the lecture on November 19th, Memphis said he had been hacked. Professor Trenton said you had to check your bank account for small charges on cards to protect against fraud. I had just reinstalled my operating system, and couldn't get my VPN TorGuard to work for a day or two. Logging in to my bank would have meant exposing my credentials to others who had access to the network.

Another thing that was a common problem in that class was for the computers to take an extremely long time to load, sometimes a half an hour. I often studied AutoCAD on off hours, and remember I believe Memphis acting exasperated it was taking so long. They like to encourage you to be frustrated and give up. I pushed through regardless.

During one class, a boy stopped by the door, looked at me on the far end, and made a motion with his hand across his neck like negating, or "cut it out." I didn't understand. He mouthed to me, "It's all a lie." And gestured to the whole room. There were maybe 15-20 students in that class, but he singled me out for that message. I didn't know him.

After my cat died, my mom posted about it and by it the story about the military's technique to get to sleep, so it seemed Brian Andrews was claiming responsibility for her death. Before the next CAD class, the professor talked about someone pouring gas on a school and lighting it on fire, perhaps to see if I was intending revenge. Gage was in the room. He said how studious I was, that I seemed to always be there studying. I see Narcissists do this simultaneous injury and friendship thing sometimes. It seems to me that it is intended to brutally damage a person, but then offer them a face-saving way to surrender. It seems they are threats thinly veiled with a moral pretense, and this rationale is what people will grasp at and vehemently defend so they do not have to face the reality of the threat beneath. Even if that pretense is fairly absurd, like an "investigation" of a "national security threat."

During the final, I was contesting some of the answers I got wrong. I wanted to take the professor's comments on them to the tech support center, but the idea of him going there seemed to bother the professor.

I continued to study AutoCAD on my own and signed up to take the AutoDesk test. I had to drive to another state, but I chose a closer location. I entered a large building with many rooms for businesses like apartments. I found a list of businesses downstairs, but could not find the name of the company who was administering the test. A man passed by, and it turns out he had just come from there and told me which room it was. Another man studied the directory after I left. I found the office, which seemed run down and shifty. The woman checked the room where I would test, and said that I would have to wait. I decided to go to the other location in a city about a half an hour from there. I paid for the test, and the payment took some time to process. I used the bathroom at the next location, and a woman opened the bathroom door while I was inside. The woman who worked there gave me a time to wait. I went out to the parking lot to look over my CAD notes text file, but my phone would not open the file. There was an issue accepting my payment, and it took much longer than it was supposed to. This began to look like it would cut into my testing time. They closed at 6 and it was around 3. The payment went through, and she started to set me up. Apparently, they did not have my test downloaded, and she had to download all of the others at the same time. I sat next to her, and commented jokingly when I saw it had downloaded 34 out of 33 tests. Eventually the test started, and seemed to function correctly. I passed. On the way back it was dark and raining, and of course I was unfamiliar with the area. Google maps would not work. I managed to find my way back anyway.

I attempted to take one class half-way through the semester taught by Kimberly. I asked her the time and days the class would be. The class time given for the first day was right after the 75% refund period would expire, meaning I would stand to lose a lot more money if I dropped the class after attending the first day.

I did drop her class. Because I signed up for that class late it required the dean's signature. After I dropped her class the dean seemed fearful of me. I spent a lot of time on campus, and would go for walks after studying for hours on end. This sometimes took me to the building where the dean was, and it seemed I always ran into him. One day, a girl stopped me as I walked down the hall, and told me I can go to the side where they are having a ribbon cutting if I want, that it is open to students. They had just built a new manufacturing lab, which was of interest to me. I said sure and checked it out. Everyone is in suit and tie. The president of the college is there, and the dean is there as well, who is of course rather freaked out. I didn't see any other students. There were probably wealthy donors present. It seemed she wanted to put me in a place where it was inappropriate and I would look bad to the leadership.

My college had a gym open to students. At first things went well. They sometimes played the radio in the gym. There was a song that would have been clear that I liked from surveillance in the car. The lyrics went "When I taste tequila..." I liked to run, and would stay on the treadmill for a while. A boy would pass me several times and check me. When I had hit my runners high or was smiling, the song about tequila would come on. After that would be a song about sex. This sort of thing happened more than once. This was likely psychological conditioning to get me to associate my positive feelings towards running with drinking and sex. That is what sexual predators do, not investigators. I have seen this sort of psychological manipulation from another narcissist. Once the woman who worked in the math lab came to exercise. As I left she followed me. There was an exit door that I passed. She stayed there and watched me for some time as I went to the woman's bathroom, where I would change. The next time I go, the sign in sheet has a legal waiver in case of injury on the top. Normally it is just a blank paper, and not a legal form. It seems to be originally intended for some team or group. I don't sign. The woman in charge of the gym enthusiastically waves to me as I enter, which she normally didn't do. She later comes in looking around for me with a panicked expression. It seemed she had very much hoped I would sign the waiver. Later, a blond girl follows me to the women's restroom. I change in the stall, and then she goes in the one I came out of immediately after. There were plenty of other stalls she could have taken, and she didn't have to wait for me.

I went to the print shop on several occasions. The man at the print shop tested me, saying he counted fewer copies than there were for me to pay for and I corrected him. He said, astonished, "So you're honest." The next time he saw me he was suspicious again. One time I attempted to print off some tax forms, and it printed something like special characters. I caught it, and they made the correction. When I went to print my resumes, the boy who worked there cut them for me incorrectly so it had to be redone. There were many cases when service people would make accidental but a bit unlikely mistakes. This is passive aggressive harassment.

At college, I regularly had computer issues, some of which I have in pictures. I often saw that the firewall is not up. Sometimes when I log off I see a notification that someone else will be logged off too. Sometimes a terminal pops up for a second. I had a notification when I attempted to open Firefox that said that Firefox was a blacklisted application. The second time it happened, I went to the library and asked tech support what that was. He said he had never heard of it but would pass on my complaint. The next several times it happened I took screen shots. I asked him later if he had heard back. He seemed frightened to talk to me. He said he hadn't, and said it was something the professor would deal with. It happened on several different computers in different classrooms, and generally the professors don't address software issues.

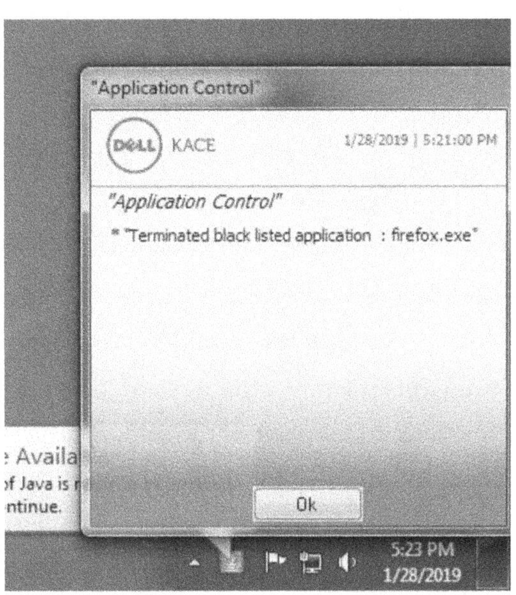

I was studying AutoCAD in the library, and for some time, I heard conversation between some librarians, including the tech support guy, about reading people and detecting lies, and a variety of things that might be designed to make working for an intelligence agency appealing. There were a number of appeals to encourage me to join the dark side, particularly when it seemed I had the advantage and it would be safer for them, or when it looked like I was about to "lose" and was being given "terms of surrender."

I went to several board meetings concerning the homeless, which were open to the public. That seemed to be an unusual thing to do. Perhaps some board members were suspicious of me. I was advised to attend the Point in Time count if I really wanted to know what was going on in the homeless community. That is a day when volunteers take to the streets, count the visibly homeless population, and fill out surveys of willing participants. We all met together beforehand for training and supplies. Several women offered to bring me on to their team. Our de facto leader worked with the homeless in healthcare. Other teams had maps, but we were told which area to look around. It was a cold January night. As we conversed, the leader turned to me, and with a changed, wary tone, asked me, "Sharon, where do you live?" I told her I wasn't homeless. I thought I should handle the supplies, but on the first street we stopped on, she handed me a pile of surveys and directed me to two men who approached us. I hadn't even read the form yet. I asked for a pen. The leader said she didn't have any, and jokingly asked the homeless guy if he had one. I asked another girl and she said she left them back at the car, but would go get them. I waited for some time and then thought to suggest she take someone with her when I saw she hadn't left. Then I saw a pen sticking out of one of the girl's hair buns. I took it, and her face flashed with realization and excitement, and after a pause, she said she had forgotten she put it there. I went back to the gentlemen. They were standing calmly, firmly, and focused, posture fully forward, one back and to the side of the other. He provided me with his name, and I searched for the name field in the form. I asked the leader, and she pointed to the top line, "Just put it there." "No, that's not the location." I answered. "Well I don't have my glasses; I left them in the car." I didn't see it around the top, so I moved on and worked through the survey with him. He answered immediately and dispassionately, even about questions of a more personal nature. Their manner was somewhat robotic. They reminded me of cops. That was the only person I interviewed. When we went back to the car, I asked the leader if she shouldn't bring her glasses so she could conduct surveys, but she didn't want to get them. We did not search very systematically for the homeless, and took the bus sometimes to keep out of the cold, approaching a few homeless as we saw them. We also passed many, and the leader didn't care to get off the bus when I pointed them out. They decided to go back rather early. The expressions of those who received us were rather grave, as was mine. After a moment, I thanked Lily for inviting me. She perked up immediately with relief. It appeared I had been intentionally set up for an undercover mental health evaluation, and that some members of the board were involved. I went the next month to the meeting. Lily was very hesitant, but seemed to gain some confidence and asserted that these meetings were in fact open to the public. Eventually she started emailing me the reminder to attend right before the meeting. I had been relying on those, and ended up missing them. During one of the meetings a member stood up and announced to the group that they were looking for people to help them build green buildings, perhaps people who felt that college had failed them. I spoke to the man afterwards. He had a cold smirk the whole time.

10

MY STALKER SPEAKS CRYPTICALLY THROUGH FACEBOOK POSTS, GETS MEAN, AND I STOP FOLLOWING

T*his is the beginning of the chronological section of my time in Tennessee.* It covers the month of July, and the last of the HONYs. As stated before, Humans of New York was a Facebook page I followed that at one point seemed to be relevant to me, as if intended to influence my behavior. After one entry, I had gone back and copied all the relevant ones and the future entries seemed to indicate Andrews knew I knew it was him, and spoke to me more directly.

July 2018

> Humans of New York - Page Liked • July 9 •
>
> "I like to shop, but I hate going to those fancy stores in midtown. They treat me like I don't have any money. They're always telling me prices when I didn't ask. Either that, or they figure I'm coming in to steal. I went to one store recently, and as soon as I walked in the door, I saw the manager lean in to the clerk and say, 'Watch her.' And so this girl starts following me around~ real close. She was acting like she wanted to help. If

I picked up an item, she'd say: 'Let me hold onto that for you.' So I thought to myself: 'I'll give you something to hold.' I walked around that entire store. I went on a real spree. By the time we were finished, she was holding 25 dresses. You could barely see her face. Then I led her up to the cash register and said, 'You know what? I changed my mind. I think I'll shop somewhere else.'"

After spending a lot of time inside studying, this was posted on the same day that I had gone out exploring and stopping off at a ton of different places seeing if it was a city I could live in.

Humans of New York - Page Liked • July 10 •

"I was in a relationship for most of my teenage years. He wasn't a bad guy, but I think long relationships can be toxic when you're that young. That's the age when you're supposed to be figuring yourself out. And that can be hard if you're completely focused on another person. I was always more worried about 'us' than I was worried about myself. I'd make decisions just to maximize our time together: the places I worked, the classes I chose, the friends I spent time with. Recently I looked through my high school photos, and I don't have a single picture when I'm not with him. And, I don't know... it feels like some of those memories should have been mine alone."

I liked this post on Facebook. Her life was, in a way, taken from her.

Humans of New York - Page Liked • July 11 •

"My mother was sick for most of my life. She had nineteen years of treatment for Hodgkin's disease. But she was the kind of mother that would come home from chemotherapy, vomit in the bathroom, and then still cook dinner for all of us. And she did this while getting a PhD in clinical psychology. She just loved being a mother. Even after the chemotherapy destroyed her ovaries, she adopted two more children. She passed away I was twenty-five. Shortly after she died, I realized that I couldn't remember her voice. I've just never been an oral person. It was maddening. It felt almost disrespectful. I had all these old videos of her, but they were silent. So I thought I'd just never know what she sounded like. Then last night, my sister found a small cassette in an old box. It was from my mother's answering machine. And she picked up the phone during one of the recordings. It was a month before she died. She was so sick at the time. But she said to the person: 'Nicholas is coming to visit me, so I stayed up late baking, and I'm waking up early to clean.'"

Humans of New York - Page Liked • July 15 •

"I feel like I had so many more stories before I came to film school. I wrote so much when I was young. I'd fill up entire journals. I was a quiet kid, so writing was my way of imagining conversations that I'd never have in real life. But it doesn't feel like I'm expressing myself anymore. It's become less about whether I like it, and more about whether my professors and classmates like it. I'm always focused on the rhythm, or the structure, or the notes I received in class, or all these rules from a long time ago that everybody uses because they work. And it just feels like I'm swapping out decorations in a house that's already been built. But I'm afraid to be more inventive, because if your work doesn't fit the rules, then people will doubt your talent. So film school has made me much better at making other people happy. But it's made me less happy. And that's not a direction that I can see myself continuing for very long."

Because I stopped journaling and don't express myself? Narcissists are extraordinarily controlling. Showing some emotions or being less than perfect or a number of normal human behaviors are routinely punished. They get as invasive and constant in their surveillance as they can. They are fully convinced that they own your soul, and depend on it. On the one hand they crave authentic expression. On the other, they exploit it.

Humans of New York

"It happened on Father's Day. I took him out to lunch, and then afterward we went to a barbecue at his family's house. He'd been drinking all day. At one point he's got our daughter in his arms, and he tells her to call me a 'biatch.' So I start yelling at him. And he hits me so hard with his fist that I had to get ten stitches. That was the last straw for me. I still think he's a great dad. I'll give him that. A lot of people ask me how I can say that, but I see it like this: when he's around my daughter, I see the love. She lights up when he walks in the room. I wanted that love for myself, but at least she gets it. And he's a good provider. He works. He just bought her a bunch of new clothes this weekend. When he dropped them off at the house, he asked me if I was going to drop the charges. I told him 'no.' Not this time."

I went shopping and a man came up behind me in line before the store opened. I got out of line and walked around for a few minutes, and then got back in line behind him casually. He looked behind him quickly and nervously three times, not looking directly at me.

After seeing this HONY, I wrote a note to myself. "It is better to be hated by King Midas than it is to be loved." This was a way to describe what would be done to the victim of narcissists. They are forced to appear perfect, but go through serious psychological damage.

> Humans of New York
>
> "Last week I was picking through the trash, looking for bottles and cans to recycle, and my social worker walked by with her family. She walked just a few feet from me. And I know she saw me. But she didn't say a thing. Not even 'hello.' I asked her about it during our next meeting, and at first she denied seeing me. But then she told me that she had been in her 'private space.' That really put a stake in my heart. Why can't you say 'hello' to me in your private space? So I'm writing her a letter. I'm using a dictionary because I want the words to be perfect. If you mess up your words, then it's easy for people to ignore what you're trying to say. And I want to be sure she knows exactly how it made me feel."

I was looking for a place and a way to build a tiny home, move out of my apartment, and live alone. It was as if he was saying he wouldn't see me as much if I could have my own house.

7/18/18

> Humans of New York
>
> "Last year I did an exploration of having a child on my own. I went to the doctor, and after she looked at my uterus, she said: 'Not only is it possible, but your uterus looks younger than its years.' Then she put me in the stirrups and did a demo to show me exactly how the procedure would work. The ultrasound screen was right next to me. I kept looking at it and wishing I could see a baby on there. But I was already 48. I was single. My income wasn't secure at the time. And I didn't have family that could take care of the child if something happened to me. So I decided not to do it. I finally closed the door for good. I cried uncontrollably for weeks. It's a gaping hole in my life that will never go away. I'll just get better at dealing with it. I wish I'd done it on my own when I was younger. I wish I'd stopped complaining about the past, and hoping for the future, and just said: '**** it. This is where I am now, and this is what I can do about it.'"

I had just received a response from Legal Shield about the legality of building a tiny home in the area. After that, I had been sitting on the edge of the bathtub crying, like a truck had run me over.

My comment on Facebook: Sometimes people can suffocate you, consuming your whole life, and you may not be able to achieve the success, love, or spirit that were once yours. It's a shame. Everyone loses. -7-20-18 ...

7/22/18

> Humans of New York
>
> "My mom left the Philippines when I was five years old. My sisters and I were very young at the time. We basically raised ourselves because my dad doesn't talk much. It must have been hard on my mother. She wasn't able to come back because of her visa status, and we didn't have the money to visit. We talked on the phone about once a month. She'd send us letters, and clothes, and toys. It took ten years of working and saving for her to finally bring us over. I think the reunion was much different than she imagined. She probably expected us to be grateful, but all of us were teenagers by then. We weren't used to being told what to do. So we were pretty awful to her. And my father divorced her soon after we arrived in America. But her sacrifice paid off. We all graduated college and have good jobs. But it wasn't until I became an adult that I realized how lonely those ten years must have been."

My mom may miss me and want me to talk to her. I may have been watching the Korean drama Call Me Mother at the time.

7/23/18

> Humans of New York
>
> "My father called me 'stupid' a lot. Even when I'd bring home good grades, he'd say things like: 'You're smart, but you don't know anything.' I just wasn't a big reader like him. He always had a book in his hand. Math was my thing. During lunch I'd go to the junior high library and sit on the floor with puzzle books. Now I'm a teacher, and I've taught every math class in the high school curriculum. A few years ago I was teaching my precalculus class, and I stumbled upon a set of numbers that generated ellipses with identical positioning in both the rectangular and polar coordinate systems. So I turned them into variables, wrote a two-page proof, and had my work published in a journal called The Mathematics Teacher. Take that, Dad."

I was studying precalculus, maybe not as hard as I should.

7/25/18

Humans of New York

"I've been on antidepressants since August of last year. I was living alone in the city at the time and feeling a lot of anxiety. So I talked to a therapist, and she recommended antidepressants. At first I was nervous about taking them. There's a bit of a stigma in the African American community. If you take any sort of medication, it's like: 'Oh, you crazy now.' So the first thing I did was look on the Internet. I'm not even sure what I searched. But somehow I ended up finding Matt's videos on YouTube. He was sort of documenting his own experience with antidepressants. He was black. He was male. He was queer. And he was doing fine. It just made me feel a lot less alone. I sent him a short message thanking him for his videos, and he started checking in on me about once a week. He's been a great friend. We actually just met in person for the first time on Saturday."

7/26/18

Humans of New York

"My son is on the computer all the time. He'll start as soon as he gets home from school and goes until bedtime. It's some sort of adventure game involving teamwork. He wears a headset and plays with his friends. His goal was to go outside more this summer but that hasn't happened. Maybe I enabled him. I held off on getting him a phone and computer, but at some point every other kid has got one. And you don't want him to fall behind with technology. He's a good kid. His grades are pretty good. His teachers love him. He's very polite. He helps his mother. I just wish he'd apply his interest in games to other things. He was in science club, but he quit that. He took some Tae Kwon Do lessons, but he quit that. I thought maybe coding classes would interest him because he loves being on the computer, but that didn't work either. I also played video games as a kid. But we'd just beat a few levels of Mario, and then we'd get a call to come outside. But that doesn't happen anymore. Because the person who'd normally call you is on the other end of the headset."

I don't get out much. I used to do Jujitsu.

7/28/18

Humans of New York

"My superpower is fire. It's inside my hands but I only use it on bullies. My dad is a superhero too. His power is minding his own business."

7/29/18

Humans of New York

"So one day I'm sitting here talking to this lady, and I'm eating a sandwich. And the lady says to me: 'There's a sparrow sitting on your sandwich.' And I think, 'Wow. That's pretty thrilling.' So I began to feed it. And that sparrow started spreading the word, and I developed a bit of a reputation in the sparrow community. And suddenly I become the sparrow guy. There's like sixty of them waiting for me every morning. All these benches are covered in ****."

There was a cat who came into my room to get pets, and there was fur all over my floor that I just left there. Brian had told me he was a bit OCD at Porcfest.

7/30/18

Humans of New York

"I took him to see Brokeback Mountain when it came out. I thought I was challenging him with the choice. But at the end of the film, he turned to me and said: 'That's me.' We'd been married for thirty years. Our kids were still young. I didn't know what to do. Do I leave? Do I stay? We were ex-pats in another country at the time, so we were all alone. I had nobody to talk to. We went to a therapist to see if it was possible to stay together, and she told us: 'I've seen it work. But only if one person is very discrete and the other is very tolerant.' So I agreed to try. It's been ten years. It's been exhausting in a lot of ways. I asked too many questions at first. I made myself miserable. Now I give him a lot of space. And I get a lot of space in return. I've been traveling alone for about two months now. I know what's going on back home but I don't ask about it. My friends ask me why I don't move on with my life. I don't know the answer. Maybe I'm just too afraid to be alone at this age. But I still feel like he's my soul mate. We have the same view of the world. We both love children. We love traveling and good food. He really is a good man. He's just gay. And we've had such a good life together, I'm just not ready to stop sharing it."

I was watching a Korean drama called Call Me Mother. There is a part near the end where the detective catches up with the kidnapper (who is rescuing a child from an abusive household) and tears the child away from a distraught "mother." Watching that scene tears just kept falling from my eyes. I had been rather stoic for a long time otherwise. After this HONY post, my mother contacted me again to chat. Note, toxic personalities consume all relationships. It was like he was saying my desire for a relationship with my mother was like cheating on him, and he was offering to be very tolerant and to let me be very discreet in having a relationship with my own mother. It's worth noting once again he misread me. I was not crying about my relationship with my mother, but with my niece.

7/31/18

> Humans of New York
>
> "I'm a single father raising a teenager. We're meeting here in a few minutes to go on a run. I'm trying to teach him discipline and focus. He's had some problems paying attention in school, but I don't want to put him on medication. His mother and I divorced when he was four. She's a good person. She's very appreciative of what I've done. She just wasn't ready to be a parent. I was in a much better place. So she didn't fight me on custody. But it scares me to think if she had. The courts are set up against men. They almost always determine that women should raise kids and men should pay child support. I don't understand it. There's a big push to see women as equal workers. Why can't men be equal parents?"

It was as though Brian wanted me to transfer the regard I had for my other loved ones to him.

August 2018

8/1/18

> Humans of New York
>
> "I love walking around the city. I catch the Metro North train at 11:40 every morning. I go to the same gym that I've been going to for forty years. Then I just start walking. If you take big strides it really stretches you out. And there are millions of other people walking around. You never feel alone. People smile at you. On weekends I'll bring my granddaughters with me and we'll tour different neighborhoods. We've seen ten or twelve so far. Sometimes I get to borrow them for the whole afternoon. But they're at sleep away camp right now so I'm missing them a lot. And that's about it. I do a little shopping at the thrift store. I stop and read the paper. I eat at outdoor restaurants. It's

simple but I found what makes me happy and I'm doing it. And when I'm heading home at night, sometimes I think: 'I just had the best day of my life.'"

I would walk all the time and go to thrift stores. This is praise for my kind of lifestyle.

8/2/18

Humans of New York

"I started my career as a teller at a community bank in Florida. I was in my early thirties. At the time I had a young child and I just needed a way to pay my rent and car payment. But I kept moving up. I wouldn't say I'm overly ambitious. It didn't come from a place of 'I need more.' I just have a lot of energy. And I'd always ask the next question or apply for the next job. So I worked my way up to CEO. It was demanding but I enjoyed the position. I was handling it quite well until a few years ago when my husband passed away. Then my mother. And then my best friend. All of this happened in a single year. I'd never even lived alone before. Suddenly I felt unanchored. I reached this place of 'what do I do now?' I couldn't go back to making more money. So I decided to make a change. I went back to college to get a Master of Public Administration. And right now I'm actually on the lunch hour for my final class. I've already got a job waiting on me back home. I'm the new Director of Broward County's Business Council on Homelessness. We're working toward getting homeless people into permanent housing. And I'm really excited. I want to do a great job. I'm in a place where I can change some lives. It feels like I've moved from success to significance."

I had just submitted a scholarship application which talked about helping the homeless. Given the way I have seen them operate, such a statement would be expected to be taken as a threat. Threatening the safety of a person's family falls under the legal definition of torture in the US. It has happened at other times in other circumstances as well. Right now someone is whistling and burping. That is usually the signal for "I'm not bothered." -2/26/20

...

8/4/18

Humans of New York

"I haven't worked with an American for three years. I'm a union drywall finisher, and my job has completely been taken over by Central and South Americans. All of them have union cards now. Can you imagine being the only one on your crew who doesn't speak Spanish? There's nobody to talk to. You have no clue what people are saying. It's isolating. And all of them stick together too. My last three foremen were from El Salvador, Paraguay, and Peru. And whenever work dries up, I'm the first one trimmed from the crew. Always. No matter how hard I work. I used to get angry about it. It felt like I'd been sold out by the mayor and the union bosses. I even started having racist thoughts. But that's not me, man. I know they aren't bad people. They're just sticking together like any of us would. How can you blame them? My parents were immigrants. I grew up in New York. I've got friends from all over the world. So I'm not going to start thinking like that. I'm not going there. That's not who I am."

This might be an unfavorable experience of someone on the "outside."

The following is in response to the next post. His tone had changed and I wanted to make sure I understood. It seemed he had decided to take off the mask once I was stuck in one place and he didn't have to pretend to be caring. Though I'm not sure why the dramatic change in tone.

My comment on Facebook: Not clearly understanding the people around you can cause a lot of problems. If he can't get a reliable channel of communication, he should look elsewhere. Confusion is not the path to success.

8/5/18

Humans of New York

"I had to take a bike ride to get away from my teenage daughter. She missed the deadline for her college application, but she lied and told me that she'd sent it in on time. I believed her. I decided to give her space and let her do it on her own. Then yesterday I found a letter saying that her application came too late. So I cooked her dinner. I let her have a nice meal. Then I served her the letter for dessert. We started arguing. She told me that she wants to take a semester off. She thinks I'm bossing her around and she wants to do things her own way. But I worked two jobs for this girl. I raised her on my own. I've given her everything. She was born at 11:58 PM, two minutes before my birthday. She looks just like me. She acts just like me. And she's stubborn like me. Whenever we butt heads I think, 'Oh my ***. I'm Angie. I'm fighting with my eighteen-year-old self.' Except I was already pregnant with her older brother by then. And I just want things to be easier for her."

My comment on Facebook: There are always curve balls. I hope she's able to focus and stay on track.

I had just successfully applied to college.

8/6/18

> Humans of New York
>
> "A few years ago I get a call from my wife, and she tells me that her aunt is going through a tough time and needs a place to stay. So I agreed to let the aunt stay with us for a few months. 'I'm doing a good deed,' I thought. But things got weird after she moved in. She was a really quiet lady. And she always seemed to be watching me. I'd be walking around downstairs, and I'd notice the aunt peering down on me from the upper level. Like I was some sort of intruder. But I think to myself: 'Just ignore it. She's going through a rough time.' Then one night I wake up at 2:30 AM and the aunt is standing over my bed, saying some sort of prayer over me. And I sleep completely naked. And I have no idea how long this woman has been there. And I wake up my wife, who starts dragging the aunt out of the room, and the whole time the woman is screaming at me: 'I know who you are! You aren't fooling anyone!' It was terrifying. My wife and I separated four months later. Things hadn't been going great, but that aunt definitely flushed the toilet."

After the 8/5 entry, I wondered if perhaps I was mistaken about the HONYs, and so I made a comment on the 8/4 entry asking to make sure I was hearing from them correctly. This post is what came next. After this, I unfollowed HONY and have not looked back.

11

I THINK MY PROFESSOR WAS A STAGE HYPNOTIST, MY FAMILY USING PSYCHOLOGICAL WARFARE ON ME, AND THEIR RESPONSE TO THIS JOURNAL ENTRY

T*his is the second part* of the chronological section of my time in Tennessee, covering August, September, and October 2018. I talk about College and Fall Break.

August 2018

Before starting college, I saw two advertisements, one not long after the other, both for shows about inappropriate videos being taken without permission and shared with the community of the victims. I took this to be an implied threat to release the footage of me in the shower to the college. I did not react. To my knowledge that never happened. -3/15/21

August 19th. I was attempting to back up my photos into a MicroSD card in my phone. When I did so, the pictures were removed off of my phone, and the card was corrupted. I looked up how to recover data on an SD card and set my laptop up for it. The program had a good track record. I was staying in my room for a long time studying so I let the program run, as I recall, for days. It ultimately did not complete the recovery.

When I went to the church, another possible example of a pastor using the pulpit as a tool for FBI harassment, the pastor gave an anecdote about how he had lost data on a card, and how enraged he was. The sermon was on anger. *This is the same church with the pastor who introduced himself twice. -3/10/21*

August 25th. I attempted to resume my efforts to recover the data. The program was supposed to be able to do that, but couldn't resume the photorec session.

Fall 2018 AC/DC Class

There were some strange things about Rasputin that showed similarities to a stage hypnotist. On the first day, he went around the room and shook every one's hand. Later, near the end of the class, he did this again, but when he came to me, he mispronounced my name, and as I took the time to explain to him what my name was, he was holding my wrist with his other hand. This could be getting a baseline heartbeat, and then checking me later on to see if I had changed.

He brought out a motor and asked me to read what the label said. He frequently drew me out with many questions. The tone he set in the class was loose and jovial. Many students who had apparently taken his class before traded barbs.

He briefly brushed aside the syllabus, saying that the basis on which we were graded would be different anyway. During the class, he would throw out new rules, like if anyone messes up their sheet on the power equations, then no one is allowed to use them during the test, and if everyone will buy a book he recommended, then everyone could use it for the test. I found these things very odd. He was using intense peer pressure to get me to do things, and he had a lot of arbitrary power over our grades. After the first class, I was unsure of what to make of this strange power dynamic, and didn't know what he might ask me to do and what I should say if I didn't feel comfortable. The whole air of the class was so light and playful that it was hard to say no to things.

Another thing that happened during the first class is he would ask my permission for things. He asked me if he could close the projector. I said, "If you wish." He told me that I was supposed to say, "Yes, you may." I did so, and at the end of the class he asked my permission again, and I said "If you wish." His brow furrowed like that is not the response he wanted. I didn't know why that would bother him, but I remember hearing one time that to make people more suggestible, you get them to say yes to you. Mr. Rory was the student who sat next to me. He and "Ras," as we were supposed to call him, had a much closer relationship. Mr. Rasputin asked Mr. Rory to confirm that he was quite a notorious teacher here, and he said, "I learned that in the second week." I wondered what happened the second week. He finished the class very early.

In the second class, he commented that he liked the trick I had for remembering my name. He seemed excited. As we began, I volunteered answers and was asked many questions. He toyed with me, asking me to pick a student who would have to answer the next question. I wasn't sure I wanted to at first. I looked around. He said that if I felt uncomfortable, all I would have to do is make eye contact with him as he passed that student, and he began to walk down the aisle gleefully. I looked at the students, and found one who I thought seemed pretty knowledgeable and open. "You're braver than I thought." He gave me some positive reinforcement for my obedience. I looked at Jace, who I had picked. He looked sick. Mr. Rasputin began to prepare his question, and he kept preparing it. Jace offered an "Uhu" in a cracked voice, unusually nervous, I thought, for how outspoken he was before. But Mr. Rasputin never did ask him a question. He just kept preparing for one and stopped like he had made some statement. He then offered Jace the chance to pick the next person. He picked a guy in the front row who hadn't spoken. Mr. Rasputin looked worried, and joked that that man showed no fear, and he didn't want to toy with people like that.

A boy appeared in the door. He was acknowledged by Mr. Rasputin as a former student, who had after graduating from his class gone on to successfully get a job. The impression I was given from that event is that Mr. Rasputin is a very great teacher and I must depend on him and what he says to succeed. I remembered Mr. Rory saying he learned how infamous Mr. Rasputin was in the second week, and here I had as well. Something felt off to me about that, and I couldn't put my finger on it.

Ras asked a student in the front who seemed to have some knowledge about electronics if he saw anything that he was doing wrong. At one point the student, Wade? tried to point something out, but he was wrong. Ras said that was okay, if someone is listening to something they are already familiar with they aren't going to pay full attention. Even he wouldn't. At the end of the class, he asked him to really tell him how he was doing as a teacher, like he needed his insight. Mr. Rasputin is supposed to be a very experienced teacher.

Mr. Rasputin was showing us some rule on the board, and asked if we accepted it, "even though it was only Mr. Rasputin saying it." "It's Ohm's law." A student added. And so Mr. Rasputin agreed that it was something we could accept. Later on, he told us a galvanometer worked just like some other tool, and asked if we accepted this. Then he directed his question to the whole back row, and just started going down the line, nodding his head as each successive person complied with a "yes." When he came to me, I said "I don't know." I really didn't. I didn't understand what it was that he had said. He laughed. He told me that I had a very good quality that his wife also has, except that she understands. He continued to teach, and asked us to clear our minds and imagine taking a break, smoking a cigarette, and drinking coffee. Then he asked me another question, which I got completely wrong. I was feeling alarmed, and wasn't paying full attention. He looked up shocked at me and exclaimed I was incorrect. Ras seemed unsettled. He kept asking Mr. Rory's permission to end the class, which he did not too long later, very early again. As I left he told me "Be safe."

It was many things, but I decided to drop that class.

September 2018

September 16th. I searched hypnotism. I remember after doing so, the next time I went to college, in front of the entrance to the building was a police car and uniformed police officer, presumably to intimidate me from retaliating against Rasputin.

October 2018

October 4th. I viewed the staff directory of the College. As I recall after this, I was tailed by their police car as I came in. In some of these cases where the police feel I am looking into them a little too much, or after they feel one of their undercover officers has been made, I get a pronounced police presence showing up to various places I go or following me. For example, after I visibly seemed suspicious of Memphis from my CAD class, or after I picked out a guy sitting across from me in a library. Sometimes they would drive by as I came out of my house, show up and stand around in the balcony in full uniform where I was singing during worship, have one tail me on the road, only to be replaced by park ranger #*redacted*, etc. Typical to be punished for their mistakes. Also, typical to meet every problem with more intimidation.

Fall Break

Wednesday, October 10th. I arrive around 1:20 am. Mom, Dad, and *redacted*, stayed up for me. Mom asks if I'm hungry. I look around. There are rules on fridge door for my niece. *They listed punishments, but not spanking. My three siblings and I were spanked growing up. We considered it condoned in the Bible. However, Brian Andrews appeared to be against corporal punishment. To be fair, as I recall I discouraged my mother from punishing my niece that way after Porcfest. However, on this day when I spoke with her, she seemed to grudgingly say they couldn't spank her. I have influence with my family, but that seemed like a bit more control than that. It seemed to me in this case and at other times my stalker was playing with my family to suit himself a great deal farther than would be useful for the "government's interests." I remember when I read my Porcfest entry to my family while they visited Tennessee in the Spring, I showed them his picture, and my father exclaimed that he could be as old as he was. My mother gave a knee jerk defense that "he could be 45." I had just explained he was an atheist who tried to kiss me twice after I was physically stopping him. It is pretty uncharacteristic for my mother to defend his viability as my romantic partner. This and many other cases suggest Andrews is using the threat of his position for his personal needs. -2/27/20*

Thursday: I show Dad my college notes. He says I have learned a lot in a few months, and his college notes were stolen when he left his briefcase behind while interviewing. *Possibly a threat.* I was quiet and awkward around Mom. She asked me questions, and wasn't sure what not to ask about. She asked me if I could smell cream to see if it is still good. *She made some comment like I know about things like that, right? It had probably never been clarified in Andrews's mind whether I knew if it was risky to eat the food that had gone bad when Ace had upset me. I imagine my mother would have taken some blame for failing to educate me. -2/27/20* She asked me about exercise. Snickers, my cat, is not well. Mom wanted me to have her put to sleep while I was there. She and Dad insist I take her to the vet. She says she doesn't want to go through the hell of taking care of an animal with worms like Blackie. I explain what I want *though I got a little emotional, which would mean Snickers' death would go on the list of vulnerabilities.* I told Mom and Dad about food going bad in Maryland, me getting sick, and how there were news stories about worms around the same time. *Including an ad with a graphic.* Mom asked if maybe something was wrong with their fridge. I said the family had food in it and was fine. She smirked and looked down. I told them about when I found my land lady's hair on my desk after I thoroughly cleaned. I talked to Dad about Narcissists and manipulators. Mom asks us to keep talking down stairs. Dad tells me about smear campaigns. *He explained a technique where you are an anonymous source to speak against someone, and then reference that source as your corroboration. He also said that it works well for them if they can be paid for a living to do these terrible things they are naturally inclined to do. -2/27/20* We talked about God as the only hope. I said you cannot just tell them to go to hell. Mom says "Exactly!" But I said you can't leave hell out for a moment. If you knew the goodness of God, you would know hell is just. God is redemptive, and dies for enemies. They destroy their friends. I talked with my brother and Mom about various things. I read descriptions of persecutions, Paul's, and in Hebrews chapter 11. I referenced the verse that said what does it profit a man if he gains the world and loses his soul? I was making an argument that as Christians, we are forbidden to be Satan to people, terrorizing and destroying people and getting them to do evil, no matter what is done to us. I worked on school with my niece, helping with a division problem, 17 divided by 3. I wanted to help her conceptualize the difference between 17/3 and 3/17, so I used 3 people, as something that isn't normally divided. *This appeared to me, when I went to a Bible study on the 12th, to lead them to interpret me as imminently plotting to kill police officers. This is something I have seen in another narcissist–a sincere belief that others are a serious physical threat. Paranoia in the hands of someone who is able to respond with destructive force is a recipe itself for a danger to public safety. -2/27/20*

I went to see my niece play volleyball. A woman asked if I was with my niece, and gave me a bag of clothes to take home for her. *It seemed my family was benefiting, during their time of financial strain, from the kindness of others. That could potentially be a way to make someone dependent. I remember Mom and my niece coming home from a restaurant with a wrap and smoothie, all while struggling to pay bills. -2/27/20*

My brother invited me to go with him for a Bible study. I went to Avery's, and they talked about free will vs predestination. One boy there brought up the comment about a guy who shot at police, disparaging him, and *Avery talked about respecting authority. He quoted a verse he used to quote very frequently, which was we are to be "wise as serpents, and harmless as doves." The boy's comment seemed placed, and Avery seemed discouraged by me. I wondered if he was told absurd things about me, like that I was plotting to kill police officers. It would be unfortunate if the perspective of a narcissist, who is seeing the world in a very skewed way due to his condition, could be taken as expert opinion, fed to the victim's connections, and kept a secret, so it will not be challenged. -2/27/20*

During bedtime, I asked the family if they would like to read the Bible with me. Mom suggested my niece's school passage, Hebrews 4. I read. Mom asked if Jesus is God, and God is not tempted, how was Jesus tempted as we are? She says he didn't lust, and started picking out which temptations he had. I say he was tempted, but didn't sin. James 1 describes that there is a difference between temptation and sin. Whatever it meant, it meant he could sympathize with her. Friendship with the world is enmity with God. We are in the world, but it doesn't drive us. ... I said "Perfect love casts out fear" used to not make sense to me. If I love something, I will fear harm to it. Fear is evidence of love. But I had come to know it was God's love for us that casts out fear. Mom says harshly the world will hate you. I agreed, if it hated Jesus, it will hate us, but we can have spiritual peace. Mom left and called my niece to come. My niece asked what a heathen is. I say "Unredeemed. Everything they do tends towards destruction.? ...

My dad and I talk about the fear of the Lord: to seek truth, and hate evil. Dad says I'm not acting normal not answering Mom's questions, and it seemed strained. He says he hopes we will come to an understanding, and I am hurting her feelings. I said I don't need to be normal and I have my reasons, and want what's best for them. But I would think about it. *I considered it best to not come forward and tell everyone I believed I was being "investigated." At the same time, the reality of an investigation would change my behavior. Largely in the beginning that meant I kept my distance from people. But I was not explaining why. This is one of the problems people in my situation face.*

Friday. Mom came to me and told me how Pawson, a preacher we both liked, said "How do you tell the difference between a backslider and an apostate? See if God takes you back." *This may have been one attempt to begin to make me think God had permanently rejected me. It is not at all in her character to do that. For the sane among us, we can take a moment to reflect on the significance of this act. This is a direct psychological attack on a person's religion, perpetrated by a government against a political dissident, namely, through a mother against her child. She does offer a possible good motive for her question posted below if she is not an informant. -2/27/20* Mom was sad. I gave her the book Hiding Place back. While we watched Sherlock Holmes together eating candy corn, she said chloroform works, but slowly. *It seemed a bit unusual for my mother to know that sort of thing.* Sherlock wasn't that good. Mom said she could see I wanted my own life and she is willing to let me go. I took a long nap. For supper we had bulgogi (meat). I didn't eat it. *I was still dealing with people trying to drug me.* Mom asked Dad how long she slept, saying it was a few hours. *Mom and I had been eating candy corn out of the same bowl. I might have assumed it was safe if an informant did it too. However, her comment could make me think my nap was due to drugs, and she had also been affected, perhaps intentionally. -2/27/20* I had to do my midterm. Mom gives me a laptop to use. At first, I think not, but Dad rushed to get me to use it. *I had suspected my mother more than my father at that point, but here he is clearly supporting her in that. This was totally uncharacteristic of him. Usually he is very calm.*

Saturday. I watched more Voltron with my niece in the afternoon. Snickers was getting bad. Her injury was not draining. I called vets and got quotes and information. Mom said they will decide what to do with Snickers before I go. I talked with my brother for several hours, reading Jeremiah 7, 9, and 17. He told me people can lose their salvation, and never be accepted again. He referenced the "three strikes" in Amos. I wondered what the application was. It is hopeless so curse God and die? *One again, perhaps an attempt to make me think God had permanently rejected me. This is totally out of character for my brother, and made no sense to bring it up in the conversation. His response is below.* I read in Judges, where God said He will not take back Israel after their many times disobeying, but has compassion when they repent and does. I referenced the unjust judge, where the persistent widow was heard, and how God will be more gracious; and Jeremiah 18, which explains God's "return policy." He asked what Paul was striving to lay hold of. I said our maturation is very important to God. He asked what having one mind means. *Not the Borg, where people can coerce others into agreement.* I said one God, one faith. If everyone is following the truth, we should arrive at the same place. Not Paul and the apostles. My brother asks about 'lend and do not expect in return.' *The passage says to give to those who ask, so it might be convenient for people with no empathy to exploit.* I point out those taking advantage of this... We must understand the reason for forbearance. Don't help people destroy themselves by taking advantage of you. He asked if I know about the verse that says we must help family, or we are worse than the unbeliever. *Basically, this appeared to be a series of attempts to use scripture as a weapon against my faith, finances, and more to come.* We talked about the homeless. I told him about harassment at Walmart and college cops. I said there are lots of reasons people are homeless, and we don't know what battles people fight. Some have kids, and are afraid CPS will take them if they seek help because they have no utilities. Some are on drugs, and are afraid to come forward. One was a pedophile. It can also be because it is the best life for them. He tells me about a church taking measures to prevent child abuse. There was a girl who was not severely abused but still had symptoms. They gave out anonymous cards for people's stories. I note they had handwriting.

Warning: sexually explicit content

A trauma of sexual abuse was one of the first things Andrews asked me about in his email. After saying in my journal at Maryland that people who are less acclimated to sex are more sensitive to it, I was sexually harassed the next morning. The first artificial dream I was given out of a long period of artificial dreams was being gang raped. After a recent dream in Quebec about child porn, unknown people kept going into my bathroom that I share with one other. It seems to be one of the highest priorities to get sexual assaults listed as a vulnerability of mine. Malignant narcissists have out of control libidos and are exploitative and sadistic, so it should be no surprise that they are sexual predators, using an also demented government program to feed their sadism. Here a brother is presenting a possible trigger which may permit a gang of sexual maniacs to get his sister to relive sexual abuse. The level of depravity that is involved in this program is one of the highest. -2/27/20

... I told him it is a sin to cause someone to sin, and read Proverbs 6, "the Lord hates... one who sows discord among brothers." I was thinking about the sorts of things informants try to get people to do. I told him about sadism, making others vulnerable so you feel less so, and the Monkey Game story. This is something I heard on YouTube. A hacker finds a website and breaks in. He sees a countdown and curtains. When the countdown ends, he enters into a chat room, and sees everyone is watching someone tied to a table. Someone is granted the opportunity to decide what to do to him next, and that person brings a saw closer to him. The hacker is horrified, but is afraid if he expresses his feelings, he may end up being the next target of this group. Then he sees someone say they have almost locked on his location, and he shuts the computer down and doesn't touch another for 4 years. *I could see recognition in his eyes, which would be a parallel to the informant's situation. It seems to me this is the fear of the informants. They act with cruelty, knowing that the action they are taking could very well be against them. In effect, they are maintaining the threat to themselves. It must be a torturous thing to be an informant. -2/27/20* He said some environments do not encourage individual thought. He said we must obey authority. *What?! What environment was he defending?* I say no. Daniel, Shadrack, Meshach, and Abednego disobeyed the king of Babylon. Peter, when told not to preach, said if the government tells you to sin, you must obey God. *My brother said, "Oh," like he had just come to a realization when I said that. -10/20/20* He said jokingly there was "being a slave to sin." "If only God had thought of that: a way to not be a slave to sin anymore," I responded sarcastically. That is exactly the point of salvation. "Judgment day is the ultimate Nuremberg trials," I added. That is to say, "Just doing my job" is no defense. Mom was also in the room. We had Bulgogi for supper. I didn't eat. *I had written this again in my original notes. Notes were written around the same time, but not necessarily the same day on this trip. We may have had the same thing twice. -2/27/20*

Sunday. I sleep in and everyone leaves. I check on Snickers. Her abscess opened, so I take care of her for several hours. My brother comes home, tells me he woke up several times, and had to pray to resolve it. I didn't say much. The family came back. My sister asked me if I'm not eating meat. I don't want to say. My niece yells "She's just curious!" *This is an example of me being automatically defensive, given attacks are couched in normal conversation. I erred on the side of not talking. This appeared to frustrate my niece. At the time it seemed to me my sister had chosen to stay out of being an informant. -2/27/20* Beef stroganoff that night. I was quiet, on the computer. Daddy had barely gotten any interviews all year, but had been contacted every day since I came. He was unemployed for over a year despite being an experienced software engineer in a booming job market. They say it was maybe six callbacks in a year he had gotten before my visit. Mom asked me if I opened Snickers' abscess or not. I say no. *Possible entrapment question. It would probably be illegal to attempt a crude surgery on a pet.* Dad got an offer and thanked God, saying it was all those prayers on Facebook. Mom notes that was a little before I came but not much. Then she gets excited and must clean Snickers' spot, wash the wall where Snickers had made a mess, and asked me eagerly if I would like a pillow to sit on. *The realization seemed to come to my mother that the whole year of my family suffering was actually about me. They didn't seem to realize that this was primarily about Andrews breaking me, and seemed to be inducted into these acts of deception and cruelty without knowing why. Her behavior was totally uncharacteristic of her. My mother does not suck up to people. She wouldn't have recognized the expectation to. The idea that she could act desperately servile to me, and that I would take that as payment and no longer harm them is totally ridiculous. That is of course par for the course in the world of narcissists. She must have taken on the change in character from them. -2/27/20* During supper, people made puns about milk. I drank milk then, and then others joined in. I spoke in American Sign Language. *Signing is a way we had semi private or overlapping conversations in my house.* My sister said quickly and alarmed that she heard a camera. Dad says it has been going for a few minutes. *It seemed it was their responsibility to not let me communicate to anyone without the prying eyes and ears of government agents. This also indicates the primary level of surveillance at that time and place was audio.* Cards afterwards. My choice—solitaire. My brother won the first hand, then me. I give Dad back the brainwashing papers, and tell him some things I've learned about hypnosis. My intention was to educate my family about some of the things I had learned about the FBI. *Something I have seen and struggled with around other victims is that it is easy to unintentionally threaten them. It seems when a possible threat is brought to their attention, the program will continue to use it against the victim until they demonstrate they are not afraid. It seems that many of those perpetrating the system are simultaneously victims themselves. It is an obstacle to exposing the criminals and bringing them to justice. They say "peace, peace" when there is no peace.* He tells me about the book Counterfeit Revival. My niece comes in, and asked me if I wanted to watch a movie, but they don't know which one. I don't want to. She looks upset, then leaves.

Monday. Dad played a video of a guy joking how dangerous preppers are. I questioned that. I said it was not dangerous to think about important things, but rather, dangerous not to. Dad says Alex Jones is rude, abrasive. "We must keep things in proportion, and focus on God," is what he said. Was I not? I noted the ad hominem logical fallacy. Regardless of what emotions Alex Jones displays, he could still be correct in his claims. *This may be a sort of gaslighting put down. If I uncovered a tactic, I may be characterized as paranoid, dangerous, or rude.* We talked about Trump. I was uninformed. Dad said I was not getting the right picture. He listed deals, the economy, and deregulation as positive things Trump has done. Downstairs, a girl said she is angry and doesn't know why. Mom told her to go run. She asked me if that isn't what I do to de-stress. I say it's one thing, but it doesn't address root problems. *It seemed to me this was put on for me. I acted slightly annoyed with Dad. I don't know in what way I would have been perceived as needing to de-stress.* Mom said something I didn't understand, "Reset your mind." I asked her what she meant by that. She said to form a new perspective, not be overwhelmed, and take it as a challenge. I packed to leave, and gave Mom a note while she is teaching my niece. "I have a comment about the 'reset your mind' to 'take things on as a challenge.' This could mean to take stupid risks because doing hard things is cool, or to reframe evil. "Temptation must come into the world, but woe to him by which it comes." "Do not do evil that good may come." Evil is objective and is never acceptable. Rather, the mindset should be to admit God's goodness and justice, serve Him regardless, and accept the outcome He gives." Then I quote Isaiah 30:15. *I had been given the impression Andrews saw his treatment of me as training me, or making me stronger. It is as if someone kicks you and then claims they were teaching you karate. It is a way he reframed his actions... so he can be as much of a villain as he likes and still be approved. It may also be standard conditioning for government slaves.* Mom comes up to the office where I am with Snickers. "You misunderstood me. This isn't what I meant at all." A pause, then she asks me annoyedly if I have anything else to do before I leave. I say it might be good to see if Snickers has another opening. Mom says she will do it, so I tell everyone goodbye and leave.

It was a Saturday after I returned from Fall Break that I went to the club. In the room were Gage and Quinn. Quinn spent a long time, maybe twenty minutes, talking about a Christian cartoon with a donkey as the main character, mocking it, and laughing at it. Gage stood behind him and laughed along. After that they mocked making puns. *Obviously, the extended conversations about Christianity and the slew of puns were what they were intending to mock. I suppose I was to feel alone and despised for my faith. It was, however, a shock to my system to give eloquent and sincere arguments, and receive childish taunts in return. I did not take the people I was dealing with to be very rational afterwards.*

I attended the human trafficking conference. There were two days to this conference. On the first day, there was a panel of high-ranking law enforcement officers, including DHS, FBI, and two from the TBI (Tennessee Bureau of Investigation). I got my name tag from a woman, who gave me a warm and pointed smile. Another woman sat in the back with me. She was holding a recording device, and seemed full of energy to the point of ADHD. Some interesting things the FBI agent said is that people think that when you leave the country the FBI can't come after you. That isn’t true. It would be more difficult, but they could. He also said, referring to men who solicit prostitutes but who otherwise have no criminal record, that they will "get them on something." This is a description of, as I understand it, normal procedure for the FBI, which is to effectively start with an enemies list, and find ways to use the powers of law enforcement to target them. He also seemed to want us to understand how in his work you always had to adapt to the target, as they kept changing how they did things to compensate for what the FBI was doing. A man from the TBI spoke. The woman who gave me a name tag was sitting next to me by now. I wrote down the address the TBI agent gave for his office, and she asked for my pen. She wrote down the man's name. She seemed to take great pride in gaining my assistance in trapping me. The thing she "caught" me doing, based on the following reaction of being trailed by uniformed officers, was presumably that I was intending violence against the agent. Another man at the conference asked a question about the homeless, and watched me afterwards, with frustrated curiosity, I suppose because I didn't take the bait and approach him. The panel was warmly thanked. However, the reality of human trafficking, which sometimes involves baiting people, making them dependent, cutting them off from their support, asserting control, giving threats or false promises, etc., is not dissimilar to what agents themselves do to bring some informants under their control.

On day two, the energetic woman who sat next to me first became even more jittery, and seemed to need to ask questions and make comments to express suspicion and outrage in every direction. She at some points became a little incoherent. I think she was behaving like a schizophrenic. *It has happened on numerous occasions when I went to a church, someone else came with me and acted crazy. -2/27/20*

After the human trafficking conference, while at the library, I hear two men conversing about what sounds like it could be a human trafficking case. I ask about it. I am told a woman is being stalked, harassed, and threatened. However, five weeks ago, she put cars in the driveway so he couldn't get to her. It is driving him crazy. One of the men was looking at me with this devious grin. I had some time before then put up a tarp over my bed, so I had a small amount of privacy from the cameras. At a later day I saw the same man in the library on a computer. He had a video paused, and was stroking the elbow of a woman on the video with black hair with his finger or mouse cruiser. He had a strange delighted smile. *Written 2/27/20*

October 31st. This morning I received two text messages from Raelynn dating 11th and 15th asking me where I had gone, if I had left town. I had not seen this notification before today.

* * *

Comments from the family:

My comment on Facebook: ... The section that talks about family begins at ++. Expected publication date is October 28th.

My mother's comment: Still presuming motives.

The narrative is fragmented (not complete sentences which leads to confusion). I'm not reading the whole thing. Your picture of our family is unrecognizable, but I'm letting go.

My comment: I'm not sure in what way it is fragmented. I left a lot of the story in so it is pretty fleshed out. I do sometimes have fragments, though. I write that way because it is natural and more conversational, but if I can find something that is confusing I can correct it.

I don't know why the picture would be unrecognizable. I wrote the account while I was there, so it is basically just what happened. I'm not lying, and I'm not generally mistaken, so unless I was completely hallucinating during these days while being able to interact with people without them realizing I was completely hallucinating, it seems that what I wrote is correct.

My perceptions are useful for people to understand. I try to be clear about the distinction between what I physically saw and heard, and what I think these things mean.

If you do not want to read or comment you are free to do so. You have the option either way. However, my motive is out of love for you and for others who are suffering and need deliverance from this tyranny.

My father's comment: This is not an exhaustive response but here are some comments on part 10:

"[He explained a technique where you are an anonymous source to speak against someone, and then reference that source as your corroboration]"

I think I was telling you about Nancy Pelosi explaining the wrap-up smear: "Nancy Pelosi explains 'wrap-up smear' tactic (June 22, 201 [youtubetube com /watch?v=9LlHU53G2Z0]

"Mom said Pawson [a preacher we both liked] said how do you tell the difference between a backslider and an apostate? See if God takes you back. [This was one attempt to begin to make me think God had [permanently] rejected me."

Did Dr. David Pawson say that? What is the "see if" and "accepts you" stuff? This sounds feeling-based.

I asked your mother about this, and she says she does not agree with everything that Dr. Pawson says. She says that you need to base your faith on what Jesus says and His faithfulness and not on your feelings.

You assert in your 02/27/2020 re-interpretation of the past, that you know what your mother's intentions were. And you say that because of your reflection, you now know it was the government directly attacking your religion through your mother. (You know that this is preposterous.) If there was an attack on your faith, why come up with nonsensical government-is-attacking-you-everywhere explanations when Scripture tells us plainly that "we do not wrestle against flesh and blood, but against principalities, against powers, against the rulers of the darkness of this age, against spiritual hosts of wickedness in the heavenly places" (Ep 6:12)?

"Mom gives me laptop to use. At first I think not, but Dad convinces me. [Dad rushed to get me to use it. I had suspected my mother more than my father at that point, but here he is clearly supporting her in that. This was totally uncharacteristic of him. Usually he is very calm. - 2/27/20]"

What??? Helping you out with a laptop is now an offense?

If you continue to call good evil and turn all people into imaginary governmental adversaries, you are doing way more evil to yourself than the few actual enemies could ever do. It may have been that a couple narcissistic gas-lighters wanted to mess with your mind. So you became suspicious of them. Then you suspected others. Then you set up your own tests to see if others were informants - such as facial expressions, presuming intentions, etc., which you decided proved your suspicions true. Now you are suspecting pretty much everyone. It seems you have eagerly volunteered to use your mind to prove everyone is an informant in order to protect yourself from all possible informants. Thus you have unwittingly joined your enemies in their effort to torment you. You are being your own worst enemy (not to mention grieving those who care about you). You must stop the wrong thinking and take up the full armor of God. God has given us all we need for life and Godliness. We are not to be overcome by evil, but are to overcome evil with good.

"He told me people can lose salvation, and never be accepted again. He referenced the 'three strikes' in Amos. I wondered what is the application. It is hopeless so curse God and die? [Once again, an attempt to make me think God had [permanently] rejected me. This is totally out of character for my brother, and made no sense to bring it up in the conversation. -2/27/20]"

I haven't heard of any 3-strikes rule. The Scripture says

'Everyone who believes in him will not be put to shame.' Romans 10:11,

'I write these things to you who believe in the name of the Son of God, that you may know that you have eternal life.' 1 Jn 5:13, and

'Now to Him who is able to keep you from stumbling, And to present you faultless Before the presence of His glory with exceeding joy, ...' Jude 24.

"and asked me eagerly if I would like a pillow to sit on." ... "Her behavior was totally uncharacteristic of her."

You say that often. Why would you say that offering you a pillow to sit on was "totally uncharacteristic"? Your mother has always been considerate of you. You are treating your mother's care and kindness with contempt.

My comment: To your first point, I don't recall you bringing up Nancy Pelosi in that conversation if you were referring to her. Regardless I think it is useful to inform the reader about this sort of technique. When you said in reference to people harassing others, that it works for them especially if they get paid for a living to do that, who were you referring to?

As for your second point, Mom made that statement out of the blue. The question is why. She wasn't disputing it, but stating it like she thought it had merit. As you just pointed out, it is not consistent with our beliefs.

When I read Eph 6:12, "not against flesh and blood" ultimately means this is a spiritual fight. The "principalities" suggests governments to me, and the "darkness" could mean secrecy. We know that "the whole world lies in the power of the evil one" (1 John 5:19), and the unsaved are slaves to Satan (Ephesians 2:2-3). So it is clear that Satan uses humans to do his evil will, which includes persecuting God's people. It is therefore a viable Biblical interpretation that the government is committing harassment campaigns, and that this would include attempts to make people doubt their faith.

Third point, the way you acted was not to help me with it, but rather when I withdrew and acted unsure of using the laptop, you rushed forward as though to strongly suggest I use it. You seemed almost desperate. This was not like you at all. Perhaps you were deeply concerned I would hurt Mom's feelings by declining to use it. Otherwise you/the family being threatened to spy on me also makes sense.

You're right, it does not serve me to overstate my case or assume the threat is greater than it is. However, as an investigator into these atrocities, I have to look at a broad range of facts and possible interpretations. I make an effort to be objective, and do see reason to suspect or believe many people are informants. That isn't an impossible reality. This happens to societies like East Germany with the Stasi.

Cont...

My comment: What *my brother* was arguing is that the three strikes rule was where people lost their salvation and could not get it back. Why would he bring that up? He did not have a response when I asked him what the application was. Why would be believe that God would reject and refuse to take back one of His lost sheep? I would be shocked if *he* believed that. And he brought it up as though to convince me of it. It is most consistent with a psychological warfare attack on my source of morale.

When Mom offered me the pillow, we were sitting in the office, relaxing and talking about how you got the job and the offers started around the time I started my visit. Mom then becomes alert and gets up quickly and rushes to the bathroom to scrub the dirty spot on the wall where Snickers made a mess, as though that had suddenly become important. She offered me the pillow in a rushed stressed way. Her behavior was not that of someone who felt like cleaning, or thought I looked uncomfortable. She was grovelling, like the narcissists who suck up to those above them. She had realized the family was being made to suffer because of me. It was an awful situation. I am not holding her in contempt for that. It is not beneath the maniacs to threaten and harm a person's family to get what they want, which in my case is sex and adoration. You can see I am making more bold perceptions in my comments made later. This is because of the greater clarity and evidence that rains down on me every day.

It is neither right nor wise to appease terrorists when they threaten third parties like my family, or make any threat at all. It is not right because I am responsible to God for my actions, not theirs. It is not wise because they are by nature bottomless pits of evil, and negotiating with or appeasing terrorists only results in giving more ground to people who will use it for harm, and teaches them that particular threat is effective. They will then have more means and motive to do worse. There is a just and peaceful way to respond, and that starts with exposing the crime.

My mother's comment: I've not been threatened.

Also, stating what someone else said - out of the blue - may have been me looking for your response to that errant belief. I have been known to criticize teachers that I usually agree with when they say something wrong, but don't think I need to tell you how wrong it is when you know better...

I'm surprised you assume I mentioned what he said meant agreement with him.

My mother's comment: If a statement surprises you as "not like me" or "not like [my brother]," why not ask about it at the time? It's always best to clarify during the discussion when it is fresh in memory.

My comment: That would be a good habit to get into, I think.

My brother's comment: Just an FYI, I have had a very busy schedule of late and have not been reading the latest.

This statement is inaccurate: "[He] tells me about [the church] looking for pedophiles". That is not what happened; they worked as a pilot for a program to educate people of the church about looking for and preventing child abuse. They've also implemented recommendations of multiple adults per area to increase accountability. A very wise move.

When it comes to scripture I like to challenge people with ideas by the Word of God itself and see where they stand as we are all called to be able to give a defense for the hope that is within us and we are to study to show ourselves approved. You have stated many assertions I've allegedly made and I disagree with the words you have put in my mouth. For example, "[He] told me people can lose salvation, and never be accepted again." This is not a view that has ever fit with my understanding of salvation at any time... The word "lose" especially paints a false picture on what Salvation even is. When I inquire about implications any particular scripture may seem to indicate I'm often leading to a discussion hoping for more scripture in return... it is not a right assessment to say I have a particular belief if I ask a leading question. The Bible does speak about us with the call to "iron sharpens iron" in Proverbs 27:17 and how else can we do this unless we challenge ideas and search the scripture for the answers.

I have not read much else in your post here. But what I did see I have written about just now. I can surmise that there are probably a lot of similar issues with the rest of your writing concerning me. But I have seen no sign of you showing any heed to the words I say in any way that would affect you sharing your opinions of old. I have no quarrel with you, I would prefer to speak only "what is good for necessary edification, that it may impart grace to the hearers" as the scripture calls us to. And by this same scripture, Eph 4:29, I ask if your goal in all this fulfills the call to do this very thing?

I have always thought you were and are blessed, and rightly so, but as of the start of you sharing all this I feel as though you have been unable to see all the good that God has done for you and His sovereignty over your life. The passage 2 Kings 6:17 comes to mind now when I think of you "And Elisha prayed, 'Open his eyes, Lord, so that he may see.' Then the Lord opened the servant's eyes, and he looked and saw the hills full of horses and chariots of fire all around Elisha." and when I think of this I pray that the Lord would open your eyes so you'd see the Good Shepherd who watches over His sheep. And "Draw near to God and He will draw near to you." From what I've read it seams as though you see only darkness and no light and according to Matt 6:22 and Luke 11:34 where the "lamp of the eye" affects the "light of the body". We are called to be a "light to the world". In these passages the eye being either good or bad can also have bad translated as either evil or unhealthy... I would say unhealthy, or a "bad eye" (meaning that one that does not work as it should) would seems to fit when a person perceives darkness in everything and does not bear testimony to the things of the light. I understand that the verses of the "lamp of the eye" are often used to refer towards seeking evil with your eyes or seeking good. But the verses as they are written aren't necessarily restricted to that view as the original words do equally translate to the health of the eye and is valid in meaning in much the same way.

Love you, God bless, I wish the best for you as always.

My comment: You claim that I was false in my first statement about the church looking for pedophiles, but then seem to clarify what you meant as including the same thing, so it does not seem I misunderstood or mischaracterized that. But it is not really relevant to my main point.

You have provided another possible explanation for why you brought up that verse about three strikes, so my stated interpretation is therefore admittedly not a given.

As far as me giving no heed to what you say, perhaps you are unable to see my responses, because I have been very thorough in responding. Unless, by giving heed, you meant automatically agreeing, which I do not necessarily do.

As far as Eph 4:29, yes, that is my intention. Many things I say are negative and offensive, but they are intended to encourage people to be who God intends. I remember Pawson explaining the word "encourage" once describing a solder pointing his sword at his soldiers, prodding them into battle. The word means 'to give courage.' People are afraid to tell the truth. How different things would be, and how quickly, if we had the courage to do so.

You have said some very good things in this last paragraph. I do bring in more scripture later on, but you are exactly right. The battle is the Lord's. We should be looking at these apparently hopeless situations from His perspective. I very much like the verse on Elijah you quoted, and I hope people take that to heart.

My comment: I am reading through your comments again, and when you talk about giving heed, it seems you are basically saying there is no way to convince me not to publish my suspicions of you. Someone else asked me what I would do if I found out my accusations were false and had already published them, what would I do? I thought it was important to allow you the opportunity to clarify and negate my interpretations and evidence in your own defense. This way your side of the story is published alongside what I think. Also anything clearly false, dangerous, or unnecessary to publish can be removed before publishing. You don't have to review and provide a defense for yourself, but I am giving you the option.

My brother's comment: Just to clarify my statement about your statement about what I said about a church I consider "bearing false witness against your brother" as you use the word "pedophile" which is a word I avoid using so you translating what I said of potential abuse into pedophilia puts a terrible slander on what is perceived but what is allegedly said. Child abuse can be simple things like locking a child away in a dark closet for prolonged periods of time. Also the statement that a church was looking for a pedophile is something I never said nor have I heard any such thing, nor am I aware of that being the case. It insinuates that there is a pedophile in the church in the first place and that those there are trying to discover the criminal. This is nothing like what I said... I said the church is a pilot for a new training program teaching how to be accountable, to be aware of potential issues of certain sins, and preventive measures.

You user phrases like "convince me not to publish my suspicions of you" in your response, I could care less about "suspicions;" but where I take great issue is where you report me as saying one thing, when that's merely how you interpretatively remembered it by the lens through which you see and understand things. You did not write those journal entries the moment I said something... rather later in the day you recalled what you believed to have been said and wrote it down. This is not accurate testimony. From what I have seen this is the common scenario for quoted situations. You're welcome to write any suspicions you have, but according to God you are accountable before His law in which He states in the ten commandments not to bear false witness against your neighbor.

Painting pictures of other people based on suspicions is also akin to slandering some one's good name. Whatever may be the case, would you willingly tear down the reputation of one who ministers the gospel to others and preaches Christ? Would you do the same towards a sinner who might receive Christ if they were to know Christ's love through the way you spoke about them... hopefully without suspicion.

You're walking a dangerous road in my mind with the words you write.

Also I've found many of the words you write to be too grievous and graphic to even even bear and grit reading through. When you write about private parts, dreams of phonographic assault nature... these are not the kind of things I would ever pick up a book to read about and I detest such writings and want to avoid them like the plague. So with no disrespect for you whom I care greatly about, you are not your writing, and I do not wish to knowingly subject myself to this indecently graphic writing. You feel you are doing right by letting us review things you write about us, but you are asking us to subject ourselves to some vile writings and I do not want any part of it.

My comment: I've modified the part where I use the word pedophile so it is more in line with what you have just clarified. As far as the reliability of a record that was written within the day or days of the event, I don't expect it to be word for word, but that is still pretty good as far as testimonies go. Even if I got your words precisely, I still wouldn't understand your schema completely. Communication is by its nature imperfect, but it is still useful and vital.

As far as defaming you, other Christians, or unbelievers, it is important to value the reputations of others, but that is not more important than protecting the innocent from harm. When there is evidence that someone, whether they preach the gospel or not, is harming another person, it does not reflect God's love for me to be nice to the offender and stay silent. It does not demonstrate the gospel to try to get sinners to like me by not exposing their ongoing crimes. That person is going to burn in hell because God LOVES their VICTIMS. That person is going to remember what I did and did not do to communicate God's love/justice to them and to the world. If I did not tell them clearly how it is, how they deserve to go to hell and will, then each of the millions of years that person in hell will be cursing me for not warning him.

As far as the sexually explicit content, it is such a constant part of my life being forced to be around perverts that I did not realize how overt I was communicating this. It is evidence, and so I am not going to obscure it. But I do want to add a warning so that people can skip over that material if they wish.

However, your sister is the victim of sexual assault. That isn't in question. I literally have surveillance footage of one event. You are offended at the appearance of sexually explicit content. May I suggest you should be more offended at the crimes. If I were being attacked right next to you, would you say you don't want to look at that because it is indecent, or would you do something about the perpetrators? What did the Samaritan do about the man robbed and left naked and bleeding on the side of the rode? Shield his eyes and be offended that the victim dare have been attacked? I am not asking for your charity. Nor am I asking you to examine each piece of evidence you are uncomfortable with. I am asking you to examine your heart.

One reason Elizabeth Smart, when she was kidnapped, did not try to be rescued was because her Christian purity culture made her think that once she had been polluted no good man would want her. She saw herself as dirty, and so she stayed away from good men who could protect her, and stayed with the filthy one. I did not ask for, and I did not consent to all the filth that has been handed to me. But I am not the one that needs to hide in shame. The shame needs to be placed on the shoulders of those who committed the acts. As the victim, it is my right to at least assert that.

And my heart breaks for the many who are enduring this quietly. They need people like me to expose the crimes. If I am holding evidence that could help them, how could I fear God and not use it?

My mother's comment: *@me* It is *just as important* not to defame someone's good name.

"A good name is of more value than great riches." Prov. 22:1

If you cannot expose the crime of one without slandering another... you are not ready to speak. Only speak what is true and verifiable. You may not have to answer in a courtroom, but you will have to answer before God.

My mother's comment: You have misrepresented our entire family.

My comment: It is not just as important to not defame than it is to stop ongoing rapes/thefts/hacking/drugging/blackmail/threats/sabotage/involuntary hypnosis etc. etc. etc.

It is not just subjecting the family to disrepute, but it is also protecting the family against said attacks, as well as others.

To voice a suspicion and to describe it as a suspicion when there is ground for suspicion is verified.

I am providing you, who I am naming, with the opportunity to refute anything I say, so that false evidence will not stand. I am doing this to protect you and the family from false accusations.

I would also answer to God for my silence.

My mother's comment: I have already told you your representation of our family is distorted, and inaccurate. It is so, on the whole.

The looks, motives, intentions presumed by you are from your own imagination. They are not based on fact.

Conversations, as you admitted, cannot be remembered perfectly, some time later. And with time, things take on nuances of your own thoughts - that may not have a basis in the event itself.

I am being kind to you, by allowing for only good motives on your part. But I do not give permission for you to speak of me as an informant or say that I had any intent of doing you harm for the sake of protecting myself. I have never been threatened by a government agency. I am only threatened by you - though I do not accuse you of malice in doing so. You are mistaken. Speaking of us in the manner you have is doing damage and it will last, as the Internet is forever. There is no undoing it once done.

Consider this a blanket refutation.

My mother's comment: As for the other matters - I only will speak to one. You mention rape, but have no evidence except pain and noises. If you had gone to the police or a doctor, you would have a basis in fact.

As it is, even this is suspect. Pain is not evidence of violation.

In this, you leave yourself and your story open to doubt and ridicule. It will not help those whom you wish to serve. Those who are really oppressed by the state.

I acknowledge that such a thing exists. The state (deep state) can oppress people.

My comment: I can understand your personal offense at me accusing you, but why do you want to try so hard to defend my accused sexual assailant? Why is this the one issue you want to dispute regardless of the evidence I have offered, when I haven't even named my attacker here?

My mother's comment: *@me* If you can name an attacker, then you saw him attack you. Having an open window, hearing a noise, and waking up in pain is not evidence. If you were attacked, you should have called the police immediately. Why did you not do this? Even if you couldn't see a doctor, you could have filled out a report. Your description sounds more like a vivid dream than reality.

My mother's comment: DNA evidence needs to be collected early, in such cases.

My mother's comment: It is very unlike you.

My comment: Many victims of sexual assault do not report it. Many do not tell anyone.

Note to the reader, this paragraph refers to events written about in Book 2. I went to the police when I had video evidence of an assault along with texts I made right after and a written account. As is consistent with my assertion that this was done by a government entity, the police first told me I didn't have to fill out the complaint form and could not receive the surveillance from me, and then left the case to sit long enough until it could no longer be prosecuted.

You have not answered the question why you want to dispute this one issue. Why do you want to defend a potential sexual assailant of your daughter?

My mother's comment: *@me* From your own story, I don't believe it happened as you think. I believe it was either a vivid dream or a demonic assault (not physical). If it were physical, there would be more than pain. There would be blood and other fluids as evidence that you could collect as proof.

My mother's comment: Regarding your attempt to contact police about the man who touched you without your permission - if one institution will not hear you, keep asking, seeking, knocking until you are heard. And I'm sure you have learned from dealing with the police, always fill out the paperwork, even if they say you don't have to. It would have been good to have legal counsel...

The infringement on your person that you got video of, is harassment, not sexual assault. Perhaps in Canada, this is not taken seriously enough to bother with (in their view). However a paper trail is helpful, should there be further offense. Then, you could likely get a restraining order.

My mother's comment: Until recently in the US, such behavior would only warrant a slap in the face of the offender, by the victim. It some locations and in certain cultures, getting "fresh" is merely showing interest. Places like Mexico... I don't know enough about Canada to speak intelligently about their standards.

My comment: It sounds like *Dad* and *my brother* have not reviewed the whole thing and I can give you more time. How about Nov 2nd?

12

BREAK-INS AND SEXUAL ASSAULTS, I TRY TO CONTACT MEDIA AND AM BLOCKED OR SABOTAGED, I THINK MY PROFESSOR IS A LAZY COP

This covers the chronological section of my notes on Tennessee from November 2018 to March 2019.

November 2018

November 1st. The radio played yesterday's weather forecast and today's as tomorrow's.

The news site Drudge Report was blocked. When I got it to work, the headline was the Pittsburgh shooting. *I believe the victims were Jewish. I wondered if it would have bothered Andrews for me to see that, as he is Jewish. -2/24/20*

November 4th. It started with the human trafficking conference and ended on November 4th. While shopping, which should have been Saturday, I noticed a police officer at the bank, which was next door to where I was shopping. I drove to the park, likely on Sunday as that is when I liked to do my outings. A police car was hugging my bumper, only to be switched right after with the park ranger truck #redacted, which had the park ranger who had seemed to intimidate me when I went to the bathroom sick. This may have happened on November 4th or October 28th: I was at church up in the balcony. As I was singing in worship "You give and take away, Lord blessed be your name," a police officer entered and stood inside the door for a while. I was in the pew closest to the door. November 4th was a Sunday. I wanted to walk along a path, which just so happened to go along a stadium where an extremely famous high-ranking politician was giving a speech in support of a candidate. After that the police presence stopped for a while. I suppose I had demonstrated they were not effective. At intimidating me. *Written 2/28/20*

Warning: sexually explicit content

Wednesday, November 21st I believe. I stay after class to work. Another CAD student tries to log on, gets frustrated at it taking so long, and moves to a computer closer to me. I can see his screen while he works. I ignore him. He lets out a strange burp/belch noise and I smile. He leaves the room for a while, comes back, and makes the same noise. I don't react. I go to the library computer and recognize a calculus student from the math lab. He sits across by the wall, a few computers down. At one point I cough or sneeze. He makes an extreme sneeze instantaneously when I do. The next morning I wake up and shower. My genitals feel a searing pain when I touch it. I thought there is no way for anyone to get through my locks and get out and put them back. Then I see the nail I use as a bolt not in the lock, but the knife is in the door, which is the other part of my lock. I test it out and find that this nail is too small to lock the door, so anyone with a key would be able to get in, but wouldn't be able to get out and completely reset it. I improve the lock.

The next Saturday, I go to the club, and Quinn's face is lit up, grinning, looking at me. He says he thinks the men's bathroom is haunted. After he used it he heard a loud noise. He puts on an anime and laughs at the picture of them eating. The woman in charge of the club tells me they have pizza and to eat a piece. Quinn says he thinks it's sexist that the girls get to eat first.

It appeared that the CAD student was demonstrating himself as a studious and capable 3D drafter. I had spent many hours focusing on drafting. His pretense of one computer not loading so he could sit nearer to me may have been so I would realize his skill and want to talk to him. The fact that he was attempting that and made the strange sound was amusing to me. But generally I ignored the attempts of informants. It seemed like Andrews saw the informant as an extension of himself, and became enraged that I was laughing at something that could be embarrassing. This was the first time I know of that he sexually assaulted me. He made sure I would know it, and made it hurt. This was an act of revenge reserved for personal injury. I got every indication he was not allowed to. He continued to try to shame me days later at the club, by apparently getting the leadership to order me to eat pizza, which likely would have had something to upset my stomach, and then by "haunting the bathroom." This continues to show the dangers of giving a narcissist that much power over someone. All I did was smile. This triggered a severe rage response that included an illegal act. Narcissists need to get as close to you as they can to feel connected, but carry deep shame, and react viciously and hysterically, even if they are misunderstanding the victim. This imposes serious pressure on the victim that at every second they must be very careful to not upset him. This legally speaking is a violation of the first amendment, to freedom of speech. The abuse that I have suffered is clearly not only political, but also personal.

When I first looked at my second room in Tennessee, there were no holes above the shower. By the time I moved in, there were two hastily placed brackets that had been put up and then moved, leaving four holes above the shower. I kept those blocked off at the beginning. On the 25th of November, I started to tighten some screws closing off some centimeter or so wide holes in the wall. There were two in the bathroom with washers and one in the ceiling on the bedroom with a hook. I also put some decorative butterflies over other holes left in the bedroom walls and electric tape in the closet. When I next looked, there were many more holes in the closet and I covered those as well. I noticed another hole in the closet beside the metal rack, which was an off place for it to be. One wouldn't support anything there. I covered this. There were two pin sized holes in the chair rail of the bedroom I thought were odd that I hadn't seen before. I plugged them up and looked over the room and baseboards again. A day later or so, there were two more pin sized holes in the baseboard behind the door. I covered those and checked. Again, a day later or so there were several indentations on the baseboard between the bedroom and bathroom doors, one of which was a through hole. I covered that as well. I believe it is very unlikely I would have missed seeing those black holes on white baseboards those several times I looked them over. On December 2nd, the chair rail itself was bent up and warped at each side. When I am not in the room, the windows and bathroom doors are mechanically blocked from the inside, and the bedroom door requires a key to enter. To my knowledge, only Remi has the other key. Raelynn is wheelchair bound and is home all day almost every day. She stays in a bedroom blocked off by a curtain next to the stairs that lead to my room, or in the open main floor or back deck. She has two dogs who alert her to visitors as well. Caretakers regularly enter the house.

December 2018

On December 1st, my cat died. On my mom's Facebook page, by the post that says that Snickers is in her last days, she posts a story about a trick the military uses to get to sleep. This is a story that I recognize from before. Given my reaction, that I knew the story had to have been specifically placed to frighten me, posting the story would have been a way to communicate that Snickers' death was done by Andrews.

I listened to music by a band called Demon Hunter. The narcissists/psychopaths could well be compared with demons. One song had the lyrics, "I am a stone unaffected, Rain hell down on to me, Flesh and bone unaffected, Your fool I will not be". I listened to that at 6:51 pm. I believe it was the next day I was told my cat died. If she was killed by Andrews, it may have been a response to me listening to this song, or because I was blocking holes for surveillance cameras, which he would have used to emotionally feed himself.

Warning: sexually explicit content

On December 7th, the air was stuffy so I opened the window around midnight. I woke up I think sometime after 6 am, with the same pain in my genitals. *I fleshed out the details of these events on 3/9/19, but had written something marking the day.*

December 8th. I downloaded Tails via torrent, attempted to write it to USB, and had an error. I reformatted the USB, then had some issue mounting it. I eventually succeeded. Then I was either unable to load the USB or to write to it. Synaptic couldn't find Unetbootin, a program that makes files of operating systems runnable off of USBs. The USB did not want to mount. Either it wouldn't show, or had "operation pending." After many clicks, I could load it and put images on it, but those disappeared. I attempted to download Tor browser. Shell couldn't find it, and the icon wouldn't do anything. I went to the website to re-download it. The page that worked before had an error message. Both 32 and 64 bit had error messages. Changing VPN server had no effect. I attempted to look up distrowatch.com. It never loaded after multiple attempts. *Tails is software designed to protect privacy. Back then it was rare for them to show themselves so obviously, however they did so whenever they felt they had to keep me under surveillance or prevent me from publishing. It isn't really a question whether I am at least being stalked attentively by capable hackers, who happen to not want me to tell people what happened at Porcfest. As I recall, Andrews acted like he wasn't good with technology.*

Warning: sexually explicit content

December 15th. My window was left open between 7 and 9 am while I slept. *When I was waking up my hips were moving, which is not something that normally happens. Playing on the car radio the next time I got in was a song I liked, "Nothing Feels Better than This." It The first two sexual assaults were out of anger. This seemed to be affectionate. -2/28/20*

December 18th. I changed my set up over my bed to more of a canopy. Only half of the "roof" was on. The next morning, all three of the covered holes over the window were uncovered, my butterfly decorations had fallen on the open side of my roof. Otherwise I have not had a problem with the butterflies coming off. *In other words, the holes where cameras could poke through and then retreat had knocked them down, as Andrews wanted to watch me sleep.*

December 19th. I attempted to log into my bank. My login page wouldn't load, but other pages on the bank's website and other websites would. I called tech support and they couldn't figure out what was wrong. I eliminated cookies and restarted my browser and WIFI and nothing worked. Then it just started working on its own.

Warning: sexually explicit content

December 25th. I had made two travel locks—one for my bedroom, and one for the bathroom. For both, a bent knife with a hole was put in the strike plate with a bolt through the hole. For the bedroom, the bolt was a nail, and a tube that slid overtop to make the bolt longer. For the bathroom, a screw was used as the bolt. I used to have to turn the screw to get it out of the hole. I noticed yesterday or the day before, the bathroom lock hole was wider. Now it just slips through. Today the nail and tube were found out of the door, but the knife left in. Were someone to break in, they wouldn't be able to leave and reset both locks completely. I have a skin condition that leaves patches on my chest. The treatment is topical lotion or a strict diet. After this I saw several ads for lotion. Remi yelled outside my door, "Mom, I think you need new lotion!" My mother messaged me that my brother had been offered a high-paying job, and if he was really good for a week, they would keep him. I go to the library shortly after, listening to a guy on the radio talk about the military. In the library, a girl talks about needing a wheat or sugar free diet. Back in my car, the same program has a guest speaker talking about a wheat free diet. Then it goes back to talking about the military. This sort of thing lasted for a few days. Over the next few months some of my favorite junk food was missing from the shelves with nothing else put in that spot. Beef Ramen at Aldis. Buttered popcorn at the Dollar Tree. One day I bought Pop Tarts and a day or two later there were zero Pop Tarts. They had been well stocked before.

Basically, my lock had been compromised again. This was on Christmas morning. I remember hearing the dogs barking around 11:30 the night before and Raelynn hushing them. It appears that Andrews decided to "open his present" on Christmas and strip me partially naked in my sleep. He also apparently wanted to get me to look better naked, and tried to get me to use the cream or to go on a diet which would have cleared it up. The fact that I was told right after that my brother had been offered a job appeared to be a reward for my "services." But he would be evaluated for the week, suggesting that was being hung over my head to compel me to whore myself out to my stalker/"investigator."

January 2019

January 2nd. I plugged around 6 new holes yesterday in the closet. I plugged two more holes in the closet corner, adjacent to the metal brackets.

January 14th. "Window was open last night." On this occasion I don't remember opening it. There was a morning, and this may have been it, when I woke up a little and heard the sound of a nut turning around 4 am. I had beefed up my lock to have a nut and bolt. I fell back asleep, and dreamed and felt a large weight slowly pressing down on the mattress next to me. I heard something like metal on metal, a turning screwdriver by the window, then Remi rushing downstairs to let the dogs out who barked vigorously. That was around 7:30 am.

During the spring semester I took one class taught by Greyson. Much of this class was trying to get personal information out of me. The first class was a list of personal questions to get to know us. The assignments would be things like, what is your budget? One week a fellow student had asked me how many classes I was taking. I asked why did he ask, and he got very apologetic for the intrusion. The next class's assignment was to write how many classes we were taking, compared to a full course load. Later on, I went to a career fair, and a math teacher with a predatory smile asked me how many classes I was taking, and if I worked, and then acted "so shocked" that I only took one. I imagine that was fuel for rumors that could be spread about me around campus.

There was a lecture devoted to public speaking for some reason, which was a written assignment about a hobby unrelated to the coursework. He was very insistent we participate. The teacher presented his job as an engineer, but when he got to the sheet metal section, he didn't want to "bore us" and skipped over it. I have work history in sheet metal, and may have been able to see if he was faking it. My presentation was about workplace culture, and how firing practices shaped it. The teacher told me he has only had to fire two people. One he almost lost his job because he didn't want to fire him. He drove to work every day with him. That sounds awfully like a patrol officer.

He told us about a trip for his company. There was a roast for the engineers, and they gave an award to the engineers who did the dumbest thing that year. One guy cashed in his 401k and invested it in pot in Colorado, and told people. One guy dragged a construction cone for some distance. One guy who redid his driveway was given a sign to hang around his neck, the "Saint of Inconvenience." It said "detour" on the other side and people would have to walk around. Him redoing his driveway doesn't sound like something other engineers would be inconvenienced by at work, but the traffic control aspect sounds like a police officer.

This class was another example of laziness, poor quality, and cheating. The professor said things were going to be easy in the first part with Word and Excel, but when we studied "programming" later in it would get difficult. The information was on a second grade level. He seemed to want to kill a lot of time. He often left class early, but was willing to stay if we had questions. He also talked about his heavy workload, as if to discourage us from keeping him. The lectures were sometimes effectively, "It's pretty self explanatory" and he didn't bother to explain a lot. I had done 45 minute or so online tutorials for Word and Excel through a staffing agency, and the quality was better by orders of magnitude that this whole class. The textbook referenced some practice Excel sheets, but we didn't have them. He said he would look into it, but later said he wasn't going to provide them, and we could look into it, and said with a drone something like "for the joy of learning."

There was a review before each test, during which he gave us most of the answers to the test. We were allowed to take notes. He also told us we could bring a page of notes to the test, but shut the door as if he didn't want to be heard. Some of the questions were things like, "Which side of the cell does the cursor appear on when you click it?" I had already read the textbook, taken notes, and watched some YouTube tutorial videos. I created a quasi AutoCAD in Excel, by recording myself drawing shapes and watching the changes in the code, then modifying the script and connecting them to a form. I showed this to whoever was there at the end of one class, which was a female classmate. She became emotional, and said it was things like this that made her feel so stupid, and she was barely getting by. I suppose I was to feel that any attempt of mine to excel would very much not be welcomed.

After my car broke down near the end of the semester, I started out taking a taxi, but upon finding the price had changed from the one I was quoted, I got out and walked. This was a very long walk. One day I walked 22 miles total. After walking for hours to get to class, the professor had not arrived. I waited in the hall with the other students. He was late, which was probably the first time he was.

January 17th. After I posted my article on ethics, I received a text about my Maryland work email asking if I wanted to log in and check something out. Paige, my former co-worker had set this up for me. I didn't know why Microsoft would associate my number with it. I took a screenshot of this. My paper said some negative things that could be construed by those in the know to be about Andrews. He seemed to not want me to publish it. I suspected this text to be either a phishing attempt, or an attempt to get me to commit hacking, by logging in to a company account I was no longer working for. This appears to be using questionable hostile legal tactics as retaliation against personal speech. I later attempted to get my paper reviewed by some writers at the writing club. The first week there was no opportunity, but I asked about it afterwards. The second week the chairs were put in a circle. The teacher said to "circle the wagons." I submitted my paper for consideration in the college publication, but I was eventually declined, and no one offered any reviews or critiques along the way. *Written 2/28/20*

January 29th. As I am logging off of my laptop, there is a dialogue box that lists programs that are taking a moment to shut down. This said "csd printer not responding." I don't own a printer.

This is a screenshot from my laptop with one of my flash drives loaded. I sometimes find I am not able to delete files off of it. There are several binary files on it I did not put there. What is interesting about this one is its modification date.

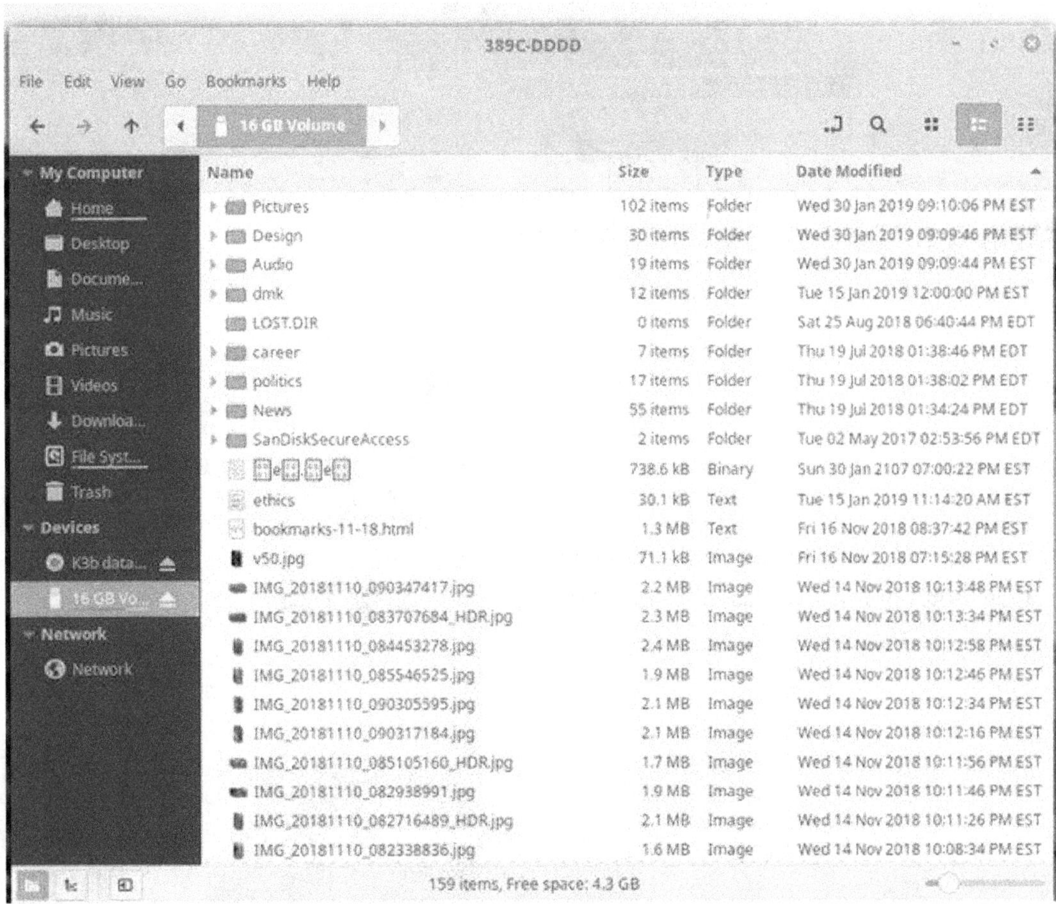

February 2019

February 21st. I attempt to register for the online forum Theologyonline.com. I had registered yesterday for a different forum and had some difficulties on my laptop, but was able to do it on my cell phone. This time neither my laptop nor my cell phone worked. While I was registering, Firefox notified me the connection was insecure, and that if I wanted to see if there was a secure version of that page, I was to type https:// in the URL bar. I did so and got to a secure page, but it still gave me the warning with the entry fields. When I requested an email verification to register, that email as of yet has not come. *After much effort I did eventually log on, and posted my Ethics Part 1 page for review. The comments largely talked about other issues tangentially related to my paper. -2/28/20*

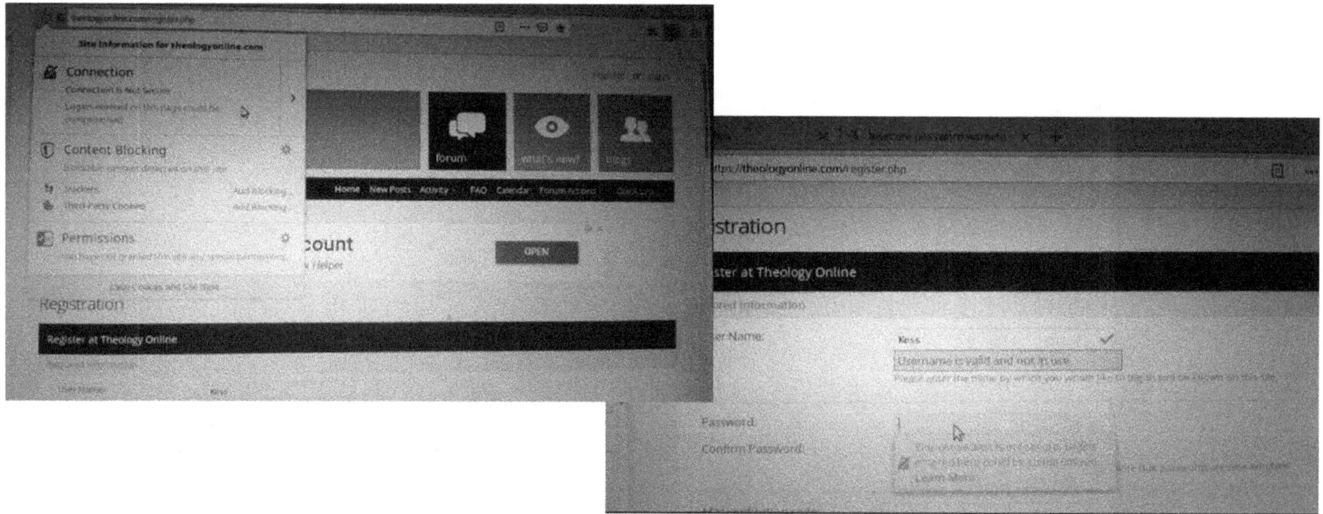

March 2019

March 9th. I took the paper with dates and a few notes of my sexual assaults and fleshed out the details. I was on my bed in a tent, so I should not have been visible.

Warning: explicit content

March 10th. I woke up at 5 am, my chest burning like I had been traumatized. I thought maybe it was dredging up those memories when I wrote about them the day before. I had some desire to take a shower. When I did, I felt the same pain in my genitals. But when I checked my locks, they were all still there. I had written that account in a covered tent in my room. When I turned on the radio they talked about the need to go to the doctor to get a checkup, and not wait till it hurts. A short time later on the radio, they talked about getting Medishare if you don't have insurance. *I did not have health insurance, and Medishare was the service that I was considering getting.* The next several nights I could barely sleep. I took other showers and ate sugar to repeat the conditions, but the pain completely went away.

This suggests that there was a way I was surveilled in my tent clearly enough to see my writing. It also means that they tried to convince me that my genital pain was due to a physical condition, and that they could count on a doctor I selected to cover for them. It means they feared me telling anyone about the sexual assaults, and treated this very differently than the other ways I was harassed. This meant that he had acted without authorization. Given that I was clearly under surveillance, it severely narrows down the possible people who could be responsible. Given the experience with Andrews, the particular concern with me publishing my account with him personally, and my mother's knee-jerk defense of him personally later on, it suggests that at least one of the members of the "investigative" team was Andrews. Given the assaults happened in the early and late morning and the cover up continued during the day, it suggests that Andrews was most likely at least aware of the assaults and the cover up. Also, it appears he had found a way to break into my room and leave my door locks in place. I do not know if I was doing this at the time, but later on I added putting a padlock on the inside of my tent zippers to my nighttime routine and checking the zippers to make sure they zipped correctly. I do not believe I have had assaults under those conditions. Getting in and leaving no trace of the break in to maintain plausible deniability would be challenging, even with something as simple as a tent. -10/21/20

March 11th. I received an email stating I would no longer be receiving paper statements. I had not created an online bank account to make it less convenient to hack, and was reviewing monthly paper statements to make sure all debit card payments were authorized. This email would require me to take additional steps to keep it as it was.

> "What to expect: Starting in mid-March, you will no longer have certain paper notices sent to you via U.S. Mail. ... If you prefer to receive all of your notices via U.S. Mail, you may select paper delivery by any of the following methods:

- Online Banking - Sign on using your user ID and password, ...
- Mobile App - Sign on using your user ID and password, click the Main Menu icon. Then select... »

In other words, I would have to log in on line allowing any hackers access to my username and password, or else not receive paper statements and not be able to notify the bank if there were unauthorized purchases before it was too late for them to address it. This prompted me to go to SunTrust and bring a little evidence that I may have been subject to hacking. I asked them to keep sending me paper statements. The employee didn't say that he was aware of a policy not to send paper statements. After looking at my file, he made some comment about talking to himself. I was followed to the bank, and that man went in the room with the employee right after I left.

To backtrack, I had set up an account over the phone (which I thought was more secure, as I wasn't using my devices) at another branch with the help of a very reluctant and complaining assistant. After that, I went to the bank, and when the employee looked at the screen with my account, her eyes got big, and she asked me with concern if I had any problems with my account. It seemed to me that the first employee had written something in my customer file which described me as a problem, apparently something like paranoid. The comment this other employee made about talking to himself is consistent with that. I could imagine how that could impact the attention they give to any legitimate complaint I had.

I went home and went to put my screen clamp in my window, which was a board visible from the backyard. It made it so I could keep my window open without compromising my security, making it harder to drug me with gasses. A caretaker came out, and while laughing, bent over to do something, and held her cell phone right up behind her back, so that apparently I could be recorded putting a board in my window. This was a threat that if I told anyone what was happening to me, they were going to say I was crazy. This is standard gaslighting.

March 15th. This was a Friday. I had gone to campus, which was mostly empty. I went to a room by myself, and pulled out a spare cell phone I had. I factory reset it as a way to wipe malware that could have possibly gotten on. I attempted, using the college's WIFI, to connect to the Intercept's website. The Intercept is a news website that has done some politically controversial stories. The site would not load. I tried to load CNN to test. It was taking a long time. I looked at my MicroSD card that I had installed, and it was corrupted, and destroyed. That evening I read a story on Ramsey Orta by the Verge. This is the man who filmed the infamous death of Eric Garner, who was choked to death by police during a stop for selling untaxed cigarettes. Eric Garner famously said "I can't breathe" as he was suffocating to death, and the slogan became a popular cry against police brutality. Ramsey Orta had been arrested on other charges shortly after he published the video, probably as retaliation for exposing police brutality. The story was about the constant abuse that he suffered in prison. When I finished the story the first time I read it, it seemed to end on a dark note. Later when I looked at the story, it continued on to a success story on filming police and holding them accountable. I suspect that the story was cut short so as to threaten me.

On Monday I went back to the college and checked another MicroSD card, which was also destroyed. When I got back in my car, there was a story about a woman who was in charge of data for MySpace. The story said she lost the data, and could have put a USB stick in a safety deposit box or something. "You had one job." The announcer said. Then, as I recall, the song "Nothing Feels Better than This." Given that I had liked this song, and it was played after I was apparently sexually assaulted on the 15th of December, it was obvious that the meaning was he believed he had destroyed my copies of the evidence, and now I had been defeated and he could have me sexually as he liked. My phone disappeared for a very long time from a bag I thoroughly searched, only to re-emerge with the pin not working, and the buttons to factory reset the device unresponsive. *It may be Andrew's intention was to destroy the evidence I had on him from Porcfest, but it appears more so later on that the authority he used was through a psychological conditioning program. In this program, anything you show concern for or fear towards can be used as a way to control you until you display no concern or fear. Meaning, if a person acts indifferently, or boldly, Andrews would not be allowed to prevent me from publishing under this pretext. It seemed to me many times other pretexts will be brought up when this is defeated. Mentions of terrorism and murder or Russian spies will be brought up, as though he has shifted to a pretext of stopping a terrorist or foreign spy. This process happens repeatedly over the years. -10/21/20*

This also shows that Andrews was using the power of his office to try to force me to have sex with him. I did not react to the song. I changed the channel to a Christian one, "Your Love Defends Me" and brightened up. This seemed to be taken as a sign that he had not routed out all of the copies. The next song that played was about forgiving each other.

I spent some time during the spring compiling some of my evidence into one document. When I had finished, I was walking in the park, and a man looks at me, gives me a thumbs up, and says "Bravo." The only way I could make sense of that was to see it as Andrews saying my evidence was sufficient. I went to a library and printed it off. The printer was buffering at one point for a long time until I turned to face the surveillance camera. There seemed to be some indications that I was welcome to join the FBI, through advertisements and the like.

I attended a church around this time where the Pastor said someone was there to speak for a few minutes. He brings up a woman to speak. She talks about Christians in other countries fleeing from their equivalent of the FBI, how they would pray and God would save them. She says she would be scared, but these people when they are stopped in one place just find another place. It seemed to me that she was acting like she was on my side, perhaps to encourage me to approach her and open up to her about my situation.

A video appeared on my Facebook page that had a guy calling for violence. Then there was Free Talk Live playing on the radio in my car, also with calls to violence. A neighbor had come outside on his porch while I was in my car listening. I responded to the video that was posted, saying you shouldn't advocate violence. Right after that it disappeared from my page, along with any other calls to violence. I also posted a verse to make it clear I could not be made to appear to advocate such things.

One day I decided to go talk to tech support at the college. I was having trouble logging on because the computer said it would run anti-virus software. I didn't want to mess with the computer's software, so I went to speak to tech support. At first, the girl's reaction was to be shocked and confused, as if I were saying something crazy. They called the woman in charge of tech support on the phone. While we were waiting for the woman in charge to answer, I pulled out my digital camera, as I had taken a picture of the screen in order to read the name of the software to her. Immediately, the other librarian pulls out a report that said they had already heard of this problem, and here was the fix tech support wanted us to do. In other words, if I were to speak out about the ridiculous things that were being done on the computers I was using, people were to think perhaps I was delusional. If I had evidence for it, they had a cover story ready.

13

THINGS START TO FALL APART AND I HEAD TO CANADA

T*his This covers the rest of the chronological section of my notes on Tennessee from April 2019 to June 2019.*

April 2019

I ended up buying a few more MicroSD cards, and using my digital camera to take pictures of the evidence and make copies. This seemed to freak Andrews out. People were extremely antsy about me possibly placing one somewhere. For example, at a library one day, I was flipping through various books. A boy kept briskly walking by and checking on me. After a little bit of time, I went to the college, and made various noises, touching various things, so if they were listening, they would not be sure if I had placed one somewhere. When I got in my car next, on the radio was a story of a woman who had given birth to a baby with no brain. The obvious indication was he was saying how stupid I was. It was like he was aware I had not hidden them. I, however, continued listening to the story with interest. It took a strong pro-life stance.

After this, it seemed Brian was probing whether or not I was pro-life, and my attitudes towards children. It may have been around this time that one of my classmates brought their child to class. I wondered why he would care if I was pro-life. It was like he wanted me to give birth to a baby if I became pregnant. I saw a news story about a police officer taking a child away. It seemed to me this was his thought, to the point that it was his primary hope of finally breaking me. This narrative continued for a long time. There seemed to be multiple attempts to find out my feelings on abortion and giving a child up, and attempts to put me in situations where I could be raped. It did not seem to me that this plot was officially sanctioned, like the sexual assaults weren't, although multiple people seemed to be involved. It dissipated for a while when after one test, I looked up a verse, which was about leaving even your children to follow Christ. *I had not written or spoken about what I was suspecting they were attempting. Once I saw they stopped, I decided there was no reason to remain silent, as I was no longer catching them in the act, and I wrote out my suspicions. After this, the threats surfaced like the rest of the threats, and continue to be brought up as an apparent high priority whenever they could be. -10/21/20*

In April, there was a sudden lull in people's concern about what I was doing in unsurveilled spaces, both at the college and other places. It was like he had seen me pretend to place them around the college, and continued to watch me in various bathrooms. I had been very tired from the sleep disruption, and would go into bathroom stalls and let my body drop forward to rest for a few minutes. Most times I did, someone would immediately come in and do something different to bother me, including a loud conversation on the phone with lots of cussing, though it seemed it made the girl uncomfortable to cuss. This reminded me of something I heard of once: a satellite that could see through buildings.

During this period, I remember seeing a commercial of a woman showing how she would act out a scene. I was drawn into it. The next commercial was some offer of surrender I don't remember, which I brushed off. That was like a conversation, testing if I understood the level of surveillance I was under, and seeing if I wanted to give up now. The surveillance technology that could see into buildings seemed to last a few weeks before normal tactics resumed.

April 3rd. Around 7 pm, as I was walking down the otherwise empty main hall in a college building, a boy came in an entrance, sighed, and walked past me holding his phone a few inches from his ear, so that the camera faced me. He was white with black hair. I followed behind him. We were the only two people there. He said nothing, and no sound came from his phone. He held it several inches away the whole time as he walked down the hall. I got a look at the screen. There was a large pink circle with the letter R in the center, small white words around the top and bottom, and a red circle near the bottom.

April 10th. I searched for the Signal app, with which I tried to communicate with the Intercept with on my regular phone. I messaged them my Porcfest entry. I never received a response. This is one of the groups I tried to reach out to.

April 11th. I searched how to fix a broken wire on a charger. My laptop battery was having issues recharging.

April 12th. I visited ProtonMail. I used this to try to contact the Rutherford Institute, but received no response.

April 13th. I searched what to do if your laptop is plugged in but not charging. I had been making various copies of my evidence. In many cases, it seemed I was not getting responses I would have expected, such as on Facebook. This led me to believe there was the ability to censor content on these platforms. One of the places I put the file was on a platform called Diaspora, which is designed to not have algorithms to hide things. One of the servers hosting a node was in Germany. After this, my laptop would not power up.

April 14th. I had a technical issue with the MEGA app. This app is for encrypted file storage. I also took video of trying to log into Theology Online, which sent me in circles.

On Sunday I went for a drive up the mountain, and hiked to a place with a waterfall. I had scheduled an appointment to meet with my campus counselor on Monday. Unfortunately, as I left my driveway and went up the second hill in my neighborhood, my transmission went out. There happened to be two utility workers there, who happened to have I believe it was transmission fluid, or something to try and help it. It did not. The two men helped push my car up the first hill, and it rolled down the other side, and with the help of a caretaker I pushed it into the driveway. College was quite far away. There were no buses that came out to that location. There weren't even sidewalks that went out all of the way. For a while I made due without. Then I arranged to have my car looked at by the local AAMCO, which, from what I had read in a book about not getting swindled by car mechanics, were extremely reliable transmission experts. I had AAA, so I had my car towed. They told me that it would cost around $2000 to repair the car. The car wasn't worth that much. I had no income. I was using it primarily to get to a college that was more like an elementary school. But more to the point, my car was hacked. I had read that transmissions were dependent on a sensor controlled by a computer to work. The way I drove on that Sunday could provide the plausible deniability to wreck it. Remi offered to give me rides. A caretaker told me her husband is a Honda expert, and when I said I thought I should have it taken into a shop, she shouted after me that it would be expensive, like she was discouraging me from doing that. I was told by the caretaker that Remi knows car people who could look at it. The informants seemed to very much not want me to take it in to the experts. Not having a car changed things dramatically for me. I had to find a place to live closer to the college.

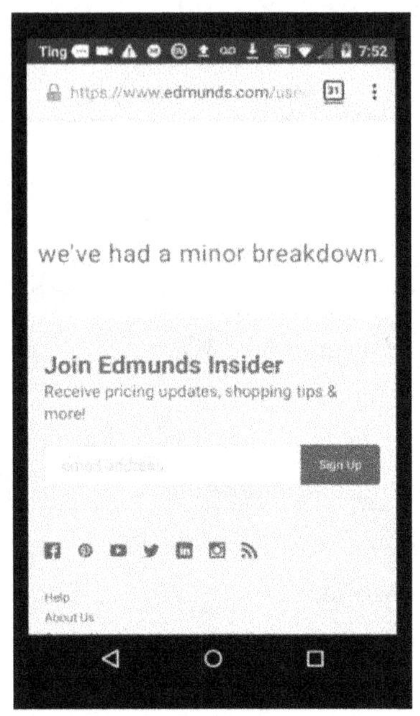

April 16th. *Around this time, I sent eight inquiries to Craigslist and got two responses, which failed my criteria. As I recall, there was one place I looked at, but before I even got to see it, the girl demanded I tell her what my sign was. I am very religious, and wasn't sure I should dabble in astrology. I looked it up, and at the time it seemed okay. This girl was looking for someone to be her buddy so I could feel coerced to open up my personal thoughts and feelings to her and do what it took for her to keep liking me. She also didn't feel comfortable with me meeting the landlord, and seemed to want to keep him out of it. I saw another location on Craigslist later on closer to the college. In the description, it said the girl was very into the new age /occult. This gave me the impression that I was to be pressured to go against my faith if I wanted to find a good place to live. -3/9/20*

My family visited me in Tennessee. They invited me to sleep over and swim at the hotel pool, and seemed very insistent that we visit a tourist attraction as one of the first things. The first two invitations had the obvious possibility of them being able to access my things that I keep with me. I had a route of my favorite places in the city planned for them. In the elevator on the way out of the hotel, I showed them a picture of the Hunger Games mug I had found, "May the odds be ever in your favor." My brother had looked away uninterested and kind of sighed. That was a little odd. I showed them the campus, and my sister asked me if I ever spent the night there. It was a bizarre question, but if they were trying to paint me as the homeless girl, it would make sense coming from her.

There was a whole episode with campus cops mistaking me as homeless as I would stay on campus for long hours studying and am very cheap. In short, I had gone late to a building which had some locked doors. The campus police officer asked me what I was doing and when I said studying, he recommended repeatedly that I stop in by the cafeteria, which has cameras. Later one day I went to the cafeteria to open some cans, pour them into a Tupperware, and heat it in the microwave. I go to the women's bathroom to rinse the cans before throwing them away, and I see him standing outside the bathroom door in the indent in the hall, as if he were listening to me in there. He walks away, and when I go to the college club, another cop stops by my car and asks me in a very predatory way what I am doing there all alone. When I say I am there for the club, he says, practically salivating, "So, you have access to the building." Later I registered to vote while under the surveillance camera by the cafeteria, and the woman verified what I had written, which included a sworn statement with my address, before submitting it, and was visibly angry. After that the first police officer passed me as I studied one night, while "talking on his phone," and said "Sorry" to me as though he was sorry for interrupting me, or perhaps for maligning me to the college. The second cop was also acting super friendly, like he was embarrassed to have treated me like what passes as an acceptable way to treat homeless people going to college. So there was apparently a rumor about me that I was homeless. It was very strange of my sister to ask that. It is pretty inexplicable that I would think of doing so, unless she herself thought I was homeless. I don't know why she would think that. But it may have been an attempt to whip up more of the rumor. -9/29/20

We were at a restaurant when my sister began to tell me about the Vic Mignogna case she is following. He was accused of doing something like sexually assaulting a girl. She continued with outrage at how incorrect it was, and how damaging it was to him. This story was sort of a parallel story to Brian and what he did at Porcfest. It appeared to me that my sister, acting as an informant, would talk about this in an attempt to discourage me from publishing my account of Andrews at Porcfest. I noted some narcissists just repeat one defense mechanism ad nauseam, and one I knew did this with threats. I said they try to cover up the things they did to you, and sometimes the things they do to cover it up are worse than the original thing. I ended up taking my family back to the car and reading them my Porcfest entry, including Andrews trying to kiss me. My brother said it was well written, and would work well in a legal case. I wondered why he thought that, and he said it was detailed, and hearing it was like he was experiencing it with me.

I showed them Brian Andrews's picture. My father said in astonishment and disgust that Brian looked as old as he was. My mother retorted defensively that he could be 45. That doesn't make much sense of my mother, to be favoring romances with atheists who try to forcibly kiss her daughter. It does make sense if she is under pressure to take his side. I explained to my family what narcissists were like, so as to prepare them. My mother made a comment, that if you broke too easily or too quickly that they would hate you. That was an interesting insight, which makes little sense unless she had more familiarity with this sort of situation. *My family seemed to not want me to admit that I was under an FBI investigation. They played stupid, like I was just telling them this so they could be aware what psychopaths were like. -9/29/20*

We went to the location with the waterfall, and I talked with my sister for a while. She was asking if I made any friends, and if I was likely to be staying in Tennessee for long. Her tone was different, and reminded me how my mom was sounding these days. I said it was strange. Here I had just told everyone about psychopaths, and how they terrorize their victims, and yet no one was concerned for me. She said coolly she knew I wanted my privacy. I said that psychopaths will go after you either directly, or through anyone around you, and so to have friends would be to put them in the "line of fire." I implied that I had kept people at a distance to protect them from the worst of it. My sister described being a people person, and how you can be worn down after a long time when you are isolated. *She said not everyone was like me, as I am very independent. -11/9/20* It seemed to me she was describing the way they had broken her. I remember seeing a selfie she took, the light gone from her eyes. I had barely recognized her. I remember seeing her during one of my visits prior to that photo, like she was frustrated and sad, and just blocking out the world around her. She always had a spark in her. But I believe what I was witnessing was the result of severe psychological trauma. I had seen it in other family members to some extent as well.

We went back to the hotel. My family seemed detached from each other, and indifferent to me. During lunch the next day, I took a picture of them, and they didn't even look up at me. My brother used a phrase, "Test you like the Devil tests you." I thought that perfectly described what the program does. On the drive back to their hotel, I kept talking to the family about scriptures like the story of Shadrach, Meshach, and Abednego, and how we are required to disobey when the government tells us to sin. My brother asked again about forgiveness. I talked about Les Misérables when the man gives Jean Val Jean the silver he had stolen, and how that act of forgiveness was so unexpected it changed his life. But the man had consideration for the soul of Jean. If you just let people wrong you and forgive them, accepting their sin and leaving them in it, how is that loving their soul? My sister showed me a picture she was drawing. She told me about a game she really liked to play. In it there was a caste system with three levels. On the top level was the Romans. They were atheistic and technologically advanced. On the second level were people who had their cities destroyed by the Romans. They were sent to foreign lands to serve. They only depended on Rome and were used as hostages against each other. They would always be second class citizens, because they had been conquered. They were polytheistic. On the third level were people who were looked down on and despised by the second level. They were considered primitive, although their abilities varied. They helped their countries. These were monotheistic.

April 29th. I took my car in to have the transmission checked out. The man told me it would be thousands of dollars to repair. I decided to scrap it, and called up the scrap company I had looked up and called before. They were to pay me $200. They arrived after some time, and when it came time to sign the title over, the boy refused to sign. He got on the phone with the owner, who seemed to suggest that is how they do business, and if I didn't like it, they had other things to do. I called up the DMV, and when I explained they had put the company name down instead of signing, the woman very urgently told me that this would not qualify, and I had to get someone to sign or else I was still liable for what happened with the car. After that call, the boy talked for a moment to his boss. He asked me if I told the woman the name of the company and said he would sign, and was now very apologetic for giving me any trouble. He said he'd never done it like that before. *Written -3/7/20*

May 2019

May 1st. I called voicemail, but did not turn off the speaker when typing in the password. Immediately it says my voicemail is not set up and I need to set a new password for it. I believe it had always worked before, and I had been getting notifications of stored messages.

May 4th. I sent out around seven emails to local churches asking if anyone had a room to rent. I got no responses. The two websites that I put the message directly into the webforms did not work. When I did this trying to move to Tennessee, I inquired at three churches, and got one or two responses.

May 6th. The Airbnb website wasn't working. It may have been May 6th, I was chopping carrots, a piece fell, and the family dog ate it. I told the caretaker and she said it was fine, they can eat carrots. The next time I came down to make food, the caretaker looked worried and guarded the water she was boiling.

May 7th. I walked to AAA and tried to load a debit card with money taken off VISA, but the website for them to put money on the card was down. The employee didn't know how to refund the money, so she called for help. They said they voided it, but she was worried and told me to check. She said it may take around five days to reimburse if it wasn't refunded. While I was walking I stopped to address a blister. A guy walks up, crouches next to my bag, and starts to preach, then asks personal questions. I said I didn't know him and wasn't comfortable. He gets up and leaves. I got an email and was checking it, then saw him approach quickly on a different street. He was looking at me and

gleaming. *The implication was that my bag could be snatched if I wasn't careful. I had been carrying around a lot of critical things, including my birth certificate.*

May 8th. Problems with the AAA app. My life was falling apart around me—car, laptop, SD cards, phones, finances, essential documents. It was clear it could be taken away from me at any time, and I wasn't sure if I would be able to build it back if they kept destroying it. It wasn't an easy decision. But I didn't have anything to stay for, and I had always thought a person should not have to live with abuse. Before I was totally incapacitated, I decided to try and escape.

May 9th. I go down to start the washing machine. Raelynn called to her dogs, "What are you doing?" even though they were not barking or disturbing at all. It was as though something had happened to the dog after he ate the carrot I dropped, and they were afraid I had drugged him.

I was looking up the possibility of attending college in Canada, but encountered some technical difficulties researching. I could not go past page six of the search results, and got video.

May 10th. The text fields to let me log in to my student portal for funding were not there. I believe I was looking to see if I had been accepted for money to pay for college.

My Airbnb app was having problems. *I would have been looking for a place to stay by myself while passing through my home town, not with my family. -3/5/20*

I put in a U-Haul rental request and it said it was expired immediately after.

May 17th. *I believe it was right after I looked up cruise ships I saw this as a recommended story: "Don't Use My Family for Your True Crime Stories." If this was to suggest a threat to harm or kill family members if I got away from him, it would violate the torture statue, and is also consistent with an obsessed psychopath. -3/5/20*

Drudge Report was blocked on two browsers though the Internet works. Drudge could be loaded in a proxy. I took video of this.

May 21st. I had just called U-Haul that morning and made a reservation. Closer towards noon, I hear there is some commotion at the neighbor's house. There are several police cars with their lights going, some blocking our driveway. There is an ambulance in the driveway of the neighbors. The police officers did not seem agitated. After a while, the ambulance slowly went away. It seemed to be there was some sort of threat because of the police presence, but not enough of an active situation for them to be agitated. There was an ambulance, but it moved away slowly, which means someone was either dead or not in critical need of getting to the hospital quickly. It seemed to me to be an unrealized threat of physical harm, and I suspected that Andrews had made threats of suicide after it became real that I was leaving. It would follow a trend of the agents staying as close by as possible, and it would make sense if he stayed in that building that he was able to sneak into my room the time I left the window open and sexually assault me. When I later told my mother about this, after a pause, she asked if I had spoken to Ace, who is the "competition." This helps to demonstrate the severity of Andrews's obsession with me. *Written 3/7/20*

Thursday, May 23rd. I arrive at my parent's house around 11 am. She kept offering to let me keep more stuff here. I asked her why and noted her attitude on that seems to have changed. She paused for a long while then said it was because they no longer thought that they had to sell the house. I tell Mom I'm going to Canada. She wonders if I'm waiting on a passport. Dad asked twice if I was taking a camera to Canada. *Given it was a means to create evidence that was not easily hackable, that was a concern of theirs.* Mom told me she had to cut off her mom from Facebook because her mom wouldn't stop worshiping Donald Trump. I talked about my conversation on justplainpolitics, and how some people refuse to listen. She excused herself to the bathroom but took no time, then shouted from there a question she had already asked about Justin Amash saying the president should be impeached. She went on about it.

She showed me something she posted on Facebook, which was about improving relationships by saying how a thing made you feel. Later Mom "urged" me to turn on the AC before bed. *Likely drugged?*

Friday, May 24th. The Internet was down all morning and early afternoon. My brother didn't want to get up to reset it. Mom said I could take her car and go to the library. I got my bike out, and then she said she had to take my niece to the library to do math anyway. Mom suggested I not leave the AC on in my room. *The Internet being down is the typical disruption routine. Mom encouraging me to take her car and then telling me I shouldn't leave the AC on, could be because I was being drugged and she was concerned about too much of a dose, meaning I would be told to drive while drugged, just like in Maryland. Also, she conveniently followed me to the library.*

My brother has gotten two call backs since I've been here. *Just like Dad got a call every day I was there before, now he is. Highly improbable.*

I showed my parents my testimony as a kid. We talked about hell. Mom said some people don't want to believe in God because they are offended by hell. *Sounds like Brian Andrews.* I said that is because they don't know that evil is evil. I said I didn't morally object to God on this. Mom argued that hell isn't eternal punishment, saying it was just academic, but she was personally invested in some way. ... As I sorted through my things, Mom asked me if I was going through every little thing. I said no, just thinning stuff out.

Saturday, May 25th. ... The Airbnb webpage was not available. Access to housing was obstructed in this and many other cases. I noticed there is a camera sitting on top of the living room TV. It was a Roku TV. I asked about it. Mom nervously says it's not taking our picture. Dad nervously says it is for lots of TV shows. I note its odd location. He says nothing. *Informants may be tasked with getting the surveillance themselves. It seems they preferred if I didn't know where. ...* My sister said Vic Mignogna tried to serve papers to the girl who accused him but she ran away, but she can still be served if it is taped to the door and a picture is taken. *Andrew's threats were nothing to me. My mind wasn't changed and I wasn't intimidated.* Mom later tells me a story on how it is polite to ghost parties and just leave without bothering people.

Sunday, May 26th. Over lunch Mom mentions someone on Facebook who needs the services of the business of the person I had just spoken with at church, as though giving me an opportunity to bring up my conversation with this person. Evening card game. Music played but Mom changes the song, "If I just lay here," because she didn't like the words. *Why not? I thought she must know about Andrews sneaking into my room and laying next to me. If his crimes were already broadly known, it is telling that he was still allowed to continue to investigate me.* We played cards and showed family slides. I stay late with my family to watch slides. *My sister had gotten up to leave earlier, and Mom had suggested the idea of leaving parties soon. –2/28/20*

Monday, May 27th. My late great grandmother Munga's photo book was out the next morning. Test: do I care about family history? Mom asks me if I need help with anything or any equipment. Test: did I stay late to suck up and get stuff? Having "ruled these out" by me not reacting, they conclude my motivation must be to spend time with my family. It is then used as a threat. Mom says she had a nightmare where she left a meeting she was running, and they voted her out while she was gone. She said those were "her people," the only Christians she fellowshipped with. It was terrible to be kicked out, and she wondered what could she do to make sure that didn't happen. Then she sits by me and tells me a student disrupts classes she teaches, and is not respectful, though the other kids are. She prepares a great class but if the student ruins it, she doesn't want to. She asks me if I have ever had that problem. I have not. She says the student doesn't listen, and it is the disdain that gets to her. She sends the student away when that happens. I tell her she used to just say to me "I'm sorry, I can't hear you when you're being disrespectful." She didn't take it personally or punish. I had suggested more delight directed learning, more choices, autonomy, project-oriented learning (her eyes lit up at this last one). *It seemed Andrews did not know what to do with me. My mother had a distant concerned look on her face. The advice I gave her of how to deal with a disrespectful student is perhaps not how Andrews would like to be told to deal with me. The note on project-oriented learning could be a useful piece of intelligence to know what I would substitute college with, and what could be disrupted next.*

Tuesday, May 28th. I drive with Dad to the bank on the way to his work and his car breaks down at a town before reaching the bank. It will not go fast, and the axle is breaking. It took around $360 to replace. We spend the afternoon walking and talking, then get back on the road to the bank when the car overheats. Daddy says that has NEVER happened to that car before. He keeps wondering since it is an older car if he should spend the thousands to repair it, or get it replaced. *Exactly like what just happened with my car.* While in that town, his voicemail stops working, like mine did a few weeks ago.

Wednesday, May 29th. Mom says she thinks her laptop is done, but she thinks it's just the wire going bad, exactly like my laptop did recently.

Thursday, May 30th. Last time I visited, when my brother mentioned Avery, I reacted. His bible study was cancelled so I couldn't meet him there, and then he was not at church on Sunday so I couldn't meet him there, or so my brother told me.

Friday, May 31st. As I am leaving the house, I brought my massive luggage with me. My dad tries to pick it up, and they insist it is too much. I get angry, and say it is fine. Dad drops me off no problem at Tysons Corner. The red line was delayed due to train issues. The lady at Greyhound won't let me on the bus with the heavy package, just like my argument with Mom that morning, so I haul my luggage around Union Station, ask, buy 3 boxes for $15, and repackage, paying $33 for extra luggage. No overweight fee, no boxes, bags, or shipping available at Greyhound, and no flexibility. The first bus is pulled over due to issues and we have an unexpected transfer. At the second transfer location, I need help moving my luggage as it has been repackaged into various smaller boxes and we had to move quickly through a large building. When I get to the bus, the man says he brought my luggage and asks for a tip. I give him one dollar. I find that the cardboard has been torn, which would have taken some effort. The second bus breaks down in the middle of the highway right outside New York City. We wait in and out for hours for a new bus. Then we have extra people so the bus driver is freaking out wondering where they came from. We all have to get off the bus to show tickets again. I make a fun video reporting it, and then the driver realizes there are fewer seats on the bus... *This is typical. I showed I wasn't bothered, so they stopped the harassment with an innocent explanation after they are done threatening.* We should have arrived at the border by around 11:40 pm, but arrived around 6:30 am instead.

Comments

My comment on Facebook: ... The whole family is mentioned in several long sections after April 18th.

Expected publication date is October 29th

My comment: I take it there are no responses.

My mother's comment: *thumbs down*

www.ingramcontent.com/pod-product-compliance
Lightning Source LLC
Chambersburg PA
CBHW081415270326
41931CB00015B/3282
9780578313047